Apache Hadoop™
YARN

Apache Hadoop™ YARN

Moving beyond MapReduce and Batch Processing with Apache Hadoop™ 2

Arun C. Murthy
Vinod Kumar Vavilapalli

Doug Eadline
Joseph Niemiec
Jeff Markham

♦♦Addison-Wesley

Upper Saddle River, NJ • Boston • Indianapolis • San Francisco
New York • Toronto • Montreal • London • Munich • Paris • Madrid
Capetown • Sydney • Tokyo • Singapore • Mexico City

Many of the designations used by manufacturers and sellers to distinguish their products are claimed as trademarks. Where those designations appear in this book, and the publisher was aware of a trademark claim, the designations have been printed with initial capital letters or in all capitals.

The authors and publisher have taken care in the preparation of this book, but make no expressed or implied warranty of any kind and assume no responsibility for errors or omissions. No liability is assumed for incidental or consequential damages in connection with or arising out of the use of the information or programs contained herein.

For information about buying this title in bulk quantities, or for special sales opportunities (which may include electronic versions; custom cover designs; and content particular to your business, training goals, marketing focus, or branding interests), please contact our corporate sales department at corpsales@pearsoned.com or (800) 382-3419.

For government sales inquiries, please contact governmentsales@pearsoned.com.

For questions about sales outside the United States, please contact international@pearsoned.com.

Visit us on the Web: informit.com/aw

Library of Congress Cataloging-in-Publication Data

Murthy, Arun C.
  Apache Hadoop YARN : moving beyond MapReduce and batch processing with Apache Hadoop 2 / Arun C. Murthy, Vinod Kumar Vavilapalli, Doug Eadline, Joseph Niemiec, Jeff Markham.
       pages   cm
  Includes index.
  ISBN 978-0-321-93450-5 (pbk. : alk. paper)
  1. Apache Hadoop. 2. Electronic data processing—Distributed processing. I. Title.
  QA76.9.D5M97 2014
  004'.36—dc23
                                                                    2014003391

ISBN-13: 978-0-321-93450-5
ISBN-10: 0-321-93450-4
Text printed in the United States on recycled paper at RR Donnelley in Crawfordsville, Indiana.
First printing, March 2014

Contents

Foreword by Raymie Stata

William Gibson was fond of saying: "The future is already here—it's just not very evenly distributed." Those of us who have been in the web search industry have had the privilege—and the curse—of living in the future of Big Data when it wasn't distributed at all. What did we learn? We learned to measure everything. We learned to experiment. We learned to mine signals out of unstructured data. We learned to drive business value through data science. And we learned that, to do these things, we needed a new data-processing platform fundamentally different from the business intelligence systems being developed at the time.

The future of Big Data is rapidly arriving for almost all industries. This is driven in part by widespread instrumentation of the physical world—vehicles, buildings, and even people are spitting out log streams not unlike the weblogs we know and love in cyberspace. Less obviously, digital records—such as digitized government records, digitized insurance policies, and digital medical records—are creating a trove of information not unlike the webpages crawled and parsed by search engines. It's no surprise, then, that the tools and techniques pioneered first in the world of web search are finding currency in more and more industries. And the leading such tool, of course, is Apache Hadoop.

But Hadoop is close to ten years old. Computing infrastructure has advanced significantly in this decade. If Hadoop was to maintain its relevance in the modern Big Data world, it needed to advance as well. YARN represents just the advancement needed to keep Hadoop relevant.

As described in the historical overview provided in this book, for the majority of Hadoop's existence, it supported a single computing paradigm: MapReduce. On the compute servers we had at the time, horizontal scaling—throwing more server nodes at a problem—was the only way the web search industry could hope to keep pace with the growth of the web. The MapReduce paradigm is particularly well suited for horizontal scaling, so it was the natural paradigm to keep investing in.

With faster networks, higher core counts, solid-state storage, and (especially) larger memories, new paradigms of parallel computing are becoming practical at large scales. YARN will allow Hadoop users to move beyond MapReduce and adopt these emerging paradigms. MapReduce will not go away—it's a good fit for many problems, and it still scales better than anything else currently developed. But, increasingly, MapReduce will be just one tool in a much larger tool chest—a tool chest named "YARN."

In short, the era of Big Data is just starting. Thanks to YARN, Hadoop will continue to play a pivotal role in Big Data processing across all industries. Given this, I was pleased to learn that YARN project founder Arun Murthy and project lead Vinod Kumar Vavilapalli have teamed up with Doug Eadline, Joseph Niemiec, and Jeff Markham to write a volume sharing the history and goals of the YARN project, describing how to deploy and operate YARN, and providing a tutorial on how to get the most out of it at the application level.

This book is a critically needed resource for the newly released Apache Hadoop 2.0, highlighting YARN as the significant breakthrough that broadens Hadoop beyond the MapReduce paradigm.

—Raymie Stata, CEO of Altiscale

Foreword by Paul Dix

No series on data and analytics would be complete without coverage of Hadoop and the different parts of the Hadoop ecosystem. Hadoop 2 introduced YARN, or "Yet Another Resource Negotiator," which represents a major change in the internals of how data processing works in Hadoop. With YARN, Hadoop has moved beyond the MapReduce paradigm to expose a framework for building applications for data processing at scale. MapReduce has become just an application implemented on the YARN framework. This book provides detailed coverage of how YARN works and explains how you can take advantage of it to work with data at scale in Hadoop outside of MapReduce.

No one is more qualified to bring this material to you than the authors of this book. They're the team at Hortonworks responsible for the creation and development of YARN. Arun, a co-founder of Hortonworks, has been working on Hadoop since its creation in 2006. Vinod has been contributing to the Apache Hadoop project full-time since mid-2007. Jeff and Joseph are solutions engineers with Hortonworks. Doug is the trainer for the popular Hadoop Fundamentals LiveLessons and has years of experience building Hadoop and clustered systems. Together, these authors bring a breadth of knowledge and experience with Hadoop and YARN that can't be found elsewhere.

This book provides you with a brief history of Hadoop and MapReduce to set the stage for why YARN was a necessary next step in the evolution of the platform. You get a walk-through on installation and administration and then dive into the internals of YARN and the Capacity scheduler. You see how existing MapReduce applications now run as an applications framework on top of YARN. Finally, you learn how to implement your own YARN applications and look at some of the new YARN-based frameworks. This book gives you a comprehensive dive into the next generation Hadoop platform.

—*Paul Dix, Series Editor*

Preface

Apache Hadoop has a rich and long history. It's come a long way since its birth in the middle of the first decade of this millennium—from being merely an infrastructure component for a niche use-case (web search), it's now morphed into a compelling part of a modern data architecture for a very wide spectrum of the industry. Apache Hadoop owes its success to many factors: the community housed at the Apache Software Foundation; the timing (solving an important problem at the right time); the extensive early investment done by Yahoo! in funding its development, hardening, and large-scale production deployments; and the current state where it's been adopted by a broad ecosystem. In hindsight, its success is easy to rationalize.

On a personal level, Vinod and I have been privileged to be part of this journey from the very beginning. It's very rare to get an opportunity to make such a wide impact on the industry, and even rarer to do so in the slipstream of a great wave of a community developing software in the open—a community that allowed us to share our efforts, encouraged our good ideas, and weeded out the questionable ones. We are very proud to be part of an effort that is helping the industry understand, and unlock, a significant value from data.

YARN is an effort to usher Apache Hadoop into a new era—an era in which its initial impact is no longer a novelty and expectations are significantly higher, and growing. At Hortonworks, we strongly believe that at least half the world's data will be touched by Apache Hadoop. To those in the engine room, it has been evident, for at least half a decade now, that Apache Hadoop had to evolve beyond supporting MapReduce alone. As the industry pours all its data into Apache Hadoop HDFS, there is a real need to process that data in multiple ways: real-time event processing, human-interactive SQL queries, batch processing, machine learning, and many others. Apache Hadoop 1.0 was severely limiting; one could store data in many forms in HDFS, but MapReduce was the only algorithm you could use to natively process that data.

YARN was our way to begin to solve that multidimensional requirement natively in Apache Hadoop, thereby transforming the core of Apache Hadoop from a one-trick "batch store/process" system into a true multiuse platform. The crux was the recognition that Apache Hadoop MapReduce had two facets: (1) a core resource manager, which included scheduling, workload management, and fault tolerance; and (2) a user-facing MapReduce framework that provided a simplified interface to the end-user that hid the complexity of dealing with a scalable, distributed system. In particular, the MapReduce framework freed the user from having to deal with gritty details of fault tolerance, scalability, and other issues. YARN is just realization of this simple idea. With YARN, we have successfully relegated MapReduce to the role of merely one of the options to process data in Hadoop, and it now sits side-by-side by other frameworks such as Apache Storm (real-time event processing), Apache Tez (interactive query backed), Apache Spark (in-memory machine learning), and many more.

Distributed systems are hard; in particular, dealing with their failures is hard. YARN enables programmers to design and implement distributed *frameworks* while sharing a common set of resources and data. While YARN lets application developers focus on their business logic by automatically taking care of thorny problems like resource arbitration, isolation, cluster health, and fault monitoring, it also needs applications to act on the corresponding signals from YARN as they see fit. YARN makes the effort of building such systems significantly simpler by dealing with many issues with which a framework developer would be confronted; the framework developer, at the same time, still has to deal with the consequences on the framework in a framework-specific manner.

While the power of YARN is easily comprehensible, the ability to exploit that power requires the user to understand the intricacies of building such a system in conjunction with YARN. This book aims to reconcile that dichotomy.

The YARN project and the Apache YARN community have come a long way since their beginning. Increasingly more applications are moving to run natively under YARN and, therefore, are helping users process data in myriad ways. We hope that with the knowledge gleaned from this book, the reader can help feed that cycle of enablement so that individuals and organizations alike can take full advantage of the data revolution with the applications of their choice.

—*Arun C. Murthy*

Focus of the Book

This book is intended to provide detailed coverage of Apache Hadoop YARN's goals, its design and architecture and how it expands the Apache Hadoop ecosystem to take advantage of data at scale beyond MapReduce. It primarily focuses on installation and administration of YARN clusters, on helping users with YARN application development and new frameworks that run on top of YARN beyond MapReduce.

Please note that this book is *not* intended to be an introduction to Apache Hadoop itself. We assume that the reader has a working knowledge of Hadoop version 1, writing applications on top of the Hadoop MapReduce framework, and the architecture and usage of the Hadoop Distributed FileSystem. Please see the book webpage (http://yarn-book.com) for a list of introductory resources. In future editions of this book, we hope to expand our material related to the MapReduce application framework itself and how users can design and code their own MapReduce applications.

Book Structure

In Chapter 1, "Apache Hadoop YARN: A Brief History and Rationale," we provide a historical account of why and how Apache Hadoop YARN came about. Chapter 2, "Apache Hadoop YARN Install Quick Start," gives you a quick-start guide for installing and exploring Apache Hadoop YARN on a single node. Chapter 3, "Apache Hadoop YARN Core Concepts," introduces YARN and explains how it expands Hadoop ecosystem. A functional overview of YARN components then appears in Chapter 4, "Functional Overview of YARN Components," to get the reader started.

Chapter 5, "Installing Apache Hadoop YARN," describes methods of installing YARN. It covers both a script-based manual installation as well as a GUI-based installation using Apache Ambari. We then cover information about administration of YARN clusters in Chapter 6, "Apache Hadoop YARN Administration."

A deep dive into YARN's architecture occurs in Chapter 7, "Apache Hadoop YARN Architecture Guide," which should give the reader an idea of the inner workings of YARN. We follow this discussion with an exposition of the Capacity scheduler in Chapter 8, "Capacity Scheduler in YARN."

Chapter 9, "MapReduce with Apache Hadoop YARN," describes how existing MapReduce-based applications can work on and take advantage of YARN. Chapter 10, "Apache Hadoop YARN Application Example," provides a detailed walk-through of how to build a YARN application by way of illustrating a working YARN application that creates a JBoss Application Server cluster. Chapter 11, "Using Apache Hadoop YARN Distributed-Shell," describes the usage and innards of distributed shell, the canonical example application that is built on top of and ships with YARN.

One of the most exciting aspects of YARN is its ability to support multiple programming models and application frameworks. We conclude with Chapter 12, "Apache Hadoop YARN Frameworks," a brief survey of emerging open-source frameworks that are being developed to run under YARN.

Appendices include Appendix A, "Supplemental Content and Code Downloads"; Appendix B, "YARN Installation Scripts"; Appendix C, "YARN Administration Scripts"; Appendix D, "Nagios Modules"; Appendix E, "Resources and Additional Information"; and Appendix F, "HDFS Quick Reference."

Book Conventions

Code is displayed in a monospaced font. Code lines that wrap because they are too long to fit on one line in this book are denoted with this symbol: ➥.

Additional Content and Accompanying Code

Please see Appendix A, " Supplemental Content and Code Downloads," for the location of the book webpage (http://yarn-book.com). All code and configuration files used in this book can be downloaded from this site. Check the website for new and updated content including "Description of Apache Hadoop YARN Configuration Properties" and "Apache Hadoop YARN Troubleshooting Tips."

Acknowledgments

We are very grateful for the following individuals who provided feedback and valuable assistance in crafting this book.

- Ron Lee, Platform Engineering Architect at Hortonworks Inc, for making this book happen, and without whose involvement this book wouldn't be where it is now.
- Jian He, Apache Hadoop YARN Committer and a member of the Hortonworks engineering team, for helping with reviews.
- Zhijie Shen, Apache Hadoop YARN Committer and a member of the Hortonworks engineering team, for helping with reviews.
- Omkar Vinit Joshi, Apache Hadoop YARN Committer, for some very thorough reviews of a number of chapters.
- Xuan Gong, a member of the Hortonworks engineering team, for helping with reviews.
- Christopher Gambino, for the target audience testing.
- David Hoyle at Hortonworks, for reading the draft.
- Ellis H. Wilson III, storage scientist, Department of Computer Science and Engineering, the Pennsylvania State University, for reading and reviewing the entire draft.

Arun C. Murthy

Apache Hadoop is a product of the fruits of the community at the Apache Software Foundation (ASF). The mantra of the ASF is "Community Over Code," based on the insight that successful communities are built to last, much more so than successful projects or code bases. Apache Hadoop is a shining example of this. Since its inception, many hundreds of people have contributed their time, interest and expertise—many are still around while others have moved on; the constant is the *community*. I'd like to take this opportunity to thank every one of the contributors; Hadoop wouldn't be what it is without your contributions. Contribution is not merely code; it's a bug report, an email on the user mailing list helping a journeywoman with a query, an edit of the Hadoop wiki, and so on.

I'd like to thank everyone at Yahoo! who supported Apache Hadoop from the beginning—there really isn't a need to elaborate further; it's crystal clear to everyone who understands the history and context of the project.

Apache Hadoop YARN began as a mere idea. Ideas are plentiful and transient, and have questionable value. YARN wouldn't be real but for the countless hours put in by hundreds of contributors; nor would it be real but for the initial team who believed in the idea, weeded out the bad parts, chiseled out the reasonable parts, and took ownership of it. Thank you, you know who you are.

Special thanks to the team behind the curtains at Hortonworks who were so instrumental in the production of this book; folks like Ron and Jim are the key architects of this effort. Also to my co-authors: Vinod, Joe, Doug, and Jeff; you guys are an amazing bunch. Vinod, in particular, is someone the world should pay even more attention to—he is a very special young man for a variety of reasons.

Everything in my life germinates from the support, patience, and love emanating from my family: mom, grandparents, my best friend and amazing wife, Manasa, and the three-year-old twinkle of my eye, Arjun. Thank you. Gratitude in particular to my granddad, the best man I have ever known and the moral yardstick I use to measure myself with—I miss you terribly now.

Cliché alert: last, not least, many thanks to you, the reader. Your time invested in reading this book and learning about Apache Hadoop and YARN is a very big compliment. Please do not hesitate to point out how we could have provided better return for your time.

Vinod Kumar Vavilapalli

Apache Hadoop YARN, and at a bigger level, Apache Hadoop itself, continues to be a healthy, community-driven, open-source project. It owes much of its success and adoption to the Apache Hadoop YARN and MapReduce communities. Many individuals and organizations spent a lot of time developing, testing, deploying and administering, supporting, documenting, evangelizing, and most of all, using Apache Hadoop YARN over the years. Here's a big thanks to all the volunteer contributors, users, testers, committers, and PMC members who have helped YARN to progress in every way possible. Without them, YARN wouldn't be where it is today, let alone this book. My involvement with the project is entirely accidental, and I pay my gratitude to lady luck for bestowing upon me the incredible opportunity of being able to contribute to such a once-in-a-decade project.

This book wouldn't have been possible without the herding efforts of Ron Lee, who pushed and prodded me and the other co-writers of this book at every stage. Thanks to Jeff Markham for getting the book off the ground and for his efforts in demonstrating the power of YARN in building a non-trivial YARN application and making it usable as a guide for instruction. Thanks to Doug Eadline for his persistent thrust toward a timely and usable release of the content. And thanks to Joseph Niemiec for jumping in late in the game but contributing with significant efforts.

Special thanks to my mentor, Hemanth Yamijala, for patiently helping me when my career had just started and for such great guidance. Thanks to my co-author, mentor, team lead and friend, Arun C. Murthy, for taking me along on the ride that is Hadoop. Thanks to my beautiful and wonderful wife, Bhavana, for all her love, support, and not the least for patiently bearing with my single-threaded span of attention while I was writing the book. And finally, to my parents, who brought me into this beautiful world and for giving me such a wonderful life.

Doug Eadline

There are many people who have worked behind the scenes to make this book possible. First, I want to thank Ron Lee of Hortonworks: Without your hand on the tiller, this book would have surely sailed into some rough seas. Also, Joe Niemiec of Hortonworks, thanks for all the help and the 11th-hour efforts. To Debra Williams Cauley of Addison-Wesley, you are a good friend who makes the voyage easier; Namaste. Thanks to the other authors, particularly Vinod for helping me understand the big and little ideas behind YARN. I also cannot forget my support crew, Emily, Marlee, Carla, and Taylor—thanks for reminding me when I raise my eyebrows. And, finally, the biggest thank you to my wonderful wife, Maddy, for her support. Yes, it is done. Really.

Joseph Niemiec

A big thanks to my father, Jeffery Niemiec, for without him I would have never developed my passion for computers.

Jeff Markham

From my first introduction to YARN at Hortonworks in 2012 to now, I've come to realize that the only way organizations worldwide can use this game-changing software is because of the open-source community effort led by Arun Murthy and Vinod Vavilapalli. To lead the world-class Hortonworks engineers along with corporate and individual contributors means a lot of sausage making, cat herding, and a heavy dose of vision. Without all that, there wouldn't even be YARN. Thanks to both of you for leading a truly great engineering effort. Special thanks to Ron Lee for shepherding us all through this process, all outside of his day job. Most importantly, though, I owe a huge debt of gratitude to my wife, Yong, who wound up doing a lot of the heavy lifting for our relocation to Seoul while I fulfilled my obligations for this project. 사랑해요!

About the Authors

Arun C. Murthy has contributed to Apache Hadoop full time since the inception of the project in early 2006. He is a long-term Hadoop committer and a member of the Apache Hadoop Project Management Committee. Previously, he was the architect and lead of the Yahoo! Hadoop MapReduce development team and was ultimately responsible, on a technical level, for providing Hadoop MapReduce as a service for all of Yahoo!—currently running on nearly 50,000 machines! Arun is the founder and architect of Hortonworks Inc., a software company that is helping to accelerate the development and adoption of Apache Hadoop. Hortonworks was formed by the key architects and core Hadoop committers from the Yahoo! Hadoop software engineering team in June 2011. Funded by Yahoo! and Benchmark Capital, one of the preeminent technology investors, Hortonworks has as its goal ensuring that Apache Hadoop becomes the standard platform for storing, processing, managing, and analyzing Big Data. Arun lives in Silicon Valley.

Vinod Kumar Vavilapalli has been contributing to Apache Hadoop project full time since mid-2007. At Apache Software Foundation, he is a long-term Hadoop contributor, Hadoop committer, member of the Apache Hadoop Project Management Committee, and a Foundation member. Vinod is a MapReduce and YARN go-to guy at Hortonworks Inc. For more than five years, he has been working on Hadoop and still has fun doing it. He was involved in Hadoop on Demand, Hadoop 0.20, Capacity scheduler, Hadoop security, and MapReduce, and now is a lead developer and the project lead for Apache Hadoop YARN. Before joining Hortonworks, he was at Yahoo! working in the Grid team that made Hadoop what it is today, running at large scale—up to tens of thousands of nodes. Vinod loves reading books of all kinds, and is passionate about using computers to change the world for better, bit by bit. He has a bachelor's degree in computer science and engineering from the Indian Institute of Technology Roorkee. He lives in Silicon Valley and is reachable at twitter handle @tshooter.

Doug Eadline, PhD, began his career as a practitioner and a chronicler of the Linux cluster HPC revolution and now documents Big Data analytics. Starting with the first Beowulf how-to document, Doug has written hundreds of articles, white papers, and instructional documents covering virtually all aspects of HPC. Prior to starting and editing the popular ClusterMonkey.net website in 2005, he served as editor-in-chief for *ClusterWorld* magazine, and was senior HPC editor for *Linux Magazine*. He has practical hands-on experience in many aspects of HPC, including hardware and software design, benchmarking, storage, GPU, cloud computing, and parallel computing. Currently, he is a writer and consultant to the HPC industry and leader of the Limulus Personal Cluster Project (http://limulus.basement-supercomputing.com). He is also author of *Hadoop Fundamentals LiveLessons* and *Apache Hadoop YARN Fundamentals LiveLessons* videos from Addison-Wesley.

Joseph Niemiec is a Big Data solutions engineer whose focus is on designing Hadoop solutions for many *Fortune 1000* companies. In this position, Joseph has worked with customers to build multiple YARN applications, providing a unique perspective on moving customers beyond batch processing, and has worked on YARN development directly. An avid technologist, Joseph has been focused on technology innovations since 2001. His interest in data analytics originally started in game score optimization as a teenager and has shifted to helping customers uptake new technology innovations such as Hadoop and, most recently, building new data applications using YARN.

Jeff Markham is a solution engineer at Hortonworks Inc., the company promoting open-source Hadoop. Previously, he was with VMware, Red Hat, and IBM, helping companies build distributed applications with distributed data. He has written articles on Java application development and has spoken at several conferences and to Hadoop user groups. Jeff is a contributor to Apache Pig and Apache HDFS.

1

Apache Hadoop YARN: A Brief History and Rationale

In this chapter we provide a historical account of why and how Apache Hadoop YARN came about. YARN's requirements emerged and evolved from the practical needs of long-existing cluster deployments of Hadoop, both small and large, and we discuss how each of these requirements ultimately shaped YARN.

YARN's architecture addresses many of these long-standing requirements, based on experience evolving the MapReduce platform. By understanding this historical context, readers can appreciate most of the design decisions that were made with YARN. These design decisions will repeatedly appear in Chapter 4, "Functional Overview of YARN Components," and Chapter 7, "Apache Hadoop YARN Architecture Guide."

Introduction

Several different problems need to be tackled when building a shared compute platform. Scalability is the foremost concern, to avoid rewriting software again and again whenever existing demands can no longer be satisfied with the current version. The desire to share physical resources brings up issues of multitenancy, isolation, and security. Users interacting with a Hadoop cluster serving as a long-running service inside an organization will come to depend on its reliable and highly available operation. To continue to manage user workloads in the least disruptive manner, serviceability of the platform is a principal concern for operators and administrators. Abstracting the intricacies of a distributed system and exposing clean but varied application-level paradigms are growing necessities for any compute platform.

Hadoop's compute layer has seen all of this and much more during its continuous and long progress. It went through multiple evolutionary phases in its architecture. We highlight the "Big Four" of these phases in the reminder of this chapter.

- "Phase 0: The Era of Ad Hoc Clusters" signaled the beginning of Hadoop clusters that were set up in an ad hoc, per-user manner.
- "Phase 1: Hadoop on Demand" was the next step in the evolution in the form of a common system for provisioning and managing private Hadoop MapReduce and HDFS instances on a shared cluster of commodity hardware.
- "Phase 2: Dawn of the Shared Compute Clusters" began when the majority of Hadoop installations moved to a model of a shared MapReduce cluster together with shared HDFS instances.
- "Phase 3: Emergence of YARN"—the main subject of this book—arose to address the demands and shortcomings of the previous architectures.

As the reader follows the journey through these various phases, it will be apparent how the requirements of YARN unfolded over time. As the architecture continued to evolve, existing problems would be solved and new use-cases would emerge, pushing forward further stages of advancements.

We'll now tour through the various stages of evolution one after another, in chronological order. For each phase, we first describe what the architecture looked like and what its advancements were from its previous generation, and then wind things up with its limitations—setting the stage for the next phase.

Apache Hadoop

To really comprehend the history of YARN, you have to start by taking a close look at the evolution of Hadoop itself. Yahoo! adopted Apache Hadoop in 2006 to replace the existing infrastructure that was then driving its WebMap application—the technology that builds a graph of the known web to power its search engine. At that time, the web-graph contained more than 100 billion nodes with roughly 1 trillion edges. The previous infrastructure, named "Dreadnaught," successfully served its purpose and grew well—starting from a size of just 20 nodes and expanding to 600 cluster nodes—but had reached the limits of its scalability. The software also didn't perform perfectly in many scenarios, including handling of failures in the clusters' commodity hardware. A significant shift in its architecture was required to scale out further to match the ever-growing size of the web. The distributed applications running under Dreadnought were very similar to MapReduce programs and needed to span clusters of machines and work at a large scale. This highlights the first requirement that would survive throughout early versions of Hadoop MapReduce, all the way to YARN—[Requirement 1] Scalability.

- **[Requirement 1] Scalability**

  The next-generation compute platform should scale horizontally to tens of thousands of nodes and concurrent applications.

For Yahoo!, by adopting a more scalable MapReduce framework, significant parts of the search pipeline could be migrated easily without major refactoring—which, in turn, ignited the initial investment in Apache Hadoop. However, although the original push for Hadoop was for the sake of search infrastructure, other use-cases started taking advantage of Hadoop much faster, even before the migration of the web-graph to Hadoop could be completed. The process of setting up research grids for research teams, data scientists, and the like had hastened the deployment of larger and larger Hadoop clusters. Yahoo! scientists who were optimizing advertising analytics, spam filtering, personalization, and content initially drove Hadoop's evolution and many of its early requirements. In line with that evolution, the engineering priorities evolved over time, and Hadoop went through many intermediate stages of the compute platform, including ad hoc clusters.

Phase 0: The Era of Ad Hoc Clusters

Before the advent of ad hoc clusters, many of Hadoop's earliest users would use Hadoop as if it were similar to a desktop application but running on a host of machines. They would manually bring up a cluster on a handful of nodes, load their data into the Hadoop Distributed File System (HDFS), obtain the result they were interested in by writing MapReduce jobs, and then tear down that cluster. This was partly because there wasn't an urgent need for persistent data in Hadoop HDFS, and partly because there was no incentive for sharing common data sets and the results of the computations. As usage of these private clusters increased and Hadoop's fault tolerance improved, persistent HDFS clusters came into being. Yahoo! Hadoop administrators would install and manage a shared HDFS instance, and load commonly used and interesting data sets into the shared cluster, attracting scientists interested in deriving insights from them. HDFS also acquired a POSIX-like permissions model for supporting multiuser environments, file and namespace quotas, and other features to improve its multitenant operation. Tracing the evolution of HDFS is in itself an interesting endeavor, but we will focus on the compute platform in the remainder of this chapter.

Once shared HDFS instances came into being, issues with the not-yet-shared compute instances came into sharp focus. Unlike with HDFS, simply setting up a shared MapReduce cluster for multiple users potentially from multiple organizations wasn't a trivial step forward. Private compute cluster instances continued to thrive, but continuous sharing of the common underlying physical resources wasn't ideal. To address some of the multitenancy issues with manually deploying and tearing down private clusters, Yahoo! developed and deployed a platform called Hadoop on Demand.

Phase 1: Hadoop on Demand

The Hadoop on Demand (HOD) project was a system for provisioning and managing Hadoop MapReduce and HDFS instances on a shared cluster of commodity hardware. The Hadoop on Demand project predated and directly influenced how the developers eventually arrived at YARN's architecture. Understanding the HOD architecture and its eventual limitations is a first step toward comprehending YARN's motivations.

To address the multitenancy woes with the manually shared clusters from the previous incarnation (Phase 0), HOD used a traditional resource manager—Torque—together with a cluster scheduler—Maui—to allocate Hadoop clusters on a shared pool of nodes. Traditional resource managers were already being used elsewhere in high-performance computing environments to enable effective sharing of pooled cluster resources. By making use of such existing systems, HOD handed off the problem of cluster management to systems outside of Hadoop. On the allocated nodes, HOD would start MapReduce and HDFS daemons, which in turn would serve the user's data and application requests. Thus, the basic system architecture of HOD included these layers:

- A ResourceManager (RM) together with a scheduler
- Various HOD components to interact with the RM/scheduler and manage Hadoop
- Hadoop MapReduce and HDFS daemons
- A HOD shell and Hadoop clients

A typical session of HOD involved three major steps: allocate a cluster, run Hadoop jobs on the allocated cluster, and finally deallocate the cluster. Here is a brief description of a typical HOD-user session:

- Users would invoke a HOD shell and submit their needs by supplying a description of an appropriately sized compute cluster to Torque. This description included:
  - The number of nodes needed
  - A description of a special head-process called the RingMaster to be started by the ResourceManager
  - A specification of the Hadoop deployment desired
- Torque would enqueue the request until enough nodes become available. Once the nodes were available, Torque started the head-process called RingMaster on one of the compute nodes.
- The RingMaster was a HOD component and used another ResourceManager interface to run the second HOD component, HODRing—with one HODRing being present on each of the allocated compute nodes.
- The HODRings booted up, communicated with the RingMaster to obtain Hadoop commands, and ran them accordingly. Once the Hadoop daemons were started, HODRings registered with the RingMaster, giving information about the daemons.
- The HOD client kept communicating with the RingMaster to find out the location of the JobTracker and HDFS daemons.
- Once everything was set up and the users learned the JobTracker and HDFS locations, HOD simply got out the way and allowed the user to perform his or her data crunching on the corresponding clusters.

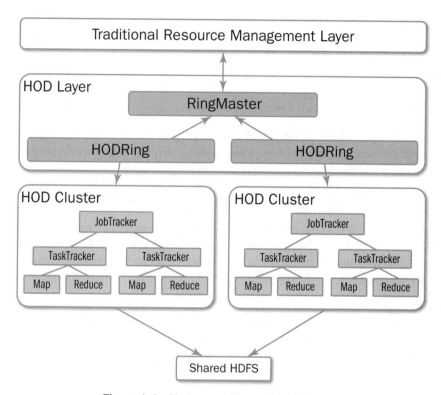

Figure 1.1 Hadoop on Demand architecture

- The user released a cluster once he or she was done running the data analysis jobs.

Figure 1.1 provides an overview of the HOD architecture.

HDFS in the HOD World

While HOD could also deploy HDFS clusters, most users chose to deploy the compute nodes across a shared HDFS instance. In a typical Hadoop cluster provisioned by HOD, cluster administrators would set up HDFS statically (without using HOD). This allowed data to be persisted in HDFS even after the HOD-provisioned clusters were deallocated. To use a statically configured HDFS, a user simply needed to point to an external HDFS instance. As HDFS scaled further, more compute clusters could be allocated through HOD, creating a cycle of increased experimentation by users over more data sets, leading to a greater return on investment. Because most user-specific MapReduce clusters were smaller than the largest HOD jobs possible, the JobTracker running for any single HOD cluster was rarely a bottleneck.

Features and Advantages of HOD

Because HOD sets up a new cluster for every job, users could run older and stable versions of Hadoop software while developers continued to test new features in isolation. Since the Hadoop community typically released a major revision every three months, the flexibility of HOD was critical to maintaining that software release schedule—we refer to this decoupling of upgrade dependencies as [Requirement 2] Serviceability.

- **[Requirement 2] Serviceability**
  The next-generation compute platform should enable evolution of cluster software to be completely decoupled from users' applications.

In addition, HOD made it easy for administrators and users to quickly set up and use Hadoop on an existing cluster under a traditional resource management system. Beyond Yahoo!, universities and high-performance computing environments could run Hadoop on their existing clusters with ease by making use of HOD. It was also a very useful tool for Hadoop developers and testers who needed to share a physical cluster for testing their own Hadoop versions.

Log Management

HOD could also be configured to upload users' job logs and the Hadoop daemon logs to a configured HDFS location when a cluster was deallocated. The number of log files uploaded to and retained on HDFS could increase over time in an unbounded manner. To address this issue, HOD shipped with tools that helped administrators manage the log retention by removing old log files uploaded to HDFS after a specified amount of time had elapsed.

Multiple Users and Multiple Clusters per User

As long as nodes were available and organizational policies were not violated, a user could use HOD to allocate multiple MapReduce clusters simultaneously. HOD provided the **list** and the **info** operations to facilitate the management of multiple concurrent clusters. The list operation listed all the clusters allocated so far by a user, and the info operation showed information about a given cluster—Torque job ID, locations of the important daemons like the HOD RingMaster process, and the RPC addresses of the Hadoop JobTracker and NameNode daemons.

The resource management layer had some ways of limiting users from abusing cluster resources, but the user interface for exposing those limits was poor. HOD shipped with scripts that took care of this integration so that, for instance, if some user limits were violated, HOD would update a public job attribute that the user could query against.

HOD also had scripts that integrated with the resource manager to allow a user to identify the account under which the user's Hadoop clusters ran. This was necessary because production systems on traditional resource managers used to manage accounts separately so that they could charge users for using shared compute resources.

Ultimately, each node in the cluster could belong to only one user's Hadoop cluster at any point of time—a major limitation of HOD. As usage of HOD grew along with its success, requirements around [Requirement 3] Multitenancy started to take shape.

- **[Requirement 3] Multitenancy**

  The next-generation compute platform should support multiple tenants to coexist on the same cluster and enable fine-grained sharing of individual nodes among different tenants.

Distribution of Hadoop Software

When provisioning Hadoop, HOD could either use a preinstalled Hadoop instance on the cluster nodes or request HOD to distribute and install a Hadoop tarball as part of the provisioning operation. This was especially useful in a development environment where individual developers might have different versions of Hadoop to test on the same shared cluster.

Configuration

HOD provided a very convenient mechanism to configure both the boot-up HOD software itself and the Hadoop daemons that it provisioned. It also helped manage the configuration files that it generated on the client side.

Auto-deallocation of Idle Clusters

HOD used to automatically deallocate clusters that were not running Hadoop jobs for a predefined period of time. Each HOD allocation included a monitoring facility that constantly checked for any running Hadoop jobs. If it detected no running Hadoop jobs for an extended interval, it automatically deallocated its own cluster, freeing up those nodes for future use.

Shortcomings of Hadoop on Demand

Hadoop on Demand proved itself to be a powerful and very useful platform, but Yahoo! ultimately had to retire it in favor of directly shared MapReduce clusters due to many of its shortcomings.

Data Locality

For any given MapReduce job, during the map phase the JobTracker makes every effort to place tasks close to their input data in HDFS—ideally on a node storing a replica of that data. Because Torque doesn't know how blocks are distributed on HDFS, it allocates nodes without accounting for locality. The subset of nodes granted to a user's JobTracker will likely contain only a handful of relevant replicas and, if the user is unlucky, none. Many Hadoop clusters are characterized by a small number of very big jobs and a large number of small jobs. For most of the small jobs, most reads will emanate from remote hosts because of the insufficient information available from Torque.

Efforts were undertaken to mitigate this situation but achieved mixed results. One solution was to spread TaskTrackers across racks by modifying Torque/Maui itself and making them rack-aware. Once this was done, any user's HOD compute cluster would be allocated nodes that were spread across racks. This made intra-rack reads of shared data sets more likely, but introduced other problems. The transfer of records between map and reduce tasks as part of MapReduce's shuffle phase would necessarily cross racks, causing a significant slowdown of users' workloads.

While such short-term solutions were implemented, ultimately none of them proved ideal. In addition, they all pointed to the fundamental limitation of the traditional resource management software—that is, the ability to understand data locality as a first-class dimension. This aspect of [Requirement 4] Locality Awareness is a key requirement for YARN.

- **[Requirement 4] Locality Awareness**

  The next-generation compute platform should support locality awareness—moving computation to the data is a major win for many applications.

Cluster Utilization

MapReduce jobs consist of multiple stages: a map stage followed by a shuffle and a reduce stage. Further, high-level frameworks like Apache Pig and Apache Hive often organize a workflow of MapReduce jobs in a directed-acyclic graph (DAG) of computations. Because clusters were not resizable between stages of a single job or between jobs when using HOD, most of the time the major share of the capacity in a cluster would be barren, waiting for the subsequent slimmer stages to be completed. In an extreme but very common scenario, a single reduce task running on one node could prevent a cluster of hundreds of nodes from being reclaimed. When all jobs in a colocation were considered, this approach could result in hundreds of nodes being idle in this state.

In addition, private MapReduce clusters for each user implied that even after a user was done with his or her workflows, a HOD cluster could potentially be idle for a while before being automatically detected and shut down.

While users were fond of many features in HOD, the economics of cluster utilization ultimately forced Yahoo! to pack its users' jobs into shared clusters. [Requirement 5] High Cluster Utilization is a top priority for YARN.

- **[Requirement 5] High Cluster Utilization**

  The next-generation compute platform should enable high utilization of the underlying physical resources.

Elasticity

In a typical Hadoop workflow, MapReduce jobs have lots of maps with a much smaller number of reduces, with map tasks being short and quick and reduce tasks being I/O heavy and longer running. With HOD, users relied on few heuristics when estimating how many nodes their jobs required—typically allocating their private HOD clusters based on the required number of map tasks (which in turn depends on the input size). In the past, this was the best strategy for users because more often than not, job latency was dominated by the time spent in the queues waiting for the allocation of the cluster. This strategy, although the best option for individual users, leads to bad scenarios from the overall cluster utilization point of view. Specifically, sometimes all of the map tasks are finished (resulting in idle nodes in the cluster) while a few reduce tasks simply chug along for a long while.

Hadoop on Demand did not have the ability to grow and shrink the MapReduce clusters on demand for a variety of reasons. Most importantly, elasticity wasn't a first-class feature in the underlying ResourceManager itself. Even beyond that, as jobs were run under a Hadoop cluster, growing a cluster on demand by starting TaskTrackers wasn't cheap. Shrinking the cluster by shutting down nodes wasn't straightforward, either, without potentially massive movement of existing intermediate outputs of map tasks that had already run and finished on those nodes.

Further, whenever cluster allocation latency was very high, users would often share long-awaited clusters with colleagues, holding on to nodes for longer than anticipated, and increasing latencies even further.

Phase 2: Dawn of the Shared Compute Clusters

Ultimately, HOD architecture had too little information to make intelligent decisions about its allocations, its resource granularity was too coarse, and its API forced users to provide misleading constraints to the resource management layer. This forced the next step of evolution—the majority of installations, including Yahoo!, moved to a model of a shared MapReduce cluster together with shared HDFS instances. The main components of this shared compute architecture were as follows:

- **A JobTracker**: A central daemon responsible for running all the jobs in the cluster. This is the same daemon that used to run jobs for a single user in the HOD world, but with additional functionality.
- **TaskTrackers**: The slave in the system, which executes one task at a time under directions from the JobTracker. This again is the same daemon as in HOD, but now runs the tasks of jobs from all users.

What follows is an exposition of shared MapReduce compute clusters. Shared MapReduce clusters working in tandem with shared HDFS instances is the dominant architecture of Apache Hadoop 1.x release lines. At the point of this writing, many organizations have moved beyond 1.x to the next-generation architecture, but at the same time multitudes of Hadoop deployments continue to the JobTracker/TaskTracker architecture and are looking forward to the migration to YARN-based Apache Hadoop 2.x release lines. Because of this, in what follows, note that we'll refer to the age of shared MapReduce-only shared clusters as *both* the past and the present.

Evolution of Shared Clusters

Moving to shared clusters from HOD-based architecture was nontrivial, and replacement of HOD was easier said than done. HOD, for all its problems, was originally designed to specifically address (and thus masked) many of the multitenancy issues occurring in shared MapReduce clusters. Adding to that, HOD silently took advantage of some core features of the underlying traditional resource manager, which eventually became missing features when the clusters evolved to being native MapReduce shared clusters. In the remainder of this section, we'll describe salient characteristics of shared MapReduce deployments and indicate how the architecture gradually evolved away from HOD.

HDFS Instances

In line with how a shared HDFS architecture was established during the days of HOD, shared instances of HDFS continue to advance. During Phase 2, HDFS improved its scalability, acquired more features such as file-append, the new FileContext API for applications, Kerberos-based security features, high availability, and other performance features such as local short-circuit to data-node files directly.

Central JobTracker Daemon

The first step in the evolution of the MapReduce subsystem was to start running the JobTracker daemon as a shared resource across jobs, across users. This started with putting an abstraction for a cluster scheduler right inside the JobTracker, the details of which we explore in the next subsection. In addition, and unlike in the phase in which HOD was the norm, both developer testing and user validation revealed numerous deadlocks and race conditions in the JobTracker that were earlier neatly shielded by HOD.

JobTracker Memory Management

Running jobs from multiple users also drew attention to the issue of memory management of the JobTracker heap. At large clusters in Yahoo!, we had seen many instances in which a user, just as he or she used to allocate large clusters in the HOD world, would submit a job with many thousands of mappers or reducers. The configured heap of the JobTracker at that time hadn't yet reached the multiple tens of gigabytes observed with HDFS's NameNode. Many times, the JobTracker would expand these very large jobs in its memory to start scheduling them, only to run into heap issues and memory thrash and pauses due to Java garbage collection. The only solution at that time once such a scenario occurred was to restart the JobTracker daemon, effectively causing a downtime for the whole cluster. Thus, the JobTracker heap itself became a shared resource that needed features to support multitenancy, but smart scheduling of this scarce resource was hard. The JobTracker heap would store in-memory representations of jobs and tasks—some of them static and easily accountable, but other parts dynamic (e.g., job counters, job configuration) and hence not bounded.

To avoid the risks associated with a complex solution, the simplest proposal of limiting the maximum number of tasks per job was first put in place. This simple solution eventually had to evolve to support more limits—on the number of jobs submitted per user, on the number of jobs that are initialized and expanded in the JobTracker's memory at any time, on the number of tasks that any job might legally request, and on the number of concurrent tasks that any job can run.

Management of Completed Jobs

The JobTracker would also remember completed jobs so that users could learn about their status once the jobs finished. Initially, completed jobs would have a memory footprint similar to that of any other running job. Completed jobs are, by definition, unbounded as time progresses. To address this issue, the JobTracker was modified to start remembering only partial but critical information about completed jobs, such as job status and counters, thereby minimizing the heap footprint per completed job. Even after this, with ever-increasing completed jobs, the JobTracker couldn't cope after sufficient time elapsed. To address this issue, the straightforward solution of remembering only the last N jobs per user was deployed. This created still more challenges: Users with a very high job-churn rate would eventually run into situations where they could not get information about recently submitted jobs. Further, the solution was a per-user limit, so given enough users; the JobTracker would eventually exhaust its heap anyway.

The ultimate state-of-the-art solution for managing this issue was to change the Job-Tracker to *not* remember *any* completed jobs at all, but instead redirect requests about completed jobs to a special server called the JobHistoryServer. This server offloaded the responsibility of serving web requests about completed jobs away from the Job-Tracker. To handle RPC requests in flight about completed jobs, the JobTracker would also persist some of the completed job information on the local or a remote file system; this responsibility of RPCs would also eventually transition to the JobHistoryServer in Hadoop 2.x releases.

Central Scheduler

When HOD was abandoned, the central scheduler that worked in unison with a traditional resource manager also went away. Trying to integrate existing schedulers with the newly proposed JobTracker-based architecture was a nonstarter due to the engineering challenges involved. It was proposed to extend the JobTracker itself to support queues of jobs. Users would interact with the queues, which are configured appropriately. In the HOD setting, nodes would be statically assigned to a queue—but that led to utilization issues across queues. In the newer architecture, nodes are no longer assigned statically. Instead, **slots** available on a node are dynamically allocated to jobs in queues, thereby also increasing the granularity of the scheduling from nodes to slots.

To facilitate innovations in the scheduling algorithm, an abstraction was put in place. Soon, several implementations came about. Yahoo! implemented and deployed the Capacity scheduler, which focused on throughput, while an alternative called the Fair scheduler also emerged, focusing on fairness.

Scheduling was done on every node's heartbeat: The scheduler would look at the free capacity on this node, look at the jobs that need resources, and schedule a task accordingly. Several dimensions were taken into account while making this scheduling decision—scheduler-specific policies such as capacity, fairness, and, more importantly, per-job locality preferences. Eventually, this "one task per heartbeat" approach was changed to start allocating multiple tasks per heartbeat to improve scheduling latencies and utilization.

The Capacity scheduler is based on allocating capacities to a flat list of queues and to users within those queues. Queues are defined following the internal organizational structure, and each queue is configured with a guaranteed capacity. Excess capacities from idle queues are distributed to queues that are in demand, even if they have already made use of their guaranteed capacity. Inside a queue, users can share resources but there is an overarching emphasis on job throughput, based on a FIFO algorithm. Limits are put in place to avoid single users taking over entire queues or the cluster.

Moving to centralized scheduling and granular resources resulted in massive utilization improvements. This brought more users, more growth to the so-called research clusters, and, in turn, more requirements. The ability to refresh queues at run time to affect capacity changes or to modify queue Access Control Lists (ACLs) was desired and subsequently implemented. With node-level isolation (described later), jobs were required to specify their memory requirements upfront, which warranted intelligent scheduling of high-memory jobs together with regular jobs; the scheduler accordingly acquired such functionality. This was done through reservation of slots on nodes for high-RAM jobs so that they do not become starved while regular jobs come in and take over capacity.

Recovery and Upgrades

The JobTracker was clearly a *single point of failure* for the whole cluster. Whenever a software bug surfaced or a planned upgrade needed to be done, the JobTracker would bring down the whole cluster. Anytime it needed to be restarted, even though the submitted job definitions were persistent in HDFS from the clients themselves, the state of running jobs would be completely lost. A feature was needed to let jobs survive JobTracker restarts. If a job was running at the time when the JobTracker restarted, along with the ability to not lose running work, the user would expect to get all information about previously completed tasks of this job transparently. To address this requirement, the JobTracker had to record and create persistent information about every completed task for every job onto highly available storage.

This feature was eventually implemented, but proved to be fraught with so many race conditions and corner cases that it eventually couldn't be pushed to production because of its instability. The complexity of the feature partly arose from the fact that JobTracker had to track and store too much information—first about the cluster state, and second about the scheduling state of each and every job. Referring to [Requirement 2] Serviceability, the shared MapReduce clusters in a way had regressed compared to HOD with respect to serviceability.

Isolation on Individual Nodes

Many times, tasks of user Map/Reduce applications would get extremely memory intensive. This could occur due to many reasons—for example, due to inadvertent bugs in the users' map or reduce code, because of incorrectly configured jobs that would unnecessarily process huge amounts of data, or because of mappers/reducers spawning children processes whose memory/CPU utilization couldn't be controlled by the task JVM. The last issue was very possible with the Hadoop streaming framework, which enabled users to write their MapReduce code in an arbitrary language that was then run under separate children processes of task JVMs. When this happened, the user tasks would start to interfere with the proper execution of other processes on the node, including tasks of other jobs, even Hadoop daemons like the DataNode and the TaskTracker. In some instances, runaway user jobs would bring down multiple DataNodes on the cluster and cause HDFS downtime. Such uncontrolled tasks would cause nodes to become unusable for all purposes, leading to a need for a way to prevent such tasks from bringing down the node.

Such a situation wouldn't happen with HOD, as every user would essentially bring up his or her own Hadoop MapReduce cluster and each node belonged to only one user at any single point of time. Further, HOD would work with the underlying resource manager to set resource limits prior to the TaskTracker getting launched. This made the entire TaskTracker process chain—the daemon itself together, with the task JVMs *and* any processes further spawned by the tasks themselves—to be bounded. Whatever system needed to be designed to throttle runaway tasks had to mimic this exact functionality.

We considered multiple solutions—for example, the host operating system facilitating user limits that are both static and dynamic, putting caps on individual tasks, and setting a cumulative limit on the overall usage across all tasks. We eventually settled on the ability to control individual tasks by killing any process trees that surpass predetermined memory limits. The TaskTracker uses a default admin configuration or a per-job user-specified configuration, continuously monitors tasks' memory usage in regular cycles, and shoots down any process tree that has overrun the memory limits.

Distributed Cache was another feature that was neatly isolated by HOD. With HOD, any user's TaskTrackers would download remote files and maintain a local cache only for that user. With shared clusters, TaskTrackers were forced to maintain this cache across users. To help manage this distribution, the concepts of a public cache, private cache, and application cache were introduced. A public cache would include public files from all users, whereas a private cache would restrict itself to be per user. An application-level cache included resources that had to be deleted once a job finished. Further, with the TaskTracker concurrently managing several caches at once, several locking problems with regard to the Distributed Cache emerged, which required a minor redesign/reimplementation of this part of the TaskTracker.

Security

Along with enhancing resource isolation on individual nodes, HOD shielded security issues with multiple users by avoiding sharing of individual nodes altogether. Even for a single user, HOD would start the TaskTracker, which would then spawn the map and reduce tasks, resulting in all of them running as the user who had submitted the HOD job. With shared clusters, however, the tasks needed to be run as the job owner for security and accounting purposes, rather than as the user running the TaskTracker daemon itself.

We tried to avoid running the TaskTracker daemon as a privileged user (such as root) to solve this requirement. The TaskTracker would perform several operations on behalf of users, and running it as a privileged user would leak a lot of surface area that was vulnerable to attacks. Ultimately, we solved this problem by creating a setuid executable called **taskcontroller** that would be owned by root but runnable only by the TaskTracker. The TaskTracker would launch this executable with appropriate commands when needed. It would first run as root, do some very basic operations, and then immediately drop privileges by using setuid POSIX call to run the remaining operations as the user. Because this was very platform-specific code, we implemented a TaskController Java abstraction and shipped an implementation for Linux called LinuxTaskController with all the platform-specific code written in C.

The directories and files used by the task also needed to have appropriate permissions. Many of these directories and files were created by the TaskTracker, but were used by the task. A few were written by the user code but then used or accessed by the daemon. For security reasons, the permissions needed to be very strict and readable/writable by only the user or the TaskTracker. This step was done by making the taskcontroller first change the permissions from the TaskTracker to the user, and then letting the task run. Any files that needed to be read by the TaskTracker after the task finished had to have been created with appropriate permissions by the tasks.

Authentication and Access Control

As Hadoop managed more tenants, diverse use-cases, and raw data, its requirements for isolation became more stringent. Unfortunately, the system lacked strong, scalable authentication and an authorization model—a critical feature for multitenant clusters. This capability was added and backported to multiple versions of Hadoop.

A user can submit jobs to one or more MapReduce clusters, but he or she should be authenticated by Kerberos or a delegation mechanism before job submission. A user can disconnect after job submission and then reconnect to get the job status by using the same authentication mechanism. Once such an authenticated user sends requests to the JobTracker, it records all such accesses in an audit log that can be postprocessed for analyzing over time—thereby creating a kind of audit trail.

Tasks run as the user need credentials to securely talk to HDFS, too. For this to happen, the user needs to specify the list of HDFS clusters for a job at job submission either implicitly by input/output paths or explicitly. The job client then uses this list to reach HDFS and obtain credentials on users' behalf. Beyond HDFS, communication with the TaskTracker for both task heartbeats and shuffle by the reduce tasks is also secured through a JobToken-based authentication mechanism.

A mechanism was needed to control who can submit jobs to a specified queue. Jobs can be submitted to only those queues the user is authorized to use. For this purpose, administrators set up **Queue ACLs** before the cluster is initialized. Administrators can dynamically change a queue's ACL to allow a specific user or group to access it at run time. Specific users and groups, called the cluster administrators and queue administrators, are able to manage the ACL on the queue as well to access or modify any job in the queue.

On top of queue-level ACLs, users are allowed to access or modify only their own MapReduce jobs or jobs to which others have given them access via **Job ACLs**. A Job

ACL governs two types of job operations: viewing a job and modifying a job. The web UI also shows information only about jobs run by the current user or about those jobs that are explicitly given access to via Job ACLs.

As one can see, MapReduce clusters acquired a lot of security features over time to manage more tenants on the same shared hardware. This [Requirement 6] Secure and Auditable Operation must be preserved in YARN.

- **[Requirement 6] Secure and Auditable Operation**

  The next-generation compute platform should continue to enable secure and auditable usage of cluster resources.

Miscellaneous Cluster Management Features

So far, we have described in great detail the evolution of the central JobTracker daemon and the individual nodes. In addition to those, HOD made use of a few other useful features in the underlying resource manager such as addition and decommissioning of nodes that needed to be reimplemented in the JobTracker to facilitate cluster management. Torque also exposed a functionality to run an arbitrary program that could dynamically recognize any issues with specific nodes. To replace this functionality, TaskTrackers would run a similar **health-check** script every so often and figure out if a node had turned bad. This information would eventually reach the JobTracker, which would in turn remove this node from scheduling. In addition to taking nodes offline after observing their (poor) health status, heuristics were implemented to track task failures on each node over time and to blacklist any nodes that failed to complete a greater-than-mean number of tasks across jobs.

Evolution of the MapReduce Framework

In addition to the changes in the underlying resource management, the MapReduce framework itself went through many changes. New MapReduce APIs were introduced in an attempt to fill some gaps in the old APIs, the algorithm for running speculative duplicate JVMs to work around slow tasks went through several iterations, and new features like reusing JVMs across tasks for performance were introduced. As the MapReduce framework was tied to the cluster management layer, this evolution would eventually prove to be difficult.

Issues with Shared MapReduce Clusters

Issues with the shared MapReduce clusters developed over time.

Scalability Bottlenecks

As mentioned earlier, while HDFS had scaled gradually over years, the JobTracker had been insulated from those forces by HOD. When that guard was removed, Map-Reduce clusters suddenly became significantly larger and job throughput increased dramatically, but issues with memory management and coarse-grained locking to support many of the features added to the JobTracker became sources of significant scalability bottlenecks. Scaling the JobTracker to clusters containing more than about 4000 nodes would prove to be extremely difficult.

Part of the problem arose from the fact that the JobTracker was keeping in memory data from user jobs that could potentially be unbounded. Despite the innumerable limits that were put in place, the JobTracker would eventually run into some other part of the data structure that wasn't limited. For example, a user job might generate so many counters (which were then not limited) that TaskTrackers would spend all their time uploading those counters. The JobTracker's RPCs would then slow down to a grinding halt, TaskTrackers would get lost, resulting in a vicious circle that ended only with a downtime and a long wild goose chase for the offending application.

This problem would eventually lead to one of the bigger design points of YARN—to not load any user data in the system daemons to the greatest extent possible.

The JobTracker could logically be extended to support larger clusters and heterogeneous frameworks, if only with significant engineering investments. Heartbeat latency could be as high as 200 ms in large clusters, leading to node heartbeat intervals of as much as 40 seconds due to coarse-grained locking of its internal data structures. This problem could be improved with carefully designed fine-grained locking. The internal data structures in the JobTracker were often inefficient but they could be redesigned to occupy less memory. Many of the functions of the JobTracker could also be offloaded to separate, multitenant daemons. For example, serving the status of historical jobs could be—and eventually was—offloaded to the separate service JobHistoryServer. In other words, evolution could ideally continue by iterating on the existing code.

Although logical in theory, this scheme proved infeasible in practice. Changes to the JobTracker had become extremely difficult to validate. The continuous push for ill-thought-out features had produced a working, scalable, but very fragile system. It was time to go back to the drawing board for a complete overhaul. Scalability targets also anticipated clusters of 6000 machines running 100,000 concurrent tasks from 10,000 concurrent jobs, and there was no way the JobTracker could support such a massive scale without a major rewrite.

Reliability and Availability

While the move to shared clusters improved utilization and locality compared to HOD, it also brought concerns for serviceability and availability into sharp focus. Instead of losing a single workflow, a JobTracker failure caused an outage that would lose all of the running jobs in a cluster and require users to manually resubmit and recover their workflows. Upgrading a cluster by deploying a new version of Hadoop in a shared cluster was a rather common event and demanded very careful planning. To fix a bug in the MapReduce implementation, operators would necessarily schedule a cluster downtime, shut down the cluster, deploy the new binaries, validate the upgrade, and then admit new jobs. Any downtime created a backlog in the processing pipelines; when the jobs were eventually resubmitted, they would put a significant strain on the JobTracker. Restarts sometimes involved manually killing users' jobs until the cluster recovered.

Operating a large, multitenant Hadoop cluster is hard. While fault tolerance is a core design principle, the surface exposed to user applications is vast. Given the various availability issues exposed by the single point of failure, it was critical to continuously monitor workloads in the cluster for offending jobs. All of these concerns may be grouped under the need for [Requirement 7] Reliability and Availability.

- **[Requirement 7] Reliability and Availability**

  The next-generation compute platform should have a very reliable user interaction and support high availability.

Abuse of the MapReduce Programming Model

While MapReduce supports a wide range of use-cases, it is not the ideal model for all large-scale computations. For example, many machine learning programs require multiple iterations over a data set to converge to a result. If one composes this flow as a sequence of MapReduce jobs, the scheduling overhead will significantly delay the result. Similarly, many graph algorithms are better expressed using a bulk-synchronous parallel model (BSP) with message passing to communicate between vertices, rather than the heavy, all-to-all communication barrier in a fault-tolerant, large-scale Map-Reduce job. This mismatch became an impediment to users' productivity, but the MapReduce-centricity in Hadoop allowed no other alternative programming model.

The evolution of the software wired the intricacies of MapReduce so deeply into the platform that it took a multiple months' effort to introduce job-level setup and cleanup tasks, let alone an alternative programming model. Users who were in dire need of such alternative models would write MapReduce programs that would spawn their custom implementations—for example, for a farm of web servers. To the central scheduler, they appeared as a collection of map-only jobs with radically different resource curves, causing poor utilization, potentially resource deadlocks, and instability. If YARN were to be the next-generation platform, it must declare a truce with its users and provide explicit [Requirement 8] Support for Programming Model Diversity.

- **[Requirement 8] Support for Programming Model Diversity**

  The next-generation compute platform should enable diverse programming models and evolve beyond just being MapReduce-centric.

Resource Model

Beyond their mismatch with emerging framework requirements, the typed slots on the TaskTrackers harmed utilization. While the separation between map and reduce capacity on individual nodes (and hence the cluster) prevented cross-task-type deadlocks, it also caused bottleneck resources.

The overlap between the map and reduce stages is configured by the user for each submitted job. Starting reduce tasks later increases cluster throughput, while starting them earlier in a job's execution reduces its latency. The number of map and reduce slots are fixed by the cluster administrators, so unused map capacity can't be used to spawn reduce tasks, and vice versa. Because the two task types can potentially (and more often than not do) complete at different rates, no configuration will ever be perfectly ideal. When either slot type becomes completely utilized, the JobTracker is forced to apply back-pressure to job initialization despite the presence of available slots of the other type. Nonstatic definition of resources on individual nodes complicates scheduling, but it also empowers the scheduler to pack the cluster more tightly.

Further, the definition of slots was purely based on jobs' memory requirements, as memory was the scarcest resource for much of this time. Hardware keeps evolving, however, and there are now many sites where CPU has become the most scarce resource, with memory being available in abundance, and the concept of slots doesn't easily accommodate this conundrum of scheduling multiple resources. This highlights the need for a [Requirement 9] Flexible Resource Model.

- **[Requirement 9] Flexible Resource Model**

  The next-generation compute platform should enable dynamic resource configurations on individual nodes and a flexible resource model.

Management of User Logs

The handling of user logs generated by applications had been one of the biggest selling points of HOD, but it turned into a pain point for shared MapReduce installations. User logs were typically left on individual nodes by the TaskTracker daemon after they were truncated, but only for a specific amount of time. If individual nodes died or were taken offline, their logs wouldn't be available at all. Runaway tasks could also fill up disks with useless logs, and there was no way to shield other tasks or the system daemons from such bad tasks.

Agility

By conflating the platform responsible for arbitrating resource usage with the framework expressing that program, one is forced to evolve both structures simultaneously. While cluster administrators try to improve the allocation efficiency of the platform, it is the users' responsibility to help incorporate framework changes into the new structure. Thus, upgrading a cluster should not require users to halt, validate, and restore their pipelines. But the exact opposite thing happened with shared MapReduce clusters: While updates typically required no more than recompilation, users' assumptions about internal framework details or developers' assumptions about users' programs occasionally created incompatibilities, wasting more software development cycles.

As stated earlier, HOD was much better at supporting this agility of user applications. [Requirement 2] Serviceability covered this need for the next-generation compute platform to enable evolution of cluster software completely decoupled from users' applications.

Phase 3: Emergence of YARN

The JobTracker would ideally require a complete rewrite to fix the majority of the scaling issues. Even if it were successful, however, this rewrite would not necessarily resolve the coupling between platform and user code, nor would it address users' appetite for non-MapReduce programming models or the dependency between careful admission control and JobTracker scalability. Absent a significant redesign, cluster availability would continue to be tied to the stability of the whole system.

Building on lessons learned by evolving Apache Hadoop MapReduce, YARN was designed to address the specific requirements stated so far (i.e., Requirement 1 through Requirement 9). However, the massive installed base of MapReduce applications, the ecosystem of related projects, the well-worn deployment practice, and a tight schedule could not tolerate a radical new user interface. Consequently, the new architecture and the corresponding implementation reused as much code from the existing framework as possible, behaved in familiar patterns, and exposed the same interfaces for the existing MapReduce users. This led to the final requirement for the YARN redesign: [Requirement 10] Backward Compatibility.

- **[Requirement 10] Backward Compatibility**

  The next-generation compute platform should maintain complete backward compatibility of existing MapReduce applications.

To summarize the requirements for YARN, we need the following features:

- **[Requirement 1] Scalability**: The next-generation compute platform should scale horizontally to tens of thousands of nodes and concurrent applications.

- **[Requirement 2] Serviceability**: The next-generation compute platform should enable evolution of cluster software to be completely decoupled from users' applications.

- **[Requirement 3] Multitenancy**: The next-generation compute platform should support multiple tenants to coexist on the same cluster and enable fine-grained sharing of individual nodes among different tenants.

- **[Requirement 4] Locality Awareness**: The next-generation compute platform should support locality awareness—moving computation to the data is a major win for many applications.

- **[Requirement 5] High Cluster Utilization**: The next-generation compute platform should enable high utilization of the underlying physical resources.

- **[Requirement 6] Secure and Auditable Operation**: The next-generation compute platform should continue to enable secure and auditable usage of cluster resources.

- **[Requirement 7] Reliability and Availability**: The next-generation compute platform should have a very reliable user interaction and support high availability.

- **[Requirement 8] Support for Programming Model Diversity**: The next-generation compute platform should enable diverse programming models and evolve beyond just being MapReduce-centric.

- **[Requirement 9] Flexible Resource Model**: The next-generation compute platform should enable dynamic resource configurations on individual nodes and a flexible resource model.
- **[Requirement 10] Backward Compatibility**: The next-generation compute platform should maintain completely backward compatibility of existing Map-Reduce applications.

Conclusion

That concludes our coverage of the history and rationale for YARN. We hope that it gives readers a perspective on the various design and architectural decisions that will appear and reappear in the remainder of this book. It should also give an insight into the evolutionary process of YARN; every major decision in YARN is backed up by a sound, if sometimes gory history.

2

Apache Hadoop YARN Install Quick Start

Apache Hadoop presents the user with a vast ecosystem of tools and applications. For those familiar with Hadoop version 1, there are two core components; the Hadoop Distributed File System and the integrated MapReduce distributed processing engine. Hadoop YARN is the new replacement for the monolithic MapReduce component found in version 1. The scheduling and resource management have been separated from the management of MapReduce pipelines. While Hadoop version 2 with YARN still provides full MapReduce capability and backwards compatibility with version 1, it also opens the door to many other "application frameworks" that are not based on MapReduce processing.

The acronym YARN is short for "Yet Another Resource Negotiator," which is a good description of what YARN actually does. Fundamentally, YARN is a resource scheduler designed to work on existing and new Hadoop clusters. The seemingly trivial split of resource scheduling from the MapReduce data flow opens up a whole new range of possibilities for Hadoop and Big Data processing. A separate scheduler allows for better utilization and scalability of the cluster, while simultaneously providing a platform for other non-MapReduce applications to take advantage of the Hadoop Distributed File System and run-time environment. A more detailed discussion of the new Hadoop YARN capabilities can be found in Chapter 3, "Apache Hadoop YARN Core Concepts."

From a larger vantage point, YARN can be viewed as a cluster-wide Operating System that provides the essential services for applications to take advantage of a large dynamic and parallel resource infrastructure. Applications written in any language can now take advantage of the combined Hadoop compute and storage assets within any size cluster.

Although motivated by the needs of large clusters, YARN is capable of running on a single cluster node or desktop machine. The instructions in this chapter will allow you to install and explore Apache Hadoop version 2 with YARN on a single machine.

Getting Started

A production Apache Hadoop system can take time to set up properly and is not necessary to start experimenting with many of the YARN concepts and attributes. This chapter provides a quick start guide to installing Hadoop version Hadoop 2.2.0 on a single machine (workstation, server, or a laptop).

A more complete description of other installation options, such as those required by a production cluster setup, is given in Chapter 5, "Installing Apache Hadoop YARN." Before we begin with the quick start, we will mention a few background details that will help with installation. These items include rudimentary knowledge of Linux, package installation, and basic system administration commands.

A basic Apache Hadoop version 2 system has two core components:

- The Hadoop Distributed File System (HDFS) for storing data
- Hadoop YARN for implementing applications to process data

Other Apache Hadoop components, such as Pig and Hive, can be added after the two core components are installed and operating properly.

Steps to Configure a Single-Node YARN Cluster

The following type of installation is often referred to as "pseudo-distributed" because it mimics some of the functionality of a distributed Hadoop cluster. A single machine is, of course, not practical for any production use, nor is it parallel. A small-scale Hadoop installation can provide a simple method for learning Hadoop basics, however.

The recommended *minimal* installation hardware is a dual-core processor with 2 GB of RAM and 2 GB of available hard drive space. The system will need a recent Linux distribution with Java installed (e.g., Red Hat Enterprise Linux or rebuilds, Fedora, Suse Linux Enterprise, OpenSuse, Ubuntu). Red Hat Enterprise Linux 6.3 is used for this installation example. A bash shell environment is also assumed. The first step is to download Apache Hadoop.

Note that the following commands and files are available for download from the book repository; see Appendix A for details.

Step 1: Download Apache Hadoop

Download the latest distribution from the Hadoop website (http://hadoop.apache.org/). For example, as root do the following:

```
# cd /root
# wget http://mirrors.ibiblio.org/apache/hadoop/common/hadoop-2.2.0/hadoop-
➥2.2.0.tar.gz
```

Next create and extract the package in /opt/yarn:

```
# mkdir -p /opt/yarn
# cd /opt/yarn
# tar xvzf /root/hadoop-2.2.0.tar.gz
```

Step 2: Set JAVA_HOME

For Hadoop 2, the recommended version of Java can be found at http://wiki.apache.
org/hadoop/HadoopJavaVersions. In general, a Java Development Kit 1.6 (or greater)
should work. For this install, we will use Open Java 1.6.0_24, which is part of Red
Hat Enterprise Linux 6.3. Make sure you have a working Java JDK installed; in this
case, it is the Java-1.6.0-openjdk RPM. To include JAVA_HOME for all bash users (other
shells must be set in a similar fashion), make an entry in /etc/profile.d as follows:

```
# echo "export JAVA_HOME=/usr/lib/jvm/java-1.6.0-openjdk-1.6.0.0.x86_64/" > /etc/
➡profile.d/java.sh
```

To make sure JAVA_HOME is defined for this session, source the new script:

```
# source /etc/profile.d/java.sh
```

Step 3: Create Users and Groups

It is best to run the various daemons with separate accounts. Three accounts (yarn,
hdfs, mapred) in the group hadoop can be created as follows:

```
# groupadd hadoop
# useradd -g hadoop yarn
# useradd -g hadoop hdfs
# useradd -g hadoop mapred
```

Step 4: Make Data and Log Directories

Hadoop needs various data and log directories with various permissions. Enter the following lines to create these directories:

```
# mkdir -p /var/data/hadoop/hdfs/nn
# mkdir -p /var/data/hadoop/hdfs/snn
# mkdir -p /var/data/hadoop/hdfs/dn
# chown hdfs:hadoop /var/data/hadoop/hdfs -R
# mkdir -p /var/log/hadoop/yarn
# chown yarn:hadoop /var/log/hadoop/yarn -R
```

Next, move to the YARN installation root and create the log directory and set the
owner and group as follows:

```
# cd /opt/yarn/hadoop-2.2.0
# mkdir logs
# chmod g+w logs
# chown yarn:hadoop . -R
```

Step 5: Configure core-site.xml

From the base of the Hadoop installation path (e.g., /opt/yarn/hadoop-2.2.0),
edit the etc/hadoop/core-site.xml file. The original installed file will have no
entries other than the <configuration> </configuration> tags. Two properties
need to be set. The first is the fs.default.name property, which sets the host and
request port name for the NameNode (metadata server for HDFS). The second is
hadoop.http.staticuser.user, which will set the default user name to hdfs. Copy
the following lines to the Hadoop etc/hadoop/core-site.xml file and remove the
original empty <configuration> </configuration> tags.

```
<configuration>
      <property>
              <name>fs.default.name</name>
              <value>hdfs://localhost:9000</value>
      </property>
      <property>
              <name>hadoop.http.staticuser.user</name>
              <value>hdfs</value>
      </property>
</configuration>
```

Step 6: Configure hdfs-site.xml

From the base of the Hadoop installation path, edit the etc/hadoop/hdfs-site.xml
file. In the single-node pseudo-distributed mode, we don't need or want the HDFS to
replicate file blocks. By default, HDFS keeps three copies of each file in the file system
for redundancy. There is no need for replication on a single machine; thus the value of
dfs.replication will be set to 1.

In hdfs-site.xml, we specify the NameNode, Secondary NameNode, and Data-
Node data directories that we created in Step 4. These are the directories used by the
various components of HDFS to store data. Copy the following lines into Hadoop
etc/hadoop/hdfs-site.xml and remove the original emptytags.

```
<configuration>
 <property>
   <name>dfs.replication</name>
   <value>1</value>
 </property>
 <property>
   <name>dfs.namenode.name.dir</name>
   <value>file:/var/data/hadoop/hdfs/nn</value>
 </property>
 <property>
   <name>fs.checkpoint.dir</name>
   <value>file:/var/data/hadoop/hdfs/snn</value>
 </property>
```

```
<property>
  <name>fs.checkpoint.edits.dir</name>
  <value>file:/var/data/hadoop/hdfs/snn</value>
</property>
<property>
  <name>dfs.datanode.data.dir</name>
  <value>file:/var/data/hadoop/hdfs/dn</value>
</property>
</configuration>
```

Step 7: Configure mapred-site.xml

From the base of the Hadoop installation, edit the etc/hadoop/mapred-site.xml file.
A new configuration option for Hadoop 2 is the capability to specify a framework
name for MapReduce, setting the mapreduce.framework.name property. In this install,
we will use the value of "yarn" to tell MapReduce that it will run as a YARN application. First, copy the template file to the mapred-site.xml.

```
# cp mapred-site.xml.template mapred-site.xml
```

Next, copy the following lines into Hadoop etc/hadoop/mapred-site.xml file and
remove the original empty <configuration> </configuration> tags.

```
<configuration>
<property>
   <name>mapreduce.framework.name</name>
   <value>yarn</value>
 </property>
</configuration>
```

Step 8: Configure yarn-site.xml

From the base of the Hadoop installation, edit the etc/hadoop/yarn-site.xml file.
The yarn.nodemanager.aux-services property tells NodeManagers that there will
be an auxiliary service called mapreduce.shuffle that they need to implement. After
we tell the NodeManagers to implement that service, we give it a class name as the
means to implement that service. This particular configuration tells MapReduce how
to do its shuffle. Because NodeManagers won't shuffle data for a non-MapReduce job
by default, we need to configure such a service for MapReduce. Copy the following
lines to the Hadoop etc/hadoop/yarn-site.xml file and remove the original empty
tags.

```
<configuration>
<property>
   <name>yarn.nodemanager.aux-services</name>
   <value>mapreduce_shuffle</value>
 </property>
<property>
   <name>yarn.nodemanager.aux-services.mapreduce.shuffle.class</name>
```

```
        <value>org.apache.hadoop.mapred.ShuffleHandler</value>
    </property>
</configuration>
```

Step 9: Modify Java Heap Sizes

The Hadoop installation uses several environment variables that determine the heap sizes for each Hadoop process. These are defined in the etc/hadoop/*-env.sh files used by Hadoop. The default for most of the processes is a 1 GB heap size; because we're running on a workstation that will probably have limited resources compared to a standard server, however, we need to adjust the heap size settings. The values that follow are adequate for a small workstation or server.

Edit the etc/hadoop/hadoop-env.sh file to reflect the following (don't forget to remove the "#" at the beginning of the line):

```
HADOOP_HEAPSIZE="500"
HADOOP_NAMENODE_INIT_HEAPSIZE="500"
```

Next, edit mapred-env.sh to reflect the following:

```
HADOOP_JOB_HISTORYSERVER_HEAPSIZE=250
```

Finally, edit yarn-env.sh to reflect the following:

```
JAVA_HEAP_MAX=-Xmx500m
```

The following line will need to be added to yarn-env.sh:

```
YARN_HEAPSIZE=500
```

Step 10: Format HDFS

For the HDFS NameNode to start, it needs to initialize the directory where it will hold its data. The NameNode service tracks all the metadata for the file system. The format process will use the value assigned to dfs.namenode.name.dir in etc/hadoop/hdfs-site.xml earlier (i.e., /var/data/hadoop/hdfs/nn). Formatting destroys everything in the directory and sets up a new file system. Format the NameNode directory as the HDFS superuser, which is typically the "hdfs" user account.

From the base of the Hadoop distribution, change directories to the "bin" directory and execute the following commands:

```
# su - hdfs
$ cd /opt/yarn/hadoop-2.2.0/bin
$ ./hdfs namenode -format
```

If the command worked, you should see the following near the end of a long list of messages:

```
INFO common.Storage: Storage directory /var/data/hadoop/hdfs/nn has been
➥successfully formatted.
```

Step 11: Start the HDFS Services

Once formatting is successful, the HDFS services must be started. There is one service for the NameNode (metadata server), a single DataNode (where the actual data is stored), and the SecondaryNameNode (checkpoint data for the NameNode). The Hadoop distribution includes scripts that set up these commands as well as name other values such as PID directories, log directories, and other standard process configurations. From the bin directory in Step 10, execute the following as user hdfs:

```
$ cd ../sbin
$ ./hadoop-daemon.sh start namenode
```

The command should show the following:

```
starting namenode, logging to /opt/yarn/hadoop-2.2.0/logs/hadoop-hdfs-namenode-
➥limulus.out
```

The secondarynamenode and datanode services can be started in the same way:

```
$ ./hadoop-daemon.sh start secondarynamenode
starting secondarynamenode, logging to /opt/yarn/hadoop-2.2.0/logs/hadoop-hdfs-
➥secondarynamenode-limulus.out
$ ./hadoop-daemon.sh start datanode
starting datanode, logging to /opt/yarn/hadoop-2.2.0/logs/hadoop-hdfs-datanode-
➥limulus.out
```

If the daemon started successfully, you should see responses that will point to the log file. (Note that the actual log file is appended with ".log," not ".out.") As a sanity check, issue a jps command to confirm that all the services are running. The actual PID (Java Process ID) values will be different than shown in this listing:

```
$ jps
15140 SecondaryNameNode
15015 NameNode
15335 Jps
15214 DataNode
```

If the process did not start, it may be helpful to inspect the log files. For instance, examine the log file for the NameNode. (Note that the path is taken from the preceding command.)

```
vi /opt/yarn/hadoop-2.2.0/logs/hadoop-hdfs-namenode-limulus.log
```

All Hadoop services can be stopped using the hadoop-daemon.sh script. For example, to stop the datanode service, enter the following (as user hdfs in the /opt/yarn/hadoop-2.2.0/sbin directory):

```
$ ./hadoop-daemon.sh stop datanode
```

The same can be done for the NameNode and SecondaryNameNode.

Step 12: Start YARN Services

As with HDFS services, the YARN services need to be started. One ResourceManager and one NodeManager must be started as user yarn (exiting from user hdfs first):

```
$ exit
logout
# su - yarn
$ cd /opt/yarn/hadoop-2.2.0/sbin
$ ./yarn-daemon.sh start resourcemanager
starting resourcemanager, logging to /opt/yarn/hadoop-2.2.0/logs/yarn-yarn-
➥resourcemanager-limulus.out
$ ./yarn-daemon.sh start nodemanager
starting nodemanager, logging to /opt/yarn/hadoop-2.2.0/logs/yarn-yarn-
➥nodemanager-limulus.out
```

As when the HDFS daemons were started in Step 1, the status of the running daemons is sent to their respective log files. To check whether the services are running, issue a jps command. The following shows all the services necessary to run YARN on a single server:

```
$ jps
15933 Jps
15567 ResourceManager
15785 NodeManager
```

If there are missing services, check the log file for the specific service. Similar to the case with HDFS services, the services can be stopped by issuing a stop argument to the daemon script:

```
./yarn-daemon.sh stop nodemanager
```

Step 13: Verify the Running Services Using the Web Interface

Both HDFS and the YARN ResourceManager have a web interface. These interfaces are a convenient way to browse many of the aspects of your Hadoop installation. To monitor HDFS, enter the following (or use your favorite web browser):

```
$ firefox http://localhost:50070
```

Connecting to port 50070 will bring up a web interface similar to Figure 2.1.

A web interface for the ResourceManager can be viewed by entering the following:

```
$ firefox http://localhost:8088
```

A webpage similar to that shown in Figure 2.2 will be displayed.

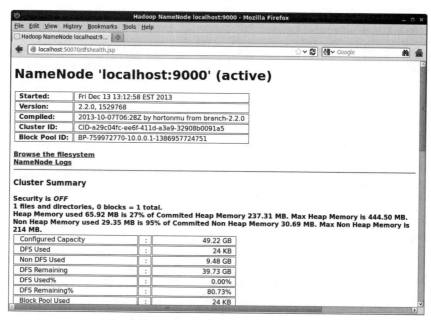

Figure 2.1   Webpage for HDFS file system

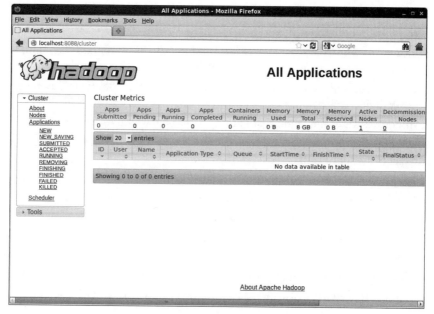

Figure 2.2   Webpage for YARN ResourceManager

Run Sample MapReduce Examples

To test your installation, run the sample "pi" program that calculates the value of pi using a quasi-Monte Carlo method and MapReduce. Change to user hdfs and run the following:

```
# su - hdfs
$ cd /opt/yarn/hadoop-2.2.0/bin
$ export YARN_EXAMPLES=/opt/yarn/hadoop-2.2.0/share/hadoop/mapreduce
$ ./yarn jar $YARN_EXAMPLES/hadoop-mapreduce-examples-2.2.0.jar pi 16 1000
```

If the program worked correctly, the following should be displayed at the end of the program output stream:

```
Estimated value of Pi is 3.14250000000000000000
```

This example submits a MapReduce job to YARN from the included samples in the share/hadoop/mapreduce directory. The master JAR file contains several sample applications to test your YARN installation. After you submit the job, its progress can be viewed by updating the ResourceManager webpage shown in Figure 2.2.

You can get a full list of examples by entering the following:

```
./yarn jar $YARN_EXAMPLES/hadoop-mapreduce-examples-2.2.0.jar
```

To see a list of options for each example, add the example name to this command. The following is a list of the included jobs in the examples JAR file.

- **aggregatewordcount**: An Aggregate-based map/reduce program that counts the words in the input files.
- **aggregatewordhist:** An Aggregate-based map/reduce program that computes the histogram of the words in the input files.
- **bbp:** A map/reduce program that uses Bailey-Borwein-Plouffe to compute the exact digits of pi.
- **dbcount**: An example job that counts the pageview counts from a database.
- **distbbp**: A map/reduce program that uses a BBP-type formula to compute the exact bits of pi.
- **grep:** A map/reduce program that counts the matches to a regex in the input.
- **join:** A job that effects a join over sorted, equally partitioned data sets.
- **multifilewc**: A job that counts words from several files.
- **pentomino:** A map/reduce tile laying program to find solutions to pentomino problems.
- **pi:** A map/reduce program that estimates pi using a quasi-Monte Carlo method.
- **randomtextwriter:** A map/reduce program that writes 10 GB of random textual data per node.

- **randomwriter**: A map/reduce program that writes 10 GB of random data per node.

- **secondarysort**: An example defining a secondary sort to the reduce.

- **sort:** A map/reduce program that sorts the data written by the random writer.

- **sudoku:** A Sudoku solver.

- **teragen:** Generate data for the terasort.

- **terasort:** Run the terasort.

- **teravalidate:** Check the results of the terasort.

- **wordcount:** A map/reduce program that counts the words in the input files.

- **wordmean:** A map/reduce program that counts the average length of the words in the input files.

- **wordmedian:** A map/reduce program that counts the median length of the words in the input files.

- **wordstandarddeviation:** A map/reduce program that counts the standard deviation of the length of the words in the input files.

Some of the examples require files to be copied to or from HDFS. For those unfamiliar with basic HDFS operation, an HDFS quick start is provided in Appendix F. If you were able to complete the preceding steps, you should now have a fully functioning Apache Hadoop YARN system running in pseudo-distributed mode.

Wrap-up

With a working installation of YARN, the concepts, examples, and applications found in this book can be explored further without the need for a large production cluster. Keep in mind that many aspects of the configuration were simplified for this single-machine installation. In particular, a single workstation/server install does not have a true parallel HDFS or parallel MapReduce environment. Additional production installation scenarios are provided in Chapter 5, "Installing Apache Hadoop YARN."

3

Apache Hadoop YARN
Core Concepts

The new Apache Hadoop YARN resource manager is introduced in this chapter. In addition to allowing non–MapReduce tasks to work within a Hadoop installation, YARN ("Yet Another Resource Negotiator") provides several other advantages over the previous version of Hadoop, including better scalability, cluster utilization, and user agility.

YARN also brings with it several new services that separate it from the standard Hadoop MapReduce model. A new ResourceManager acting purely as a resource scheduler is the sole arbitrator of cluster resources. User applications, including Map-Reduce jobs, ask for specific resource requests via the new ApplicationMaster component, which in turn negotiates with the ResourceManager to create an application container within the cluster.

By incorporating MapReduce as a YARN framework, YARN also provides full backward compatibility with existing MapReduce tasks and applications.

Beyond MapReduce

The Apache Hadoop ecosystem continues to grow beyond the simple MapReduce job. Although MapReduce remains at the core of many Hadoop 1.0 tasks, the introduction of YARN has expanded the capability of a Hadoop environment to move beyond the basic MapReduce process.

The basic structure of Hadoop with Apache Hadoop MapReduce version 1 (MRv1) can be seen in Figure 3.1. The two core services, Hadoop File System (HDFS) and MapReduce, form the basis for almost all Hadoop functionality. All other components are built around these services and must use MapReduce to run Hadoop jobs.

Apache Hadoop provides a basis for large-scale MapReduce processing and has spawned a Big Data ecosystem of tools, applications, and vendors. While MapReduce methods enable users to focus on the problem at hand rather than the underlying

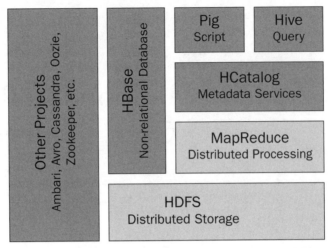

Figure 3.1   The Hadoop 1.0 ecosystem. MapReduce and HDFS are the core components, while other components are built around the core.

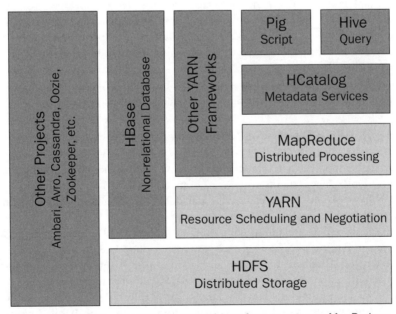

Figure 3.2   YARN adds a more general interface to run non-MapReduce jobs within the Hadoop framework

processing mechanism, they do limit some of the problem domains that can run in the Hadoop framework.

To address these needs, the YARN project was started by the Apache Hadoop community to give Hadoop the ability to run non-MapReduce jobs within the Hadoop framework. YARN provides a generic resource management framework for implementing distributed applications. Starting with Apache Hadoop version 2.0, MapReduce has undergone a complete overhaul; it is now architected as an application on YARN to be called MapReduce version 2 (MRv2). YARN provides both full compatibility with existing MapReduce applications and new support for virtually any distributed application. Figure 3.2 illustrates how YARN fits into the new Hadoop ecosystem.

The introduction of YARN does not change the ability of Hadoop to run MapReduce jobs. It does, however, position MapReduce as merely one of the application frameworks within Hadoop, which works the same way as it did in MRv1. The new capability offered by YARN is the use of new non–MapReduce frameworks that add many new features to the Hadoop ecosystem.

The MapReduce Paradigm

The MapReduce processing model consists of two separate steps. The first step is an embarrassingly parallel map phase, in which input data is split into discrete chunks that can be processed independently. The second step is a reduce phase, in which the output of the map phase is aggregated to produce the desired result. The simple, and fairly restricted, nature of the programming model lends itself to very efficient and extremely large-scale implementations across thousands of low-cost commodity servers (or nodes). When MapReduce is paired with a distributed file system such as Apache Hadoop HDFS, which can provide very high aggregate I/O bandwidth across a large cluster of commodity servers, the economics of the system become extremely compelling—a key factor in the popularity of Hadoop.

One of the keys to Hadoop performance is the *lack of data motion*, such that compute tasks are moved to the servers on which the data reside and not the other way around (i.e., large data movement to compute servers is minimized or eliminated). Specifically, the MapReduce tasks can be scheduled on the same physical nodes on which data reside in HDFS, which exposes the underlying storage layout across the cluster. This design significantly reduces the network I/O patterns and keeps most of the I/O on the local disk or on a neighboring server within the same server rack.

Apache Hadoop MapReduce

To understand the new YARN process flow, it is helpful to review the original Apache Hadoop MapReduce design. As part of the Apache Software Foundation, Apache Hadoop MapReduce has evolved and improved as an open-source project. This project is an implementation of the MapReduce programming paradigm described previously. The Apache Hadoop MapReduce project itself can be broken down into the following major facets:

- The end-user MapReduce API for programming the desired MapReduce application
- The MapReduce run-time, which is the implementation of various phases such as the map phase, the sort/shuffle/merge aggregation, and the reduce phase
- The MapReduce framework, which is the back-end infrastructure required to run the user's MapReduce application, manage cluster resources, and schedule thousands of concurrent jobs, among other things

This separation of concerns has significant benefits, particularly for end-users where they can completely focus on their application via the API and let the combination of the MapReduce run-time and the framework deal with the complex details such as resource management, fault tolerance, and scheduling.

The current Apache Hadoop MapReduce system is composed of several high-level elements, as shown in Figure 3.3. The master process is the JobTracker, which serves as the clearinghouse for all MapReduce jobs on in the cluster. Each node has a Task-Tracker process that manages tasks on the individual node. The TaskTrackers communicate with and are controlled by the JobTracker.

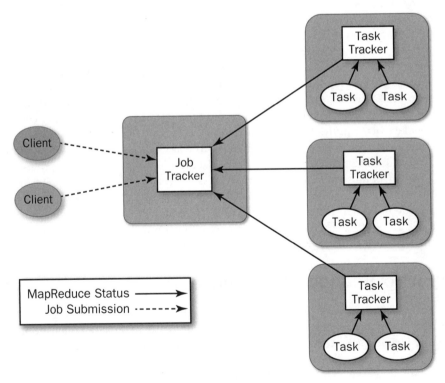

Figure 3.3 Current Hadoop MapReduce control elements

The JobTracker is responsible for *resource management* (managing the worker server nodes—that is, the TaskTrackers), *tracking resource consumption/availability,* and *job life-cycle management* (e.g., scheduling individual tasks of the job, tracking progress, providing fault tolerance for tasks).

The TaskTracker has simple responsibilities—launch/tear down tasks on orders from the JobTracker and provide task status information to the JobTracker periodically.

As described in Chapter 1, the Apache Hadoop MapReduce framework has exhibited some growing pains. In particular, with regard to the JobTracker, several aspects, including scalability, cluster utilization, ability of users to control upgrades to the stack (i.e., user agility), and support for workloads other than MapReduce itself, have been identified as desirable features.

The Need for Non-MapReduce Workloads

MapReduce is great for many applications, but not everything; other programming models better serve requirements such as graph processing (e.g., Google Pregel/Apache Giraph) and iterative modeling using the Message Passing Interface (MPI). As is often the case, much of the enterprise data is already available in Hadoop HDFS, and having multiple paths for processing is critical and a clear necessity. Furthermore, given that MapReduce is essentially batch oriented, support for real-time and near-real-time processing has become an important issue for the user base. A more robust computing environment within Hadoop will enable organizations to see an increased return on their Hadoop investments by lowering operational costs for administrators, reducing the need to move data between Hadoop HDFS and other storage systems, and providing other such efficiencies.

Addressing Scalability

The processing power available in data centers continues to increase rapidly. As an example, consider the additional hardware capability offered by a commodity server over a three-year period:

- 2009: 8 cores, 16 GB of RAM, 4 × 1 TB disk
- 2012: 16+ cores, 72 GB of RAM, 12 × 3 TB of disk

These new servers are often available at the same price point as those of previous generations. In general, servers are twice as capable today as they were two to three years ago—on every dimension. Apache Hadoop MapReduce is known to scale to production deployments of approximately 5000 server nodes of 2009 vintage. Thus, for the same price, the number of CPU cores, amount of RAM, and local storage available to the user will put continued pressure on the scalability of new Apache Hadoop installations.

Improved Utilization

In the current system, the JobTracker views the cluster as composed of nodes (managed by individual TaskTrackers) with distinct map slots and reduce slots, which are not *fungible*. As discussed in Chapter 1, utilization issues occur because maps slots might be "full," while reduce slots are empty (and vice versa). Improving this situation is necessary to ensure the entire system could be used to its maximum capacity for high utilization and applying resources when needed.

User Agility

In real-world deployments, Hadoop is very commonly offered as a shared, multitenant system. As a result, changes to the Hadoop software stack affect a large cross-section of the enterprise, if not the entire enterprise. Against that backdrop, users are very keen to control upgrades to the software stack, as such upgrades have a direct impact on their applications. Thus, allowing multiple, if limited, number of versions of the MapReduce framework is critical for Hadoop.

Apache Hadoop YARN

The fundamental idea of YARN is to split the two major responsibilities of the Job-Tracker—that is, resource management and job scheduling/monitoring—into separate daemons: a global ResourceManager and a per-application ApplicationMaster (AM). The ResourceManager and per-node slave, the NodeManager (NM), form the new, and *generic,* operating system for managing applications in a distributed manner.

The ResourceManager is the ultimate authority that arbitrates division of resources among all the applications in the system. The per-application ApplicationMaster is, in effect, a *framework-specific* entity and is tasked with negotiating for resources from the ResourceManager and working with the NodeManager(s) to execute and monitor the component tasks.

The ResourceManager has a pluggable scheduler component, which is responsible for allocating resources to the various running applications subject to the familiar constraints of capacity, queues, and other factors. The Scheduler is a *pure scheduler* in the sense that it performs no monitoring or tracking of status for the application, offering no guarantees on restarting tasks that are not carried out due to either application failure or hardware failure. The scheduler performs its scheduling function based on the *resource requirements* of an application by using the abstract notion of a *resource container,* which incorporates resource dimensions such as memory, CPU, disk, and network.

The NodeManager is the per-machine slave, which is responsible for launching the applications' containers, monitoring their resource usage (CPU, memory, disk, network), and reporting the same to the ResourceManager.

The per-application ApplicationMaster is responsible for negotiating appropriate resource containers from the Scheduler, tracking their status, and monitoring their progress. From the system perspective, the ApplicationMaster runs as a normal *container.* An architectural view of YARN is provided in Figure 3.4.

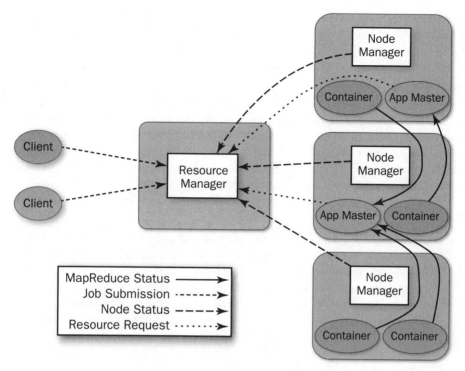

Figure 3.4 New YARN control elements

One of the crucial implementation details for MapReduce within the new YARN system is the reuse of the existing MapReduce framework without any major surgery. This step was very important to ensure compatibility for existing MapReduce applications and users.

YARN Components

By adding new functionality, YARN brings new components into the Apache Hadoop workflow. These components provide finer-grained control for the end-user and simultaneously offer more advanced capabilities to the Hadoop ecosystem.

ResourceManager

As mentioned earlier, the YARN ResourceManager is primarily a *pure scheduler*. It is strictly limited to arbitrating requests for available resources in the system made by the competing applications. It optimizes for cluster utilization (i.e., keeps all resources in use all the time) against various constraints such as capacity guarantees, fairness, and service level agreements (SLAs). To allow for different policy constraints, the ResourceManager has a *pluggable scheduler* that enables different algorithms such as those focusing on capacity and fair scheduling to be used as necessary.

ApplicationMaster

An important new *concept* in YARN is the ApplicationMaster. The ApplicationMaster is, in effect, an *instance* of a *framework-specific library* and is responsible for negotiating resources from the ResourceManager and working with the NodeManager(s) to execute and monitor the containers and their resource consumption. It has the responsibility of negotiating for appropriate resource containers from the ResourceManager, tracking their status, and monitoring progress.

The ApplicationMaster design enables YARN to offer the following important new features:

- Scale: The ApplicationMaster provides much of the job-oriented functionality of the JobTracker so that the entire system can scale more dramatically. Simulations have shown that jobs may scale to 10,000 node clusters composed of modern hardware without significant issue. As a pure scheduler, the ResourceManager does not, for example, have to provide fault tolerance for resources across the cluster. By shifting fault tolerance to the ApplicationMaster instance, control becomes local, rather than global. Furthermore, because an instance of an ApplicationMaster is made available per application, the ApplicationMaster itself is rarely a bottleneck in the cluster.

- Openness: Moving all application framework-specific code into the Application-Master generalizes the system so that it can now support multiple frameworks such as MapReduce, MPI, and Graph Processing.

These features were the result of some key YARN design decisions:

- Move all complexity (to the extent possible) to the ApplicationMaster, while providing sufficient functionality to allow application framework authors sufficient flexibility and power.

- Because it is essentially user code, do not trust the ApplicationMaster(s). In other words, no ApplicationMaster is a privileged service.

- The YARN system (ResourceManager and NodeManager) has to protect itself from faulty or malicious ApplicationMaster(s) and resources granted to them at all costs.

In reality, every application has its own instance of an ApplicationMaster. However, it's completely feasible to implement an ApplicationMaster to manage a set of applications (e.g., ApplicationMaster for Pig or Hive to manage a set of MapReduce jobs). Furthermore, this concept has been stretched to manage long-running services, which manage their own applications (e.g., launching HBase in YARN via a special HBaseAppMaster).

Resource Model

YARN supports a very general resource model for applications. An application (via the ApplicationMaster) can request resources with highly specific requirements, such as the following:

- Resource name (including hostname, rackname, and possibly complex network topologies)
- Amount of memory
- CPUs (number/type of cores)
- Eventually resources such as disk/network I/O, GPUs, and more

ResourceRequests and Containers

YARN is designed to allow individual applications (via the ApplicationMaster) to utilize cluster resources in a shared, secure, and multitenant manner. It also remains aware of cluster topology so that it can efficiently schedule and optimize data access (i.e., reduce data motion for applications to the extent possible).

To meet those goals, the central Scheduler (in the ResourceManager) maintains extensive information about an application's resource needs, which allows it to make better scheduling decisions across all applications in the cluster. This leads us to the ResourceRequest and the resulting container.

Essentially, an application can ask for specific resource requests via the Application-Master to satisfy its resource needs. The Scheduler responds to a resource request by allocating a container, which satisfies the requirements laid out by the Application-Master in the initial ResourceRequest.

A ResourceRequest has the following form:

```
<resource-name, priority, resource-requirement, number-of-containers>
```

These components are described as follows:

- resource-name is either hostname, rackname where the resource is desired, or * to indicate no preference. Future plans may support even more complex topologies for virtual machines on a host, more complex networks, and other features.
- priority is intra-application priority for this request (not across multiple applications). This orders various ResourceRequests within a given application.
- resource-requirement is the required capabilities such as the amount of memory or CPU time (currently YARN supports only memory and CPU).
- number-of-containers is just a multiple of such containers. It limits the total number of containers as specified in the ResourceRequest.

Essentially, the container is the resource allocation, which is the successful result of the ResourceManager granting a specific ResourceRequest. A container grants rights to an application to use a specific amount of resources (e.g., memory, CPU) on a specific host.

The ApplicationMaster must take the container and present it to the NodeManager managing the host, on which the container was allocated, to use the resources for launching its tasks. For security reasons, the container allocation is verified, in the secure mode, to ensure that ApplicationMaster(s) cannot fake allocations in the cluster.

Container Specification

While a container, as described previously, is merely the *right* to use a specified amount of resources on a specific machine (NodeManager) in the cluster, the Application-Master must provide considerably more information to the NodeManager to actually *launch* the container. YARN allows applications to launch any process and, unlike existing Hadoop MapReduce, this ability isn't limited to Java applications.

The YARN container launch specification API is platform agnostic and contains the following elements:

- Command line to launch the process within the container
- Environment variables
- Local resources necessary on the machine prior to launch, such as jars, shared-objects, and auxiliary data files
- Security-related tokens

This design allows the ApplicationMaster to work with the NodeManager to launch containers ranging from simple shell scripts to C/Java/Python processes on UNIX/Windows to full-fledged virtual machines.

Wrap-up

The release of Apache Hadoop YARN provides many new capabilities to the existing Hadoop Big Data ecosystem. While the scalable MapReduce paradigm has enabled previously intractable problems to be efficiently managed on large clustered systems, YARN provides a framework for managing both MapReduce and non-MapReduce tasks of greater size and complexity. YARN provides the framework to apply low-cost commodity hardware to virtually any Big Data problem.

4

Functional Overview of YARN Components

Yarn relies on three main components for all of its functionality. The first component is the ResourceManager (RM), which is the arbitrator of all cluster resources. It has two parts: a pluggable scheduler and an ApplicationManager that manages user jobs on the cluster. The second component is the per-node NodeManager (NM), which manages users' jobs and workflow on a given node. The central Resource-Manager and the collection of NodeManagers create the unified computational infrastructure of the cluster. The third component is the ApplicationMaster, a user job life-cycle manager. The ApplicationMaster is where the user application resides. Together, these three components provide a very scalable, flexible, and efficient environment to run virtually any type of large-scale data processing jobs.

Architecture Overview

The central ResourceManager runs as a standalone daemon on a dedicated machine and acts as the central authority for allocating resources to the various competing applications in the cluster. The ResourceManager has a central and global view of all cluster resources and, therefore, can provide fairness, capacity, and locality across all users. Depending on the application demand, scheduling priorities, and resource availability, the ResourceManager dynamically allocates resource containers to applications to run on particular nodes. A container is a logical bundle of resources (e.g., memory, cores) bound to a particular cluster node. To enforce and track such assignments, the ResourceManager interacts with a special system daemon running on each node called the NodeManager. Communications between the ResourceManager and NodeManagers are heartbeat based for scalability. NodeManagers are responsible for local monitoring of resource availability, fault reporting, and container life-cycle management (e.g., starting and killing jobs). The ResourceManager depends on the NodeManagers for its "global view" of the cluster.

User applications are submitted to the ResourceManager via a public protocol and go through an admission control phase during which security credentials are validated and various operational and administrative checks are performed. Those applications that are accepted pass to the scheduler and are allowed to run. Once the scheduler has enough resources to satisfy the request, the application is moved from an accepted state to a running state. Aside from internal bookkeeping, this process involves allocating a container for the ApplicationMaster and spawning it on a node in the cluster. Often called "container 0," the ApplicationMaster does not get any additional resources at this point and must request and release additional containers.

The ApplicationMaster is the "master" user job that manages all life-cycle aspects, including dynamically increasing and decreasing resources consumption (i.e., containers), managing the flow of execution (e.g., in case of MapReduce jobs, running reducers against the output of maps), handling faults and computation skew, and performing other local optimizations. The ApplicationMaster is designed to run arbitrary user code that can be written in any programming language, as all communication with the ResourceManager and NodeManager is encoded using extensible network protocols (i.e., Google Protocol Buffers, http://code.google.com/p/protobuf/).

YARN makes few assumptions about the ApplicationMaster, although in practice it expects most jobs will use a higher-level programming framework. By delegating all these functions to ApplicationMasters, YARN's architecture gains a great deal of scalability, programming model flexibility, and improved user agility. For example, upgrading and testing a new MapReduce framework can be done independently of other running MapReduce frameworks.

Typically, an ApplicationMaster will need to harness the processing power of multiple servers to complete a job. To achieve this, the ApplicationMaster issues resource requests to the ResourceManager. The form of these requests includes specification of locality preferences (e.g., to accommodate HDFS use) and properties of the containers. The ResourceManager will attempt to satisfy the resource requests coming from each application according to availability and scheduling policies. When a resource is scheduled on behalf of an ApplicationMaster, the ResourceManager generates a lease for the resource, which is acquired by a subsequent ApplicationMaster heartbeat. A token-based security mechanism guarantees its authenticity when the ApplicationMaster presents the container lease to the NodeManager. In MapReduce, the code running in the container can be a map or a reduce task. Commonly, running containers will communicate with the ApplicationMaster through an application-specific protocol to report status and health information and to receive framework-specific commands. In this way, YARN provides a basic infrastructure for monitoring and life-cycle management of containers, while application-specific semantics are managed independently by each framework. This design is in sharp contrast to the original Hadoop version 1 design, in which scheduling was designed and integrated around managing only MapReduce tasks.

Figure 4.1 illustrates the relationship between the application and YARN components. The YARN components appear as the large outer boxes (ResourceManager and NodeManagers), and the two applications appear as smaller boxes (Containers), one

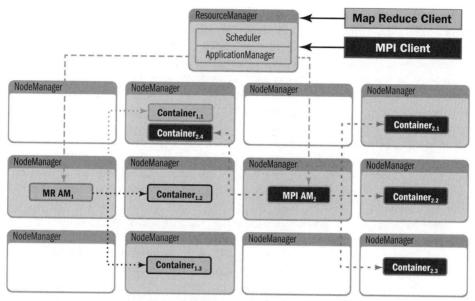

Figure 4.1 YARN architecture with two clients (MapReduce and MPI).
The client MPI AM$_2$ is running an MPI application and the client MR AM$_1$ is
running a MapReduce application.

dark and one light. Each application uses a different ApplicationMaster; the darker client is running a Message Passing Interface (MPI) application and the lighter client is running a MapReduce application.

ResourceManager

As previously described, the ResourceManager is the master that arbitrates all the available cluster resources, thereby helping manage the distributed applications running on the YARN system. It works together with the per-node NodeManagers and the per-application ApplicationMasters.

In YARN, the ResourceManager is primarily limited to scheduling—that is, it allocates available resources in the system among the competing applications but does not concern itself with per-application state management. The scheduler handles only an overall resource profile for each application, ignoring local optimizations and internal application flow. In fact, YARN completely departs from the static assignment of map and reduce slots because it treats the cluster as a resource pool. Because of this clear separation of responsibilities coupled with the modularity described previously, the ResourceManager is able to address the important design requirements of scalability and support for alternative programming paradigms.

In contrast to many other workflow schedulers, the ResourceManager also has the ability to symmetrically request back resources from a running application. This situation typically happens when cluster resources become scarce and the scheduler decides to reclaim some (but not all) of the resources that were given to an application.

In YARN, ResourceRequests can be strict or negotiable. This feature provides ApplicationMasters with a great deal of flexibility on how to fulfill the reclamation requests—for example, by picking containers to reclaim that are less crucial for the computation, by checkpointing the state of a task, or by migrating the computation to other running containers. Overall, this scheme allows applications to preserve work, in contrast to platforms that kill containers to satisfy resource constraints. If the application is noncollaborative, the ResourceManager can, after waiting a certain amount of time, obtain the needed resources by instructing the NodeManagers to forcibly terminate containers.

ResourceManager failures remain significant events affecting cluster availability. As of this writing, the ResourceManager will restart running ApplicationMasters as it recovers its state. If the framework supports restart capabilities—and most will for routine fault tolerance—the platform will automatically restore users' pipelines.

In contrast to the Hadoop 1.0 JobTracker, it is important to mention the tasks for which the ResourceManager is not responsible. Other than tracking application execution flow and task fault tolerance, the ResourceManager will not provide access to the application status (servlet; now part of the ApplicationMaster) or track previously executed jobs, a responsibility that is now delegated to the JobHistoryService (a daemon running on a separated node). This is consistent with the view that the ResourceManager should handle only live resource scheduling, and helps YARN central components scale better than Hadoop 1.0 JobTracker.

YARN Scheduling Components

YARN has a pluggable scheduling component. Depending on the use case and user needs, administrators may select either a simple FIFO (first in, first out), capacity, or fair share scheduler. The scheduler class is set in `yarn-default.xml`. Information about the currently running scheduler can be found by opening the ResourceManager web UI and selecting the Scheduler option under the Cluster menu on the left (e.g., http://your_cluster:8088/cluster/scheduler). The various scheduler options are described briefly in this section.

FIFO Scheduler

The original scheduling algorithm that was integrated within the Hadoop version 1 JobTracker was called the *FIFO* scheduler, meaning "first in, first out." The FIFO scheduler is basically a simple "first come, first served" scheduler in which the Job-Tracker pulls jobs from a work queue, oldest job first. Typically, FIFO schedules have no sense of job priority or scope. The FIFO schedule is practical for small workloads, but is feature-poor and can cause issues when large shared clusters are used.

Capacity Scheduler

The Capacity scheduler is another pluggable scheduler for YARN that allows for multiple groups to securely share a large Hadoop cluster. Developed by the original Hadoop team at Yahoo!, the Capacity scheduler has successfully been running many of the largest Hadoop clusters.

To use the Capacity scheduler, an administrator configures one or more queues with a predetermined fraction of the total slot (or processor) capacity. This assignment guarantees a minimum amount of resources for each queue. Administrators can configure soft limits and optional hard limits on the capacity allocated to each queue. Each queue has strict ACLs (Access Control Lists) that control which users can submit applications to individual queues. Also, safeguards are in place to ensure that users cannot view or modify applications from other users.

The Capacity scheduler permits sharing a cluster while giving each user or group certain minimum capacity guarantees. These minimums are not given away in the absence of demand. Excess capacity is given to the most starved queues, as assessed by a measure of running or used capacity divided by the queue capacity. Thus, the fullest queues as defined by their initial minimum capacity guarantee get the most needed resources. Idle capacity can be assigned and provides elasticity for the users in a cost-effective manner.

Queue definitions and properties such as capacity and ACLs can be changed, at run time, by administrators in a secure manner to minimize disruption to users. Administrators can add additional queues at run time, but queues cannot be deleted at run time. In addition, administrators can stop queues at run time to ensure that while existing applications run to completion, no new applications can be submitted.

The Capacity scheduler currently supports memory-intensive applications, where an application can optionally specify higher memory resource requirements than the default. Using information from the NodeManagers, the Capacity scheduler can then place containers on the best-suited nodes.

The Capacity scheduler works best when the workloads are well known, which helps in assigning the minimum capacity. For this scheduler to work most effectively, each queue should be assigned a minimal capacity that is less than the maximal expected workload. Within each queue, multiple applications are scheduled using hierarchical FIFO queues similar to the approach used with the stand-alone FIFO scheduler. Capacity Scheduler is covered in more detail in Chapter 8, "Capacity Scheduler in YARN."

Fair Scheduler

The Fair scheduler is a third pluggable scheduler for Hadoop that provides another way to share large clusters. Fair scheduling is a method of assigning resources to applications such that all applications get, on average, an equal share of resources over time.

> **Note**
>
> In Hadoop version 1, the Fair scheduler uses the term "pool" to refer to a queue. Starting with the YARN Fair scheduler, the term "queue" will be used instead of "pool." To provide backward compatibility with the original Fair scheduler, "queue" elements can be named as "pool" elements.

In the Fair scheduler model, every application belongs to a queue. YARN containers are given to the queue with the least amount of allocated resources. Within the queue, the application that has the fewest resources is assigned the container. By default, all users share a single queue, called "default." If an application specifically lists a queue in a container resource request, the request is submitted to that queue. It is also possible to configure the Fair scheduler to assign queues based on the user name included with the request. The Fair scheduler supports a number of features such as weights on queues (heavier queues get more containers), minimum shares, maximum shares, and FIFO policy within queues, but the basic idea is to share the resources as uniformly as possible.

Under the Fair scheduler, when a single application is running, that application may request the entire cluster (if needed). If additional applications are submitted, resources that are free are assigned "fairly" to the new applications so that each application gets roughly the same amount of resources. The Fair scheduler also applies the notion of preemption, whereby containers can be requested back from the ApplicationMaster. Depending on the configuration and application design, preemption and subsequent assignment can be either friendly or forceful.

In addition to providing fair sharing, the Fair scheduler allows guaranteed minimum shares to be assigned to queues, which is useful for ensuring that certain users, groups, or production applications always get sufficient resources. When a queue contains waiting applications, it gets at least its minimum share; in contrast, when the queue does not need its full guaranteed share, the excess is split between other running applications. To avoid a single user flooding the clusters with hundreds of jobs, the Fair scheduler can limit the number of running applications per user and per queue through the configurations file. Using this limit, user applications will wait in the queue until previously submitted jobs finish.

The YARN Fair scheduler allows containers to request variable amounts of memory and schedules based on those requirements. Support for other resource specifications, such as type of CPU, is under development. To prevent multiple smaller memory applications from starving a single large memory application, a "reserved container" has been introduced. If an application is given a container that it cannot use immediately due to a shortage of memory, it can reserve that container, and no other application can use it until the container is released. The reserved container will wait until other local containers are released and then use this additional capacity (i.e., extra

RAM) to complete the job. One reserved container is allowed per node, and each node may have only one reserved container. The total reserved memory amount is reported in the ResourceManager UI. A larger number means that it may take longer for new jobs to get space.

A new feature in the YARN Fair scheduler is support for hierarchical queues. Queues may now be nested inside other queues, with each queue splitting the resources allotted to it among its subqueues in a fair scheduling fashion. One use of hierarchical queues is to represent organizational boundaries and hierarchies. For example, Marketing and Engineering departments may now arrange a queue structure to reflect their own organization. A queue can also be divided into subqueues by job characteristics, such as short, medium, and long run times.

The Fair scheduler works best when there is a lot of variability between queues. Unlike with the Capacity scheduler, all jobs make progress rather than proceeding in a FIFO fashion in their respective queues.

Containers

At the fundamental level, a container is a collection of physical resources such as RAM, CPU cores, and disks on a single node. There can be multiple containers on a single node (or a single large one). Every node in the system is considered to be composed of multiple containers of minimum size of memory (e.g., 512 MB or 1 GB) and CPU. The ApplicationMaster can request any container so as to occupy a multiple of the minimum size.

A container thus represents a resource (memory, CPU) on a single node in a given cluster. A container is supervised by the NodeManager and scheduled by the ResourceManager.

Each application starts out as an ApplicationMaster, which is itself a container (often referred to as container 0). Once started, the ApplicationMaster must negotiate with the ResourceManager for more containers. Container requests (and releases) can take place in a dynamic fashion at run time. For instance, a MapReduce job may request a certain amount of mapper containers; as they finish their tasks, it may release them and request more reducer containers to be started.

NodeManager

The NodeManager is YARN's per-node "worker" agent, taking care of the individual compute nodes in a Hadoop cluster. Its duties include keeping up-to-date with the ResourceManager, overseeing application containers' life-cycle management, monitoring resource usage (memory, CPU) of individual containers, tracking node health, log management, and auxiliary services that may be exploited by different YARN applications.

On start-up, the NodeManager registers with the ResourceManager; it then sends heartbeats with its status and waits for instructions. Its primary goal is to manage application containers assigned to it by the ResourceManager.

YARN containers are described by a container launch context (CLC). This record includes a map of environment variables, dependencies stored in remotely accessible storage, security tokens, payloads for NodeManager services, and the command necessary to create the process. After validating the authenticity of the container lease, the NodeManager configures the environment for the container, including initializing its monitoring subsystem with the resource constraints' specified application. The NodeManager also kills containers as directed by the ResourceManager.

ApplicationMaster

The ApplicationMaster is the process that coordinates an application's execution in the cluster. Each application has its own unique ApplicationMaster, which is tasked with negotiating resources (containers) from the ResourceManager and working with the NodeManager(s) to execute and monitor the tasks. In the YARN design, MapReduce is just one application framework; this design permits building and deploying distributed applications using other frameworks. For example, YARN ships with a Distributed-Shell application that allows a shell script to be run on multiple nodes on the YARN cluster.

Once the ApplicationMaster is started (as a container), it will periodically send heartbeats to the ResourceManager to affirm its health and to update the record of its resource demands. After building a model of its requirements, the ApplicationMaster encodes its preferences and constraints in a heartbeat message to the ResourceManager. In response to subsequent heartbeats, the ApplicationMaster will receive a lease on containers bound to an allocation of resources at a particular node in the cluster. Depending on the containers it receives from the ResourceManager, the ApplicationMaster may update its execution plan to accommodate the excess or lack of resources. Container allocation/deallocation can take place in a dynamic fashion as the application progresses.

YARN Resource Model

In earlier Hadoop versions, each node in the cluster was statically assigned the capability of running a predefined number of map slots and a predefined number of reduce slots. The slots could not be shared between maps and reduces. This static allocation of slots wasn't optimal because slot requirements vary during the MapReduce application life cycle. Typically, there is a demand for map slots when the job starts, as opposed to the need for reduce slots toward the end of the job.

The resource allocation model in YARN addresses the inefficiencies of static allocations by providing for greater flexibility. As described previously, resources are requested in the form of containers, where each container has a number of nonstatic attributes. YARN currently has attribute support for memory and CPU. The general-ized attribute model can also support things like bandwidth or GPUs. In the future resource management model, only a minimum and a maximum for each attribute are defined, and ApplicationManagers can request containers with attribute values as mul-tiples of the minimum.

Client Resource Request

A YARN application starts with a client resource request. Figure 4.2 illustrates the initial step in which a client communicates with the ApplicationManager compo-nent of the ResourceManager to initiate this process. The client must first notify the ResourceManager that it wants to submit an application. The ResourceManager responds with an ApplicationID and information about the capabilities of the cluster that will aid the client in requesting resources. This process is shown in Steps 1 and 2 in Figure 4.2.

ApplicationMaster Container Allocation

Next the client responds with a "Application Submission Context" in Step 3. The Application Submission context contains the ApplicationID, user, queue, and other information needed to start the ApplicationMaster. In addition a "Container Launch

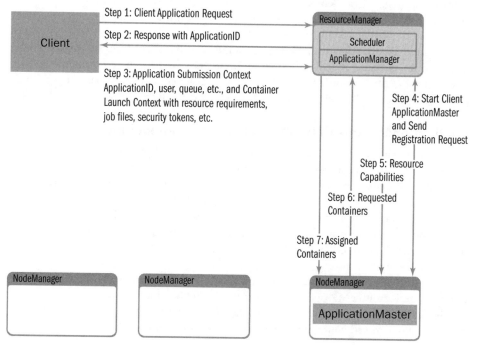

Figure 4.2   Example client resource request to ResourceManager

Context" (CLC) is sent to the ResourceManager. The CLC provides resource requirements (memory/CPU), job files, security tokens, and other information needed to launch an ApplicationMaster on a node. Once the application has been submitted, the client can also request that the ResourceManager kill the application or provide status reports about the application.

When the ResourceManager receives the application submission context from a client, it schedules an available container for the ApplicationMaster. This container is often called "container 0" because it is the ApplicationMaster, which must request additional containers. If there are no applicable containers, the request must wait. If a suitable container can be found, then the ResourceManager contacts the appropriate NodeManager and starts the ApplicationMaster (Step 4 in Figure 4.2). As part of this step, the ApplicationMaster RPC port and tracking URL for monitoring the application's status will be established.

In response to the registration request, the ResourceManager will send information about the minimum and maximum capabilities of the cluster (Step 5 in Figure 4.2). At this point the ApplicationMaster must decide how to use the capabilities that are currently available. Unlike some resource schedulers in which clients request hard limits, YARN allows applications to adapt (if possible) to the current cluster environment.

Based on the available capabilities reported from the ResourceManager, the ApplicationMaster will request a number of containers (Step 6 in Figure 4.2). This request can be very specific, including containers with multiples of the resource minimum values (e.g., extra memory). The ResourceManager will respond, as best as possible based on scheduling policies, to this request with container resources that are assigned to the ApplicationMaster (Step 7 in Figure 4.2).

As a job progresses, heartbeat and progress information is sent from the ApplicationMaster to the ResourceManager (shown in Figure 4.3). Within these heartbeats, it is possible for the ApplicationMaster to request and release containers. When the job finishes, the ApplicationMaster sends a Finish message to the ResourceManager and exits.

ApplicationMaster–Container Manager Communication

At this point, the ResourceManager has handed off control of assigned NodeManagers to the ApplicationMaster. The ApplicationMaster will independently contact its assigned node managers and provide them with a Container Launch Context that includes environment variables, dependencies located in remote storage, security tokens, and commands needed to start the actual process (refer to Figure 4.3). When the container starts, all data files, executables, and necessary dependencies are copied to local storage on the node. Dependencies can potentially be shared between containers running the application.

Once all containers have started, their status can be checked by the ApplicationMaster. The ResourceManager is absent from the application progress and is free to schedule and monitor other resources. The ResourceManager can direct the NodeManagers to kill containers. Expected kill events can happen when the

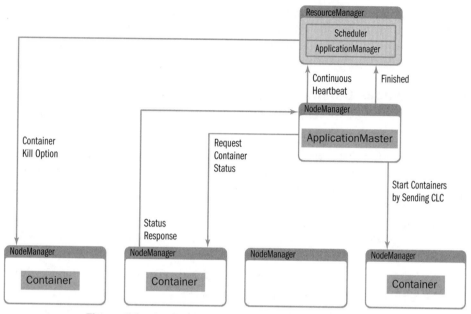

Figure 4.3 ApplicationMaster NodeManager interaction.

ApplicationMaster informs the ResourceManager of its completion, or the Resource-Manager needs nodes for another applications, or the container has exceeded its limits. When a container is killed, the NodeManager cleans up the local working directory. When a job is finished, the ApplicationMaster informs the ResourceManager that the job completed successfully. The ResourceManager then informs the NodeManager to aggregate logs and clean up container-specific files. The NodeManagers are also instructed to kill any remaining containers (including the ApplicationMaster) if they have not already exited.

Managing Application Dependencies

In YARN, applications perform their work by running containers that map to pro-cesses on the underlying operating system. Containers have dependencies on files for execution, and these files are either required at start-up or may be needed one or more times during application execution. For example, to launch a simple Java program as a container, we need a collection of classes and/or a file and potentially more jar files as dependencies. Instead of forcing every application to either access (mostly for reading) these files remotely every time or manage the files themselves, YARN gives the appli-cations the ability to *localize* these files.

When starting a container, an ApplicationMaster can specify all the files that a container will require and, therefore, that should be localized. Once these files are specified, YARN takes care of the localization and hides all the complications involved in securely copying, managing, and later deleting these files.

In the remainder of this section, we'll explain the basic concepts underlying this functionality.

LocalResources Definitions

We will begin with some definitions that will aid in the discussion of application dependencies.

- **Localization:** The process of copying or downloading remote resources onto the local file system. Instead of always accessing a resource remotely, that resource is copied to the local machine, so it can then be accessed locally from that point of time.

- **LocalResource:** The file or library required to run a container. The Node-Manager is responsible for localizing the resource prior to launching the container. For each LocalResource, applications can specify the following:

  - URL: A remote location from where a LocalResource must be downloaded.

  - Size: The size in bytes of the LocalResource.

  - TimeStamp: The last modification of the resource on the remote file system before container start.

  - LocalResourceType: A specific type of a resource localized by the Node-Manager—FILE, ARCHIVE, or PATTERN.

  - Pattern: The pattern that should be used to extract entries from the archive (used only when the type is PATTERN).

  - LocalResourceVisibility: The specific visibility of a resource localized by the NodeManager. The visibility can be either PUBLIC, PRIVATE, or APPLICATION.

A container can request and use any kind of files for localization, provided they are used as read-only by the containers. Typical examples of LocalResources include the following:

- Libraries required for starting the container, such as a jar file.

- Configuration files required to configure the container once started (e.g., remote service URLs, application default configurations).

- A static dictionary file.

The following are some examples of bad candidates for LocalResources:

- Shared files that external components may potentially update in the future and for which current containers wish to track these changes.
- Files that applications themselves directly want to update.
- Files through which an application plans to share the updated information with external services.
- **LocalCache:** The NodeManager maintains and manages several local caches of all the files downloaded. The resources are uniquely identified based on the remote URL originally used while copying that file.

LocalResource Timestamps

As mentioned earlier, NodeManager tracks the last-modification timestamp of each LocalResource before a container starts. Before downloading them, the NodeManager checks that the files haven't changed in the interim. This check ensures a consistent view at the LocalResources—an application can use the very same file contents all the time it runs without worrying about data corruption issues due to concurrent writers to the same file.

Once the file is copied from its remote location to one of the NodeManager's local disks, it loses any connection to the original file other than the URL (used while copying). Any future modifications to the remote file are *not* tracked; hence, if an external system has to update the remote resource, it should be done via versioning. YARN will cause containers that depend on modified remote resources to fail, in an effort to prevent inconsistencies.

Note that the ApplicationMaster specifies the resource timestamps to a Node-Manager while starting any container on that node. Similarly, for the container running the ApplicationMaster itself, the client must populate the timestamps for all the resources that ApplicationMaster needs.

In case of a MapReduce application, the MapReduce JobClient determines the modification timestamps of the resources needed by the MapReduce Application-Master. The ApplicationMaster itself then sets the timestamps for the resources needed by the MapReduce tasks.

LocalResource Types

Each LocalResource can be of one of the following types:

- FILE: A regular file, either textual or binary.
- ARCHIVE: An archive, which is automatically unarchived by the Node-Manager. As of now, NodeManager recognizes jar, tar, tar.gz, and .zip files.

- PATTERN: A hybrid of ARCHIVE and FILE types. The original file is retained, and at the same time (only) part of the file is unarchived on the local file system during localization. Both the original file and the extracted files are put in the same directory. Which contents have to be extracted from the ARCHIVE and which shouldn't be are determined by the pattern field in the LocalResource specification. Currently, only jar files are supported under PATTERN type; all others are treated as a regular ARCHIVE.

LocalResource Visibilities

LocalResources can be of three types depending on their specified LocalResource-Visibility—that is, depending on how visible/accessible they are on the original storage/file system.

PUBLIC

All the LocalResources (remote URLs) that are marked PUBLIC are accessible for containers of any user. Typically PUBLIC resources are those that can be accessed by anyone on the remote file system and, following the same ACLs, are copied into a public LocalCache. If in the future a container belonging to this or any other application (of this or any user) requests the same LocalResource, it is served from the Local-Cache and, therefore, not copied or downloaded again if it hasn't been evicted from the LocalCache by then. All files in the public cache will be owned by "yarn-user" (the user that NodeManager runs as) with world-readable permissions, so that they can be shared by containers from all users whose containers are running on that node.

PRIVATE

LocalResources that are marked PRIVATE are shared among all applications of the same user on the node. These LocalResources are copied into the specific user's (the user who started the container—that is, the application submitter) private cache. These files are accessible to all the containers belonging to different applications, but all started by the same user. These files on the local file system are owned by the user and are not accessible by any other user. Similar to the public LocalCache, even for the application submitters, there aren't any write permissions; the user cannot modify these files once localized. This feature is intended to avoid accidental write operations to these files by one container that might potentially harm other containers. All containers expect each LocalResource to be in the same state as originally specified (mirroring the original timestamp and/or version number).

APPLICATION

All the resources that are marked as having the APPLICATION scope are shared only among containers of the same application on the node. They are copied into the application-specific LocalCache that is owned by the user who started the container (application submitter). All of these files are owned by the user with read-only permissions.

Specifying LocalResource Visibilities

The ApplicationMaster specifies the visibility of a LocalResource to a NodeManager while starting the container; the NodeManager itself doesn't make any decisions or classify resources. Similarly, for the container running the ApplicationMaster itself, the client has to specify visibilities for all the resources that the ApplicationMaster needs.

In case of a MapReduce application, the MapReduce JobClient decides the resource type which the corresponding ApplicationMaster then forwards to a NodeManager.

Lifetime of LocalResources

As mentioned previously, different types of LocalResources have different life cycles:

- PUBLIC LocalResources are not deleted once the container or application finishes, but rather are deleted only when there is pressure on each local directory for disk capacity. The threshold for local files is dictated by the configuration property __yarn.nodemanager.localizer.cache.target-size-mb__, as described later in this section.
- PRIVATE LocalResources follow the same life cycle as PUBLIC resources.
- APPLICATION-scoped LocalResources are deleted immediately after the application finishes.

For any given application, we may have multiple ApplicationAttempts, and each attempt may start zero or more containers on a given NodeManager. When the first container belonging to an ApplicationAttempt starts, NodeManager localizes files for that application as requested in the container's launch context. If future containers request more such resources, then all of them will be localized. If one Application-Attempt finishes or fails and another is started, ResourceLocalizationService doesn't do anything with respect to the previously localized resources. However, when the application finishes, the ResourceManager communicates that information to NodeManagers which in turn clear the application LocalCache. In summary, APPLI-CATION LocalResources are truly application scoped and not ApplicationAttempt scoped.

Wrap-up

The three main yarn components work together to deliver a new level of functionality to Apache Hadoop. The ResourceManager acts as a pure scheduler controlling the use of cluster resources in the form of resource containers (e.g., CPUs, memory). User applications are under the control of an application-specific ApplicationMaster (itself a container) that must negotiate the use of additional containers with the Resource-Manager at run time. Once the ApplicationMaster has been given resources, it works with the per-node NodeManagers to start and monitor containers on the cluster nodes. Containers are flexible and can be released and requested as the application progresses.

To ensure best utilization of the cluster, administrators have three scheduling options: FIFO, capacity, and fair share. These schedulers are used by the Resource-Manager to best match the user needs with the available cluster resources.

LocalResources are new and are a very useful feature that application writers can exploit to declare their start-up and run-time dependencies.

In this new YARN environment, MapReduce does not hold a special place in the workflow because it is "just an application framework" directed by an Application-Master. Other frameworks are available or under development for use in the YARN environment.

5

Installing Apache Hadoop YARN

A cluster-wide installation of Hadoop 2 YARN is necessary to harness the parallel processing capability of the Hadoop ecosystem. HDFS and YARN form the core components of Hadoop version 2. The familiar MapReduce process is still part of YARN, but it has become its own application framework. The installation methods described in this chapter enable you to fully install the base components needed for YARN functionality. Recall that in YARN, the JobTracker has been replaced by the ResourceManager and the per-node TaskTrackers have been replaced by the Node-Manager. The basic HDFS installation using a NameNode and DataNodes remains unchanged.

We describe two methods of installation here: a script-based install and a GUI-based install using Apache Ambari. In both cases, a certain minimum amount of user is input required for successful installation.

The Basics

Of all the many ways to install Hadoop version 2, one of the more involved ways is to simply download the distribution from the Apache Software Foundation (ASF) site. This process requires the creation of a few directories, possibly creation and editing of the configuration files, and maybe even creation of your own scripts. Such a process is a great way to learn the basics of Hadoop administration, but for those wanting a fast and flexible route to Hadoop installation, we present two methods of automated installation in this chapter.

The system requirements for a Hadoop installation are somewhat basic. The installation of the ASF distribution still relies on a Linux file system such as ext3, ext4, or xfs. A Java Development Kit 1.6 (or greater) is required as well. The OpenJDK that comes with most popular Linux distributions should work for most installation procedures. Production systems should have processors, memory, disk, and network sufficient for the production use cases of each organization. To just get started, however, all we need are Linux servers and the right version of Java.

Hadoop 2 offers significant improvements beyond YARN—namely, improvements in the HDFS (Hadoop File System) that can influence infrastructure decisions. Whether to use NameNode federation and NameNode HA (high availability) are the two important decisions that must be made by most organizations. NameNode federation significantly improves the scalability and performance of HDFS by introducing the ability to deploy multiple NameNodes for a single cluster. In addition, HDFS introduces built-in high availability for the NameNode via a new feature called the Quorum Journal Manager (QJM). QJM-based HA features an active NameNode and a standby NameNode. The standby NameNode can become active either by a manual process or automatically. Automatic failover works in coordination with ZooKeeper. Hadoop 2 HDFS introduces the ZKFailoverController, which uses ZooKeeper's election functionality to determine the active NameNode. Other features are also available in HDFS, but a complete description of HDFS installation and configuration is beyond the scope of this book. More information on HDFS options can be found at http://hadoop.apache.org/docs/stable/hdfs_user_guide.html.

For the purposes of describing the YARN installation process, a simple HDFS installation familiar to Hadoop 1 users will be used. It consists of a single NameNode, a SecondaryNameNode, and multiple DataNodes.

System Preparation

Once your system requirements are confirmed and you have downloaded the latest version of Hadoop 2, you will need some information that will make the scripted installation easier. The workhorse of this method is the open-source tool Parallel Distributed Shell (http://sourceforge.net/projects/pdsh), commonly referred to as simply pdsh, which describes itself as "an efficient, multithreaded remote shell client which executes commands on multiple remote hosts in parallel." In simple terms, pdsh will execute commands remotely on hosts specified either on the command line or in a file. As Hadoop is a distributed system that potentially spans thousands of hosts, pdsh can be a very valuable tool for managing systems. Also included in the pdsh distribution is the pdcp command, which performs distributed copying of files. We'll use both the pdsh and pdcp commands to install Hadoop 2.

> **Note**
> The following procedure describes an RPM (Red Hat)-based installation. The scripts described here are available for download from the book repository (see Appendix A), along with instructions for Ubuntu installation.

Step 1: Install EPEL and pdsh

The pdsh tool is easily installed using an existing RPM package. It is also possible to install pdsh by downloading prebuilt binaries or by compiling the tool from its source files. In most cases, this tool will be available through your system's existing software installation or update mechanism. For Red Hat–based systems, this is the yum RPM repository; for SUSE systems, it is the zypper RPM repository.

For the purposes of this installation, we will use Red Hat RPM-based system. A version of the pdsh package is distributed in the Extra Packages for Enterprise Linux (EPEL) repository. EPEL has extra packages not in the standard RPM repositories for distributions based on Red Hat Linux. The following steps, performed as root, are needed to install the EPEL repository the pdsh RPM.

```
# rpm -Uvh http://download.fedoraproject.org/pub/epel/6/i386/epel-release-6-
➥8.noarch.rpm
...
# yum install pdsh
```

Step 2: Generate and Distribute ssh Keys

For pdsh to work effectively, we need to configure "password-less" ssh (secure shell). When pdsh executes remote commands, it will attempt to do so without the need for a password, similar to a user executing an ssh command. The first step is to generate the public and private keys for any user executing pdsh commands (at a minimum, for the root user). On Linux, the OpenSSH package is generally used for this task. This package includes the ssh-keygen command shown later in this subsection. For the easiest installation, as root we execute the ssh-keygen command and accept all the defaults, making sure not to enter a passphrase. If we did specify a passphrase, we would need to enter this passphrase every time we used pdsh or any other tool that accessed the private key.

After generating the keys, we need to copy the public key to the hosts to which we want to log in via ssh without a password. While this might seem like a painstaking task, OpenSSH has the tools to make things easier. The OpenSSH clients package, which is usually installed by default, provides ssh-copy-id, a command that copies a public key to another host and adds the host to the ssh known_hosts file. During an installation using pdsh, we'll want to use the host's fully qualified domain name (FQDN), as this is also the hostname we'll use in Hadoop configuration files.

```
# ssh-keygen -t rsa
...
# ssh-copy-id -i /root/.ssh/id_rsa.pub my.fqdn.tld
...
```

Once pdsh is installed and password-less ssh is working, the following type of command should be possible. See the pdsh man page for more information.

```
# pdsh -w my.fqdn.tld hostname
```

One feature of pdsh that will be useful to us is the ability to use host lists. For example, if we create a file called all_hosts and include the FQDNs of all the nodes in the cluster, then pshd can use this list as follows:

```
# pdsh -w ^all_hosts uptime
```

This feature will be used extensively in the installation script.

Script-based Installation of Hadoop 2

To simplify the installation process, we will use an installation script to perform the series of tasks required for a typical Hadoop 2 installation. The script is available for review in Appendix B, and can serve as a guide to the steps necessary to install Hadoop 2. The script and all other files are also available from the book repository; see Appendix A for details. The installation script is designed to be flexible and customizable to your needs. Modification for your specific needs is encouraged.

Before we begin, there are some assumptions and some prerequisites that you will need to provide. First, we assume that all nodes have a current Red Hat distribution installed (or Red Hat–like distribution). Second, we assume that adequate memory, cores, network, and disk space are available to meet your needs. Best practices for selecting hardware can be found on the web: http://hortonworks.com/blog/best-practices-for-selecting-apache-hadoop-hardware. Finally, we assume that pdsh is working across the cluster.

You will need to choose a version of Hadoop. As of this book's writing, version 2.2.0 was the most current version available from Apache Hadoop's website. To obtain the current version, go to http://hadoop.apache.org/releases.html and follow the links to the current version. For this install, we downloaded hadoop-2.2.0.tar.gz (there is no need to use the "src" version).

JDK Options

There are two options for installing a Java JDK. The first is to install the OpenJDK that is part of the distribution. You can test whether the OpenJDK is installed by issuing the following command. If the OpenJDK is installed, the packages will be listed.

```
# rpm -qa|grep jdk
java-1.6.0-openjdk-devel-1.6.0.0-1.62.1.11.11.90.el6_4.x86_64
java-1.6.0-openjdk-1.6.0.0-1.62.1.11.11.90.el6_4.x86_64
```

Both the base and devel versions should be installed. The other recommended JVM is jdk-6u31-linux-x64-rpm.bin from Oracle. This version can be downloaded from http://www.oracle.com/technetwork/java/javasebusiness/downloads/java-archive-downloads-javase6-419409.html.

If you choose to use the Oracle version, make sure you have removed the OpenJDK from all your systems using the following command:

```
# rpm -e java-1.6.0-openjdk-devel java-1.6.0-openjdk-devel
```

You may need to add the "--nodeps" option to remove the packages. Keep in mind that if there are dependencies on the OpenJDK, you may need to change some settings to use the Oracle JDK.

Step 1: Download and Extract the Scripts

The install scripts and supporting files are available from the book repository (see Appendix A). You can simply use `wget` to pull down the `hadoop2-install-scripts.tgz` file.

As root, extract the file move to the `hadoop2-install-scripts` working directory:

```
# tar xvzf hadoop2-install-scripts.tgz
# cd hadoop2-install-scripts
```

If you have not done so already, download your Hadoop version and place it in this directory (do not extract it). Also, if you are using the Oracle SDK, place it in this directory as well.

Step 2: Set the Script Variables

The main script is called `install-hadoop2.sh`. The following is a list of the user-defined variables that appear at the beginning of this script. You will want to make sure your version matches the `HADOOP_VERSION` variable. You can also change the install path by changing `HADOOP_HOME` (in this case, the path is `/opt`). Next, there are various directories that are used by the various services. The following example assumes that `/var` has sufficient capacity to hold all the Hadoop 2 data and log files. These paths can also be changed to suit your hardware. It is a good idea to keep the default values for `HTTP_STATIC_USER` and `YARN_PROXY_PORT`. Finally, `JAVA_HOME` needs to be defined. If you are using the OpenJDK, make sure this definition corresponds to the OpenJDK path. If you are using the Oracle JDK, then download `jdk-6u31-linux-x64-rpm.bin` to this directly and define `JAVA_HOME` as empty: `JAVA_HOME=""`.

```
# Basic environment variables. Edit as necessary
HADOOP_VERSION=2.2.0
HADOOP_HOME="/opt/hadoop-${HADOOP_VERSION}"
NN_DATA_DIR=/var/data/hadoop/hdfs/nn
SNN_DATA_DIR=/var/data/hadoop/hdfs/snn
DN_DATA_DIR=/var/data/hadoop/hdfs/dn
YARN_LOG_DIR=/var/log/hadoop/yarn
HADOOP_LOG_DIR=/var/log/hadoop/hdfs
HADOOP_MAPRED_LOG_DIR=/var/log/hadoop/mapred
YARN_PID_DIR=/var/run/hadoop/yarn
HADOOP_PID_DIR=/var/run/hadoop/hdfs
HADOOP_MAPRED_PID_DIR=/var/run/hadoop/mapred
HTTP_STATIC_USER=hdfs
YARN_PROXY_PORT=8081
# If using local OpenJDK, it must be installed on all nodes.
# If using jdk-6u31-linux-x64-rpm.bin, then
# set JAVA_HOME="" and place jdk-6u31-linux-x64-rpm.bin in this directory
JAVA_HOME=/usr/lib/jvm/java-1.6.0-openjdk-1.6.0.0.x86_64/
```

Step 3: Provide Node Names

Once you have set the options, it is time to perform the installation. Keep in mind that the script relies heavily on `pdsh` and `pdcp`. If these two commands are not working across the cluster, then the installation procedure will not work. You can get help for the script by running

```
# ./install-hadoop2.sh -h
```

The script offers two options: file based or interactive. In file-based mode, the script needs the following list of files with the appropriate node names for your cluster:

- `nn_host`: HDFS NameNode hostname
- `rm_host`: YARN ResourceManager hostname
- `snn_host`: HDFS SecondaryNameNode hostname
- `mr_history_host`: MapReduce Job History server hostname
- `yarn_proxy_host`: YARN Web Proxy hostname
- `nm_hosts`: YARN NodeManager hostnames
- `dn_hosts`: HDFS DataNode hostnames, separated by a space

If you use the interactive method, the files will be created automatically. If you choose the file-based method, you can edit the files yourself. With exception of `nm_hosts` and `dn_hosts`, all of the files require one hostname. Depending on your installation, some of these hosts may be the same physical machine. The `nm_hosts` and `dn_hosts` files take a space-delimited list of hostnames, which will identify HDFS data nodes and/or YARN worker nodes.

Step 4: Run the Script

After you have checked over everything, you can run the script as follows, using `tee` to keep a record of the install:

```
# ./install-hadoop2.sh -f |tee install-hadoop2-results
```

Some steps may take longer than others. If everything worked correctly, a MapReduce job (the classic "calculate pi" example) will be run. If it is successful, the installation process is complete. You may wish to install other tools like Pig, Hive, or HBase as well. For your reference, the script does the following:

1. Copies the Hadoop tar file to all hosts.
2. Optionally copies and installs Oracle JDK 1.6.0_31 to all hosts.
3. Sets the `JAVA_HOME` and `HADOOP_HOME` environment variables on all hosts.
4. Extracts the Hadoop distribution on all hosts.
5. Creates system accounts and groups on all hosts (Group: hadoop, Users: yarn, hdfs, and mapred).
6. Creates HDFS data directories on the NameNode host, SecondaryNameNode host, and DataNode hosts.

7. Creates log directories on all hosts.

8. Creates pid directories on all hosts.

9. Edits Hadoop environment scripts for log directories on all hosts.

10. Edits Hadoop environment scripts for pid directories on all hosts.

11. Creates the base Hadoop XML config files (core-site.XML, hdfs-site.XML, mapred-site.XML, yarn-site.XML).

12. Copies the base Hadoop XML config files to all hosts.

13. Creates configuration, command, and script links on all hosts.

14. Formats the NameNode.

15. Copies start-up scripts to all hosts (hadoop-datanode, hadoop-historyserver, hadoop-namenode, hadoop-nodemanager, hadoop-proxyserver, hadoop-resourcemanager, and hadoop-secondarynamenode).

16. Starts Hadoop services on all hosts.

17. Creates MapReduce Job History directories.

18. Runs the YARN pi MapReduce job.

Step 5: Verify the Installation

There are a few points in the script-based installation process where problems may occur. One important step is formatting the NameNode (Step 14 in the preceding list). The results of this command will show up in the script output. Make sure there were no errors with this command.

If you note other errors, such as when starting the Hadoop daemons, check the log files located under $HADOOP_HOME/logs. The final part of the script runs the following example "pi" MapReduce job command.

```
hadoop jar \
$HADOOP_HOME/share/hadoop/mapreduce/hadoop-mapreduce-examples-$HADOOP_VERSION.jar \
pi -Dmapreduce.clientfactory.class.name=org.apache.hadoop.mapred.YarnClientFactory \
-libjars $HADOOP_HOME/share/hadoop/mapreduce/hadoop-mapreduce-client-jobclient-
➥$HADOOP_VERSION.jar \
16 10000
```

If this test is successful, you should see the following at the end of the output. (Your run-time time will vary.)

```
Job Finished in 25.854 seconds
Estimated value of Pi is 3.14127500000000000000
```

You can also examine the HDFS file system using the following command:

```
# hdfs dfs -ls /
Found 6 items
drwxr-xr-x   - hdfs   hdfs        0 2013-02-06 21:17 /apps
drwxr-xr-x   - hdfs   hadoop      0 2013-02-06 22:26 /benchmarks
```

```
drwx------   - mapred hdfs       0 2013-04-25 16:20 /mapred
drwxr-xr-x   - hdfs   hdfs       0 2013-05-16 11:53 /system
drwxrwxr--   - hdfs   hadoop     0 2013-05-14 14:54 /tmp
drwxrwxr-x   - hdfs   hadoop     0 2013-04-26 02:00 /user
```

Similar to Hadoop version 1, many aspects of Hadoop version 2 are available via the built-in web UI. The web UI can be accessed by directly accessing the following URL in your favorite browser or by issuing the following command as the user hdfs (using your local *hostname*):

```
$ firefox http://hostname:8088/cluster
```

An example of the UI is shown in Figure 5.1.

The test job should be listed in the UI window. You can find out about the job history by clicking the History link on the right side of the job summary. When you do so, the window shown in Figure 5.2 should be displayed.

To check the status of the your parallel file system, enter *hostname*:50070 into the browser. A page similar to Figure 5.3 should be displayed.

> **Note**
>
> The output with Hadoop version 2.2.0 may look slightly different than it does in Figures 5.1, 5.2, and 5.3.

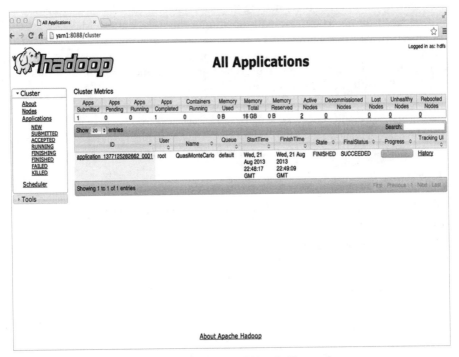

Figure 5.1 YARN web UI

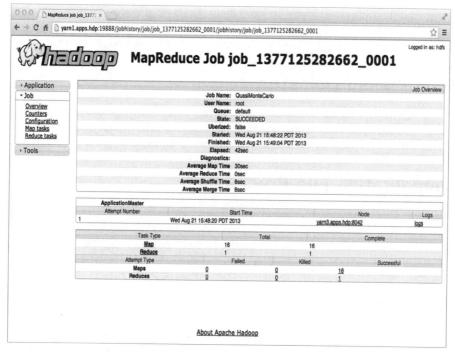

Figure 5.2   YARN pi example job history

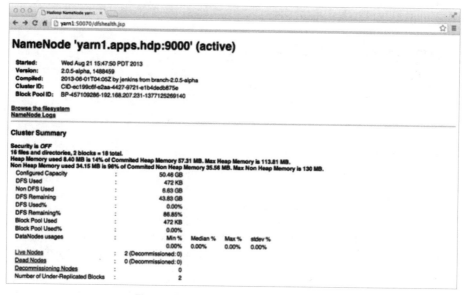

Figure 5.3   HDFS NameNode web UI

If the HDFS file system looks fine and there are no dead nodes, then your Hadoop cluster should be fully functional. You can investigate other aspects of your Hadoop 2 cluster by exploring some of the links on both the HDFS and YARN UI pages.

Script-based Uninstall

To uninstall the Hadoop2 installation, use the `uninstall-hadoop2.sh` script. Make sure any changes you made to the `install-hadoop2.sh` script, such as the Hadoop version number (`HADOOP_VERSION`), are copied to the uninstall script.

Configuration File Processing

The install script provides some commands that you will find useful for processing Hadoop XML files. If you examine the `install-hadoop2.sh` script, you should notice that several commands are used to create the Hadoop XML configuration files:

```
create_config() --file filename
put_config --file filename --property-property pname --value pvalue
del_config()--file filename --property-property pname
```

where `filename` is the name of the XML file, `pname` is the property to be defined, and `pvalue` is the actual value. The functions are defined in `hadoop-xml-conf.sh`, which is part of the `hadoop2-install-scripts.tgz` archive. See the book repository (Appendix A) for download instructions. Basically, these scripts facilitate the creation of Hadoop XML configuration files. If you want to customize the installation or make changes to the XML files, these scripts may be useful.

Configuration File Settings

The following is a brief description of the settings specified in the Hadoop configuration files by the installation script. These files are located in `$HADOOP_HOME/etc/hadoop`.

core-site.xml

In this file, we define two essential properties for the entire system.

```
hdfs://$nn:9000 --> fs.default.name
$HTTP_STATIC_USER --> hadoop.http.staticuser.user
```

First, we define the name of the default file system we wish to use. Because we are using HDFS, we will set this value to `hdfs://$nn:9000` ($nn is the NameNode

we specified in the script and 9000 is the standard HDFS port). Next we add the
`hadoop.http.staticuser.user` (hdfs) that we defined in the install script. This login
is used as the default user for the built-in web user interfaces.

hdfs-site.xml

The `hdfs-site.xml` file holds information about the Hadoop HDFS file system. Most
of these values were set at the beginning of the script. They are copied as follows:

```
$NN_DATA_DIR --> dfs.namenode.name.dir
$SNN_DATA_DIR --> fs.checkpoint.dir
$SNN_DATA_DIR --> fs.checkpoint.edits.dir
$DN_DATA_DIR --> dfs.datanode.data.dir
```

The remaining two values are set to the standard default port numbers ($nn is the
NameNode and $snn is the SecondaryNameNode we input to the script):

```
$nn:50070 --> dfs.namenode.http-address
$snn:50090 --> dfs.namenode.secondary.http-address
```

mapred-site.xml

Users who are familiar with Hadoop version 1 may notice that this is a known configuration file. Given that MapReduce is just another YARN framework, it needs its
own configuration file. The script specifies the following settings:

```
yarn --> mapreduce.framework.name
$mr_hist:10020 --> mapreduce.jobhistory.address
$mr_hist:19888 --> mapreduce.jobhistory.webapp.address
/mapred --> yarn.app.mapreduce.am.staging-dir
```

The first property is `mapreduce.framework.name`. For this property, there are three
valid values: local (default), classic, or yarn. Specifying "local" for this value means
that the MapReduce Application is run locally in a process on the client machine,
without using any cluster resources. This local process will execute the map and
reduce tasks for a given job; because it is local, it doesn't need to shuffle data from map
task output on one server to reduce task input on another server. Typically, this means
that there will be one map task and one reduce task.

Specifying "classic" for the `mapreduce.framework.name` property is appropriate
when there is a Hadoop 1.x JobTracker running in your cluster where Hadoop can
submit the job. This property exists to accommodate unforeseen situations where there
are backward-compatibility problems with users' MapReduce jobs and the need for a
classic job submission process to a JobTracker is unavoidable.

As we are interested in using yarn, we will set `mapreduce.framework.name` to
"yarn" and use the new MapReduce framework provided by YARN.

The next two properties, `mapreduce.jobhistory.address` and `mapreduce`
`.jobhistory.webapp.address`, may seem similar but have some subtle differences. The `mapreduce.jobhistory.address` property is the host and port where
the MapReduce application will send job history via its own internal protocol. The
`mapreduce.jobhistory.webapp.address` is where an administrator or a user can view
the details of MapReduce jobs that have completed.

Finally, we specify a property for a MapReduce staging directory. When a Map-
Reduce job is submitted to YARN, the MapReduce ApplicationMaster will create
temporary data in HDFS for the job and will need a staging area for this data. The
property `yarn.app.mapreduce.am.staging-dir` is where we designate such a directory in HDFS (i.e., `/mapred`).

This staging area will also be used by the job history server. The installation
script will make sure that the proper permissions and subdirectories are created (i.e.,
`/mapred/history/done_intermediate`).

yarn-site.xml

The final configuration file is `yarn-site.xml`. The script sets the following values:

```
mapreduce.shuffle --> yarn.nodemanager.aux-services
org.apache.hadoop.mapred.ShuffleHandler --> yarn.nodemanager.aux-
➥services.mapreduce.shuffle.class
$yarn_proxy:$YARN_PROXY_PORT --> yarn.web-proxy.address
$rmgr:8030 --> yarn.resourcemanager.scheduler.address
$rmgr:8031 --> yarn.resourcemanager.resource-tracker.address
$rmgr:8032 --> yarn.resourcemanager.address
$rmgr:8033 --> yarn.resourcemanager.admin.address
$rmgr:8088 --> yarn.resourcemanager.webapp.address
```

The `yarn.nodemanager.aux-services` property tells the NodeManager that a
MapReduce container will have to do a shuffle from the map tasks to the reduce tasks.
Previously, the shuffle step was part of the monolithic MapReduce TaskTracker. With
YARN, the shuffle is an auxiliary service and must be set in the configuration file.
In addition, the `yarn.nodemanager.aux-services.mapreduce.shuffle.class` property tells YARN which class to use to do the actual shuffle. The class we use for the
shuffle handler is `org.apache.hadoop.mapred.ShuffleHandler`. Although it's possible
to write your own shuffle handler by extending this class, it is recommended that the
default class be used.

The next property is the `yarn.web-proxy.address`. This property is part of the
installation process because we decided to run the YARN Proxy Server as a separate
process. If we didn't configure it this way, the Proxy Server would run as part of the
ResourceManager process. The Proxy Server aims to lessen the possibility of security
issues. An ApplicationMaster will send to the ResourceManager a link for the application's web UI but, in reality, this link can point anywhere. The YARN Proxy Server
lessens the risk associated with this link, but it doesn't eliminate it.

The remaining settings are the default ResourceManager port addresses.

Start-up Scripts

The Hadoop distribution includes a lot of convenient scripts to start and stop services such as the ResourceManager and NodeManagers. In a production cluster, however, we want the ability to integrate our scripts with the system's services management. On most Linux systems today, that means integrating with the init system.

Instead of relying on the built-in scripts that ship with Hadoop, we provide a set of init scripts that can be placed in /etc/init.d and used to start, stop, and monitor the Hadoop services. The files are as follows, with each service being identified by name:

```
hadoop-namenode
hadoop-datanode
hadoop-secondarynamenode
hadoop-resourcemanager
hadoop-nodemanager
hadoop-proxyserver
hadoop-historyserver
```

Of course, not all services run on all nodes; thus the installation script places the correct files on the requisite nodes. Before starting the service, the script also registers each service with chkconfig. Once these services are installed, they can be easily managed with commands like the following:

```
# service hadoop-namenode start
# hadoop-resourcemanager status
# hadoop-proxyserver restart
# hadoop-historyserver stop
```

Installing Hadoop with Apache Ambari

A script-based manual Hadoop installation can turn out to be a challenging process as it scales out from tens of nodes to thousands of nodes. Because of this complexity, a tool with the ability to manage installation, configuration, and monitoring of the Hadoop cluster became a much-needed addition to the Hadoop ecosystem. Apache Ambari provides the means to handle these simple, yet highly valuable tasks by utilizing an agent on each node to install required components, change configuration files, and monitor performance or failures of nodes either individually or as an aggregate. Both administrators and developers will find many of the Ambari features useful.

Installation with Ambari is faster, easier, and less error prone than manually setting up each service's configuration file. As an example, a 12-node cluster install of Hortonworks HDP2.X services (HDFS, MRv2, YARN, Hive, Sqoop, ZooKeeper, HCatalog, Oozie, HBase, and Pig) was accomplished in less than one hour with this tool. Ambari can dramatically cut down on the number of people required to install large clusters and increase the speed with which development environments can be created.

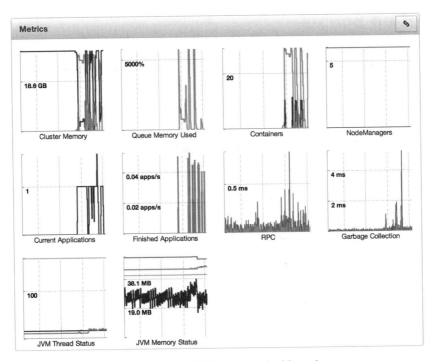

Figure 5.4   YARN metrics dashboard

Configuration files are maintained by an Ambari server acting as the primary inter-face to make changes to the cluster. Ambari guarantees that the configuration files on all nodes are the same by automatically redistributing them to the nodes every time a service's configuration changes. From an operational perspective, this approach pro-vides peace of mind; you know that the entire cluster—from 10 to 4000-plus nodes—is always in sync. For developers, it allows for rapid performance tuning because the configuration files can be easily manipulated.

Monitoring encompasses the starting and stopping of services, along with reporting on whether a service is up or down, network usage, HDFS, YARN, and a multitude of other load metrics. Ganglia and Nagios report back to the Ambari server monitor-ing cluster health on issues ranging from utilization of services such as HDFS storage to failures of stack components or entire nodes. Users can also take advantage of the ability to monitor a number of YARN metrics such as cluster memory, total contain-ers, NodeManagers, garbage collection, and JVM metrics. An example of the Ambari dashboard is shown in Figure 5.4.

Performing an Ambari-based Hadoop Installation

Compared to a manual installation of Hadoop 2, when using Ambari there are signifi-cantly fewer software requirements and operating system tasks like creating users or groups and directory structures to perform. To manage the cluster with Ambari, we install two components:

1. The Ambari-Server, which should be its own node separate from the rest of the cluster

2. An Ambari-Agent on each node of the rest of the cluster that requires managing

For the purposes of this installation, we will reference the HDP 2.0 (Hortonworks Data Platform) documentation for the Ambari Automated Install (see http://docs. hortonworks.com/#2.0 for additional information). In addition, although Ambari may eventually work with other Hadoop installations, we will use the freely available HDP version to ensure a successful installation.

Step 1: Check Requirements

As of this writing, RHEL 5 and 6, CentOS 5 and 6, OEL (Oracle Enterprise Linux) 5 and 6, and SLS 11 are supported by HDP 2, however Ubuntu is not supported at this time. Ensure that each node has yum, rpm, scp, curl, and wget. Additionally, ntpd should be running. Hive/HCatalog, Oozie, and Ambari all require their own internal databases; we can control these databases during installation, but they will need to be installed. If your cluster nodes do not have access to the Internet, you will have to mirror the HDP repository and set up your own local repositories.

Step 2: Install the Ambari Server

Perform the following actions to download the Ambari repository, add it to your existing yum.repos.d on the server node, and install the packages:

```
# wget http://public-repo-1.hortonworks.com/ambari-beta/centos6/1.x/beta/ambari.repo
# cp ambari.repo /etc/yum.repos.d
# yum -y install ambari-server
```

Next we set up the server. At this point, you can decide whether you want to customize the Ambari-Server database; the default is PostgreSQL. You will also be prompted to accept the JDK license unless you specify the --java-home option with the path of the JDK on all nodes in the cluster. For this installation, we will use the default values as signified by the silent install option. If the following command is successful, you should see "Ambari Server 'setup' completed successfully."

```
# ambari-server setup --silent
```

Step 3: Install and Start Ambari Agents

Most of today's current enterprise security divisions have a hard time accepting some of Hadoop's more unusual requirements, such as root password-less ssh between all nodes in the cluster. Root password-less ssh is used only to automate installation of the Ambari agents and is not required for day-to-day operation. To stay within many security guidelines, we will be performing a manual install of the Ambari-Agent on each node in the cluster. Be sure to set up the repository files on each node as described in Step 2. Optionally, you can use `pdsh` and `pdcp` with password-less root to help automate the installation of Ambari agents across the cluster. To install the agent, enter the following for each node:

```
# yum -y install ambari-agent
```

Next, configure the Ambari-Agent ini file with the FQDN of the Ambari-Server. By default, this value is localhost. This task can be done using `sed`.

```
# sed -i 's/hostname=localhost/hostname=yourAmbariServerFQDNhere/g' /etc/ambari-
➥agent/conf/ambari-agent.ini
```

On all nodes, start Ambari with the following command:

```
# ambari-agent start
```

Step 4: Start the Ambari Server

To start the Ambari-Server, enter

```
# ambari-server start
```

Log into the Ambari-Server web console using http://AmbariServerFQDN:8080. If everything is working properly, you should see the login screen shown in Figure 5.5. The default login is username = admin and password = admin.

Figure 5.5 Ambari sign-in screen

Step 5: Install an HDP2.X Cluster

The first task is to name your cluster.

1. Enter a name for your cluster and click the green "Next" button (see Figure 5.6).

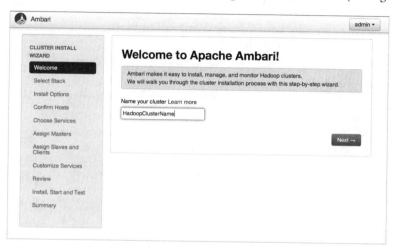

Figure 5.6   Enter a cluster name

2. The next option is to select the version of the HDP software stack. Currently the options include only the recent version of HDP. Select the 2.X stack option and click Next as shown in Figure 5.7.

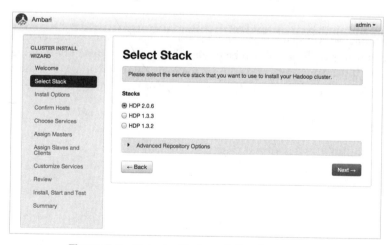

Figure 5.7   Select a Hadoop 2.X software stack

3. Next, Ambari will ask for your list of nodes, one per line, and ask you to select manual or private key registration. In this installation, we are using the manual method (see Figure 5.8).

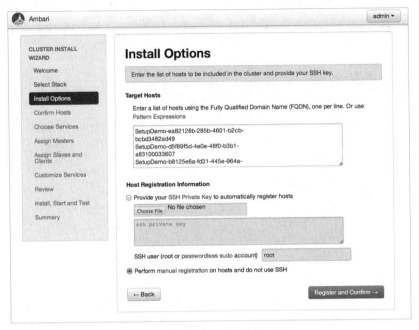

Figure 5.8   Hadoop install options

The installed Ambari-Agents should register with the Ambari-Server at this point. Any install warnings will also be displayed here, such as ntpd not running on the nodes. If there are issues or warnings, the registration window will indicate these as shown in Figure 5.9. Note that the example is installing a "cluster" of one node.

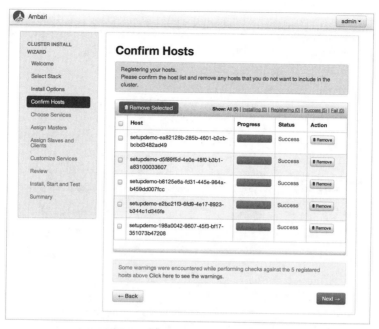

Figure 5.9   Ambari host registration screen

If everything is set correctly, your window should look like Figure 5.10.

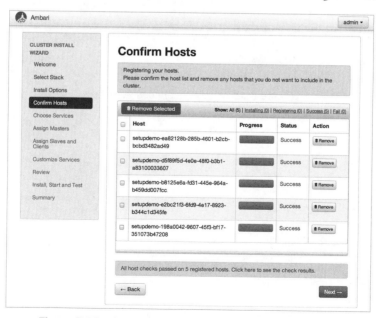

Figure 5.10   Successful Ambari host registration screen

4. The next step is to select which components of the HDP2.X stack you want
   to install. At the very least, you will want to install HDFS, YARN, and
   MapReduceV2. In Figure 5.11, we will install everything.

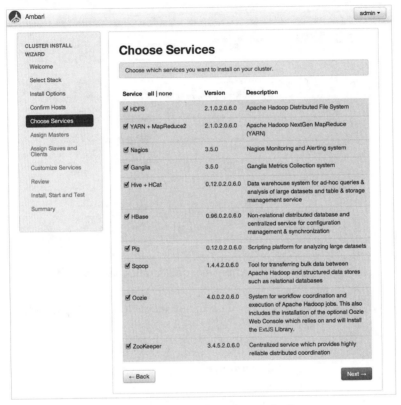

Figure 5.11 Ambari services selection

5. The next step is to assign functions to the various nodes in your cluster (see Figure 5.12). The Assign Masters window allows for the selection of master nodes—that is, NameNode, ResourceManager, HBaseMaster, Hive Server, Oozie Server, etc. All nodes that have registered with the Ambari-Server will be available in the drop-down selection box. Remember that the ResourceManager has replaced the JobTracker from Hadoop version 1 and in a multi-node installation should always be given its own dedicated node.

Figure 5.12   Ambari host assignment

6. In this step, you assign NodeManagers (which run YARN containers), Region-Servers, and DataNodes (HDFS). Remember that the NodeManager has replaced the TaskTracker from Hadoop version 1, so you should always co-locate one of these node managers with a DataNode to ensure that local data is available for YARN containers. The selection window is shown in Figure 5.13. Again, this example has only a single node.

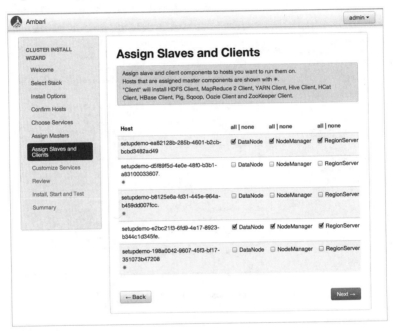

Figure 5.13   Ambari slave and client component assignment

7. The next set of screens allows you to define any initial parameter changes and usernames for the services selected for installation (i.e., Hive, Oozie, and Nagios). Users are required to set up the database passwords and alert reporting email before continuing. The Hive database setup is pictured in Figure 5.14.

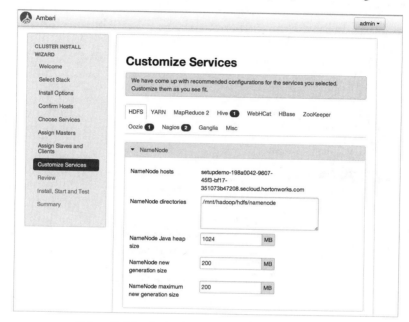

Figure 5.14   Ambari customized services window

8. The final step before installing Hadoop is a review of your configuration. Figure 5.15 summarizes the actions that are about to take place. Be sure to double-check all settings before you commit to an install.

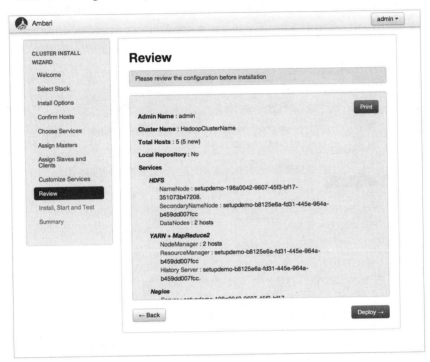

Figure 5.15   Ambari final review window

9. During the installation step shown in Figure 5.16, the cluster is actually provisioned with the various software packages. By clicking on the node name, you can drill down into the installation status of every component. Should the installation encounter any errors on specific nodes, these errors will be highlighted on this screen.

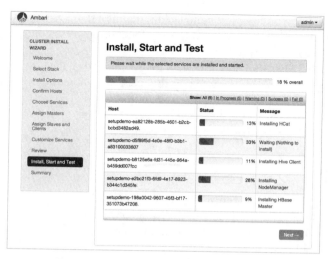

Figure 5.16 Ambari deployment process

10. Once the installation of the nodes is complete, a summary window similar to Figure 5.17 will be displayed. The screen indicates which tasks were completed and identifies any preliminary testing of cluster services.

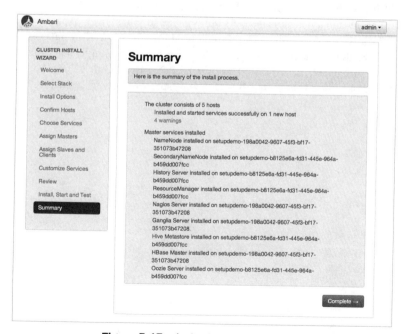

Figure 5.17 Ambari summary window

Congratulations! You have just completed installing HDP2.X with Ambari. Consult the online Ambari documentation (http://docs.hortonworks.com/#2) for further details on the installation process.

If you are using Hive and have a FQDN longer than 60 characters (as is common in some cloud deployments), please note that this can cause authentication issues with the MySQL database that Hive installs by default with Ambari. To work around this issue, start the MySQL database with the "--skip-name-resolve" option to disable FQDN resolution and authenticate based only on IP number.

Wrap-up

It is possible to perform an automated script-based install of moderate to very large clusters. The use of parallel distributed shell and copy commands (pdsh and pdcp, respectively) makes a fully remote installation on any number of nodes possible. The script-based install process is designed to be flexible, and users can easily modify it for their specific needs on Red Hat (and derivative)–based distributions.

In addition to the install script, some useful functions for creating and changing the Hadoop XML property files are made available to users. To aid with start-up and shutdown of Hadoop services, the scripted install also provides SysV init scripts for Red Hat–based systems.

Finally, a graphical install process using Apache Ambari was described in this chapter. With Ambari, the entire Hadoop installation process can be automated with a powerful point-and-click interface. As we will see in Chapter 6, "Apache Hadoop YARN Administration," Ambari can also be used for administration purposes.

Installing Hadoop 2 YARN from scratch is also easy. The single-machine installation outlined in Chapter 2, "Apache Hadoop YARN Install Quick Start," can be used as a guide. Again, in custom scenarios, pdsh and pdcp can be very valuable.

## 6

Apache Hadoop YARN Administration

Administering a YARN cluster involves many things. Those familiar with Hadoop 1 may know that there are many configuration properties and that their values are listed in the Hadoop documentation. Instead of repeating that information here and coming up with different explanations of each property, what we'll do here is to give practical examples of how you can use open-source tools to manage and understand a complex environment like a YARN cluster.

To effectively administer YARN, we will use the bash scripts and init system scripts developed in Chapter 5, "Installing Apache Hadoop YARN." Also, YARN and Hadoop in general comprise a distributed data platform written in Java. Naturally, this means that there will be many Java processes running on your servers, so it's a good idea to know some of the basics concerning those processes and the process for analyzing them should the need arise.

We will not cover Hadoop File System (HDFS) administration in this chapter. It is assumed that most readers are familiar with HDFS operations and can navigate the file system. For those unfamiliar with HDFS, see Appendix F for a short introduction. In addition, further information on HDFS can be found on the Apache Hadoop website: http://hadoop.apache.org/docs/stable/hdfs_user_guide.html. In this chapter, we cover some basic YARN administration scenarios, introduce both Nagios and Ganglia for cluster monitoring, discuss JVM monitoring, and introduce the Ambari management interface.

Script-based Configuration

In Chapter 5, "Installing Apache Hadoop YARN," we presented some bash scripts to help us install and configure Hadoop. If you haven't read that chapter, we suggest you examine it to get an idea of how we'll reuse the scripts to manage our cluster once it's up and running. If you've already read Chapter 5, you'll recall that we use a script called `hadoop-xml-conf.sh` to do XML file processing. We can reuse these commands to create an administration script that assists us in creating and pushing out Hadoop configuration changes to our cluster. This script, called `configure-hadoop2.sh`, is part of the `hadoop2-install-scripts.tgz` tar file from the book's repository (see Appendix A). A listing of the administration script is also available in Appendix C.

The `configure-hadoop2.sh` script is designed to push (and possibly delete) configuration properties to the cluster and optionally restart various services within the cluster. Since the bulk of our work for these scripts was presented in Chapter 5, we will use these scripts as a starting point. You will need to set your version of Hadoop in the beginning of the script.

```
HADOOP_VERSION=2.2.0
HADOOP_HOME="/opt/hadoop-${HADOOP_VERSION}"
```

The script also sources `hadoop-xml-conf.sh`, which contains the basic file manipulation commands. We also need to decide whether we want to restart and refresh the Hadoop cluster. The default is `refresh=false`.

We can reuse our scripts to create a function that adds or overwrites a configuration property.

```
put()
{
        put_config --file $file --property $property --value $value
}
```

The `put_config` function from `hadoop-xml-conf.sh` can be used in the same way as was shown in Chapter 5. In a similar fashion, we can add a function to delete a property.

```
delete()
{
        del_config --file $file --property $property
}
```

Next, we enlist the help of `pdcp` to push the file out to the cluster in a single command. We've kept the `all_hosts` file on our machine from the installation process, but in the event you deleted this file, just create a new one with the fully qualified domain names of every host on which you want the configuration file to reside.

```
deploy()
{
        echo "Deploying $file to the cluster..."
pdcp -w ^all_hosts "$file" $HADOOP_HOME/etc/hadoop/
}
```

We've gotten good use out of our existing scripts to modify configuration files, so all we need is a way to restart Hadoop. We need to be careful as to how we bring down the services on each node, because the order in which the services are brought down and the order in which they're brought back up makes a difference. The follow-ing code will accomplish this task.

```
restart_hadoop()
{
        echo "Restarting Hadoop 2..."
        pdsh -w ^dn_hosts "service hadoop-datanode stop"
        pdsh -w ^snn_host "service hadoop-secondarynamenode stop"
        pdsh -w ^nn_host "service hadoop-namenode stop"
        pdsh -w ^mr_history_host "service hadoop-historyserver stop"
        pdsh -w ^yarn_proxy_host "service hadoop-proxyserver stop"
        pdsh -w ^nm_hosts "service hadoop-nodemanager stop"
        pdsh -w ^rm_host "service hadoop-resourcemanager stop"

        pdsh -w ^nn_host "service hadoop-namenode start"
        pdsh -w ^snn_host "service hadoop-secondarynamenode start"
        pdsh -w ^dn_hosts "service hadoop-datanode start"
        pdsh -w ^rm_host "service hadoop-resourcemanager start"
        pdsh -w ^nm_hosts "service hadoop-nodemanager start"
        pdsh -w ^yarn_proxy_host "service hadoop-proxyserver start"
        pdsh -w ^mr_history_host "service hadoop-historyserver start"
}
```

As you can see, we use the init scripts we introduced in Chapter 5 to make restart-ing Hadoop easier. While each of the scripts has a restart function, Hadoop must be restarted across the cluster in an orderly fashion. The correct order is given in the restart_hadoop() function shown above.

The complete script is listed in the Appendix C and is available in the book reposi-tory. The possible script arguments, shown in the following listing, can be found by using the –h argument.

```
configure-hadoop2.sh [options]


OPTIONS:
  -o, --operation      Valid values are 'put' and 'delete'. A 'put'
                       operation writes the property and value if it
                       doesn't exist and overwrites it if it does.
                       exist. A 'delete' operation removes the property
  -f, --file           The name of the configuration file.
  -p, --property       The name of the Hadoop configuration property.
  -v, --value          The value of the Hadoop configuration property.
                       Required for a 'put' operation; ignored for a
                       'delete' operation.
  -r, --restart        Flag to restart Hadoop. Configuration files are
                       deployed to the cluster automatically to
                       $HADOOP_HOME/etc/hadoop.
  -h, --help           Show this message.
```

As an example, let's pick a configuration property that would be a good test candidate. Recall that in Chapter 5 we tested the freshly installed Hadoop cluster by running a simple job. If we wanted to navigate in the YARN web user interface (UI) to obtain the test job details, we would be able to view the details of the job through the MapReduce History server we configured in Chapter 5.

In Figure 6.1, we see the summary information for the test in the YARN web UI. We can look at some of the details of this job by clicking on the link for the one successful reduce task, which should result in Figure 6.2.

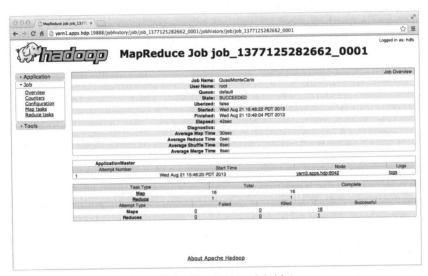

Figure 6.1   MapReduce job history

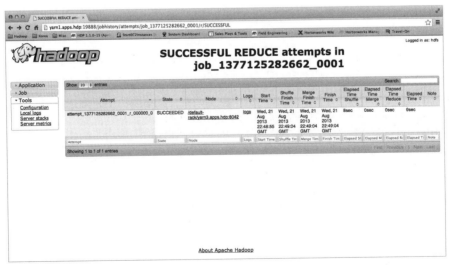

Figure 6.2   MapReduce reduce task information

So far, the information looks normal, but let's see what happens if we drill down further into the task clicking on the "logs" link in the "Logs" column. The result appears in Figure 6.3.

We don't see the log file contents, but we do see a message that "Aggregation is not enabled." If we check the Hadoop 2 documentation (see the discussion of user log aggregation later in this chapter), we see a property called yarn.log-aggregation-enable in the yarn-site.xml file, which has a default value of "false." We also note the property called yarn.nodemanager.remote-app-log-dir, which has a default value of /tmp/logs. Additionally, the directory we designate for log aggregation must reside in HDFS, which is then accessible to all NodeManagers. Depending on the aggregation directory, we need to either check the permissions for that directory if it exists or create a new directory with appropriate permissions. These steps are accomplished as follows:

```
# su - hdfs -c "hadoop fs -mkdir -p /yarn/logs"
# su - hdfs -c "hadoop fs -chown -R yarn:hadoop /yarn/logs"
# su - hdfs -c "hadoop fs -chmod -R g+rw /yarn/logs
```

To complete the setting, we will use the configure-hadoop2.sh script described previously. First we set the location of the logs (yarn.nodemanager.remote-app-log-dir) to /yarn/logs; next we enable the log aggregation (yarn.log-aggregation-enable). Also note the -r option, which will restart the Hadoop installation with the new setting.

```
# ./configure-hadoop2.sh -o put -f yarn-site.xml \
-p yarn.nodemanager.remote-app-log-dir \
-v /yarn/logs -f

# ./configure-hadoop2.sh -o put -f yarn-site.xml \
-p yarn.log-aggregation-enable -v true -r
```

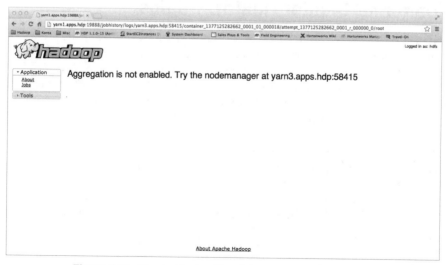

Figure 6.3   Viewing logs without log aggregation enabled

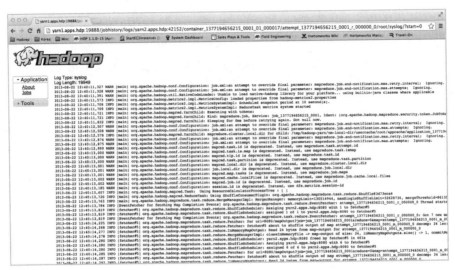

Figure 6.4 Example of aggregated log output

Once Hadoop has restarted, we can resubmit the test job and consult the web UI to see if the logs are now available. If the setting worked, you should see something similar to Figure 6.4.

Other Hadoop properties can be changed in a similar fashion. The `configure-hadoop2.sh` script provides a simple method to change Hadoop XML files across the entire cluster without the repetitive need to log into individual nodes. It also helps with an orderly restart of the whole cluster.

Monitoring Cluster Health: Nagios

A popular open-source monitoring tool is Nagios (http://www.nagios.org). Nagios monitors your infrastructure with a number of built-in and community-developed plug-ins. It is also possible to write your own plug-ins using a number of different methods, in different languages like C, Python, and shell scripts. We've been using bash shell scripts to show installation and configuration, so we'll stick with that method to show you how to begin to monitor your Hadoop cluster using Nagios. In our example, we'll use a small, three-node cluster.

The first step is to choose a server in your cluster that will be the Nagios server. This server will act as the hub in our monitoring system. On the machine you choose to be the Nagios server, we recommend you install Nagios using your native package management system. For Red Hat–based systems, this would be done as follows. (Note: This step assumes you have enabled the EPEL repository as explained in Chapter 5.)

```
# yum install nagios
```

Other distributions may use different tools (e.g., apt for Debian-based systems).

Once the Nagios RPM is installed, there are a few configuration steps. First, you may want to add your email address to the /etc/nagios/objects/contacts.cfg file. If you want to remotely view the Nagios web UI, you may need to modify the "Allow from" line in the /etc/httpd/conf.d/nagios.conf. Also, check your iptables, in case your firewall is blocking access. It is also a good idea to set a Nagios password by issuing the following command:

```
# htpasswd -c /etc/nagios/passwd nagiosadmin
```

Finally, make sure that both the httpd and nagios services are running. Use chk-config to ensure they start on the next reboot. At this point, you should be able to bring up the Nagios web UI by pointing your local browser to http://localhost/nagios.

Once you have the Nagios server installed, you'll be able to define a large number of objects—such as hosts, host groups, and services—that can be monitored. Although there are other things worth monitoring in the cluster, we will focus on installing and configuring Nagios for monitoring YARN.

Since we will add our own entry for the local host, edit the file /etc/nagios/ nagios.cfg and comment out (add # in front of the line) the following line:

```
cfg_file=/etc/nagios/objects/localhost.cfg
```

To set up our Hadoop 2 cluster monitoring, we first tell Nagios about our servers by creating a file in /etc/nagios/conf.d called hadoop-cluster.cfg. By default, Nagios is configured to look in this directory for files with the *.cfg extension. Listing 6.1 shows us how to define a host so that it becomes available to Nagios.

Listing 6.1 **Nagios host definition**

```
define host{
        use                     linux-server
        host_name               yarn1.apps.hdp
        alias                   yarn1.apps.hdp
        address                 192.168.207.231
        }
```

Nagios uses templates that allow the administrator to set up a configuration quickly. One such template is linux-server, as shown in Listing 6.1. It is assigned to the "use" directive and instructs Nagios to use the standard Linux monitoring template. The rest of the directives are obvious and include host_name, alias, and address. The alias is used by the Nagios web UI. We also need a host entry for the other two nodes in our cluster (yarn2.apps.hdp and yarn3.apps.hdp).

Once we have all our hosts defined with a define host block, it is very convenient to define a host group for similar nodes in the hadoop-cluster.cfg file. Our host group will look like the definition in Listing 6.2, where we add all the nodes in our Hadoop cluster.

Listing 6.2 **Nagios host group definition**

```
define hostgroup{
        hostgroup_name  hadoop-cluster
        alias           Hadoop
        members         yarn1.apps.hdp,yarn2.apps.hdp,yarn3.apps.hdp
        }
```

Monitoring Basic Hadoop Services

In Chapter 5, we deployed scripts to start and stop all of the Hadoop services on the cluster. Nagios can easily monitor these services and display the results of that monitoring on a convenient web interface. The first step is to create a script that will do the service monitoring. According to the Nagios documentation, the following return codes are expected as the result of each command or script that's run to determine a service state:

```
OK = 0
Warning = 1
Critical = 2
Unknown = 3
```

As an example, we will write a plug-in to monitor the state of the ResourceManager. The full listing for the plug-in appears in Appendix D and can be found in the book repository. For this plug-in, we'll keep things simple and reuse the init scripts that we created in Chapter 5. First, because the ResourceManager is running or stopped, we will use only two return codes.

```
# Exit codes
STATE_OK=0
STATE_CRITICAL=2
```

As with the other scripts we've created, we need code to parse the arguments passed to the script as well as the arguments passed to the help and usage output functions. This code can be found in the full script in Appendix D. The heart of the script is as follows:

```
status=$(/sbin/service hadoop-resourcemanager status)

if echo "$status" | grep --quiet running ; then
    echo "ResourceManager OK - $status"
    exit $STATE_OK
else
    echo "ResourceManager CRITICAL - $status"
    exit $STATE_CRITICAL
fi
```

The script is fairly simple. We are using the init scripts from Chapter 5 that return one of two responses to the "status" requests (running or stopped).

```
# service hadoop-resourcemanager status
Hadoop YARN ResourceManager daemon (pid  36772) is running...

# service hadoop-resourcemanager status
Hadoop YARN ResourceManager daemon is stopped
```

We can use `grep` to confirm the "running" response or assume the service is stopped otherwise. Once we're satisfied with the script, we name it `check_resource_manager.sh` and put it in the Nagios plug-in directory (e.g., `/usr/lib64/nagios/plugins`). We tell Nagios about this plug-in by adding the following lines to our `hadoop-cluster.cfg` file:

```
define command{
        command_name check_resource_manager
        command_line /usr/lib64/nagios/plugins/check_resource_manager.sh
        }
```

Defining the command is pretty simple: We give the fully qualified path and file names for the actual command and give the command a name that will be used elsewhere in our configuration file.

The next step is to define a Nagios service that uses our new command in the `hadoop-cluster.cfg` file.

```
define service{
        use                     local-service
        host_name               yarn1.apps.hdp
        service_description     ResourceManager
        check_command           check_resource_manager
        }
```

The service definition uses a template like the block we used earlier to define a host. This template is called `local-service` and, as the name suggests, it defines a service local to the Nagios server. The `host_name` and `service_description` are self-explanatory. We run this service only on the node that runs the ResourceManager. The `check_command` is where we see the `command_name` in the `define command` block created previously (these names must match).

The next step is to define a service and command entry for each of the other services. To save time, these are provided in Appendix D and online.

To use the new configuration, we need to restart Nagios as follows:

```
# service nagios restart
```

If everything is working correctly, the new service should be available on the Nagios web UI for `yarn1.apps.hdp`.

The assumption so far has been that Nagios will monitor local services on the same machine as the Nagios server. Obviously, Hadoop is a distributed system that requires cluster-wide monitoring. Nagios has a few methods available for providing cluster-wide functionality, but the easiest way is with the Nagios Remote Plugin Executor

(NRPE). Assuming that the NodeManagers and DataNodes are on remote servers, we need to install the Nagios NRPE on each of these remote servers as follows. (Note: pdsh can be helpful here.)

```
# yum install nrpe nagios-plug-ins
```

The default configuration for NRPE is to trust only communication from the local host. Thus the first thing to do in an NRPE installation is to tell it where the Nagios server is by specifying its IP address in the /etc/nagios/nrpe.cfg file on the cluster nodes. (Your IP address may be different.)

```
allowed_hosts=127.0.0.1,192.168.207.231
```

We can use the Nagios script plug-ins found in Appendix D to check the Node-Manager and DataNode state. These scripts should be placed in the plug-in directories of the remote machines (/usr/lib64/nagios/plug-ins). When this step is complete, we define the command in the nrpe.cfg file.

```
command[check_node_manager]=/usr/lib64/nagios/plugins/check_node_manager.sh
command[check_data_node]=/usr/lib64/nagios/plugins/check_data_node.sh
```

Once we've set up the remote servers via NRPE, we can go back to our hadoop-cluster.cfg file on the Nagios server and add the following commands and services:

```
define command{
 command_name check_nrpe
 command_line /usr/lib64/nagios/plugins/check_nrpe -H $HOSTNAME$ -c $ARG1$
     }

define service{
        use                 local-service
        host_name           yarn2.apps.hdp,yarn3.apps.hdp
        service_description NodeManager
        check_command       check_nrpe!check_node_manager
        }

define service{
        use                 local-service
        host_name           yarn2.apps.hdp,yarn3.apps.hdp
        service_description DataNode
        check_command       check_nrpe!check_data_node
        }
```

The NRPE command uses command variable substitution in Nagios. In the define command block, we see several variables that, in Nagios terms, are called macros. The $HOSTNAME$ macro is expanded by Nagios with the host_name value in the service definition. If more than one host is defined, Nagios executes the command remotely on each host specified. The $ARG1$ macro is expanded with the values delimited by the "!" character in the check_command line, which is also found in the service definition.

You may wish to add other services from the Nagios plug-ins (e.g., check_local_load) for all nodes by using the hostgroup_name. In this case, add the service block to the hadoop-cluster.cfg as follows:

```
define service {
        use                       generic-service
        hostgroup_name            hadoop-cluster
        service_description       Current Load
        check_command             check_local_load!5.0,4.0,3.0!10.0,6.0,4.0
        }
```

Monitoring the JVM

So far, we have defined some basic services that simply monitor the started/stopped state of the various Hadoop daemons. An example of a slightly more complex service is one that monitors a specific portion of the Java Virtual Machine heap space for the ResourceManager process. To create this monitor, we will utilize the command-line tool that ships with the Java Development Kit we installed in Chapter 5.

To write this service, we will take advantage of a tool called jstat. The jstat tool is found in the JDK's bin directory and displays a large number of JVM statistics. Almost all JDKs provide the jstat tool as part of their installation; for instance, it is available in both the Linux OpenJDK and the Oracle JDK packages. As an example, we will monitor the JVM's old space utilization as a percentage of the old space's capacity. The command to do this and its output are shown here:

```
# $JAVA_HOME/bin/jstat -gcutil $(cat /var/run/hadoop/yarn/yarn-yarn-
➥resourcemanager.pid)
  S0     S1      E      O       P     YGC      YGCT    FGC    FGCT     GCT
  0.00 100.00  40.85  11.19  99.35      9     0.044      0   0.000    0.044
```

According to the jstat documentation, the column with the heading "O" identifies the percentage of old space used in the JVM based on the old space's capacity (in this case, 11.19% of capacity). We use the following lines to create the desired monitor:

```
pct=$("$JAVA_HOME"/bin/jstat -gcutil $(cat "$PIDFILE") | awk 'FNR == 2 {print $4}')

if [ "$pct" > "$critical" ] ; then
    printf "ResourceManager Heap Old Space %% used %s - %g" CRITICAL "$pct"
    exit $STATE_CRITICAL
elif [ "$pct" > "$warn" ]; then
    printf "ResourceManager Heap Old Space %% used %s - %g" WARN "$pct"
    exit $STATE_WARNING
else
    printf "ResourceManager Heap Old Space %g%% used is %s" "$pct" OK
    exit $STATE_OK
fi
```

In the previous code snippet, the `awk` command is used to parse the tabular output of the `jstat` command. In defining the bash "pct" variable, we simply pipe the output of the `jstat` command to `awk`, and then tell `awk` to get the fourth column in the second row of the output. The script snippet assumes the appropriate files have been included via the "source" function so that we have access to the JAVA_HOME variable. You can find the complete script in Appendix D.

Unlike in the previous examples, we may have situations that can pass with a warning instead of meeting a critical threshold. If the "Old Space Percentage Used" passes these thresholds, then Nagios can send the appropriate message.

To use the service, we need to add the following command and service definitions in our `hadoop-cluster.cfg` file:

```
define command{
    command_name check_resource_manager_old_space_pct
    command_line /usr/lib64/nagios/plugins/check_resource_manager_old_space_pct.
➥sh -w $ARG1$ -c $ARG2$
    }

define service{
    use                    local-service
    host_name              yarn1.apps.hdp
    service_description    ResourceManager Old Space Pct Used
    check_command          check_resource_manager_old_space_pct!50!75
    }
```

In the `define command` section, the option values of -w and -c are used to signify the warning and critical levels and are reserved for use by Nagios. In our example, we're using 50% as a warning value and 75% as a critical value; these values are appended to the `check_resource_manager_old_space_pct` command we created earlier.

Nagios also has many publicly available plug-ins that are found in `/usr/lib64/nagios/plug-ins` (assuming a 64-bit server platform). If you are using a Red Hat–based system, you can issue the following command to see which plug-ins are available:

```
# yum search nagios
```

One widely used tool is `ping`. As the name implies, it pings servers in your infrastructure to see if they can respond to a basic ping. If you install the `ping` plug-in (e.g., `#yum install nagios-plug-ins-ping`), you'll find it in the plug-in directory as a command called `check_ping`.

Putting it all together, when we have our monitoring scripts written, and our Hadoop cluster hosts, commands, and services defined in a configuration file available to Nagios, we are able to monitor our cluster as shown in Figure 6.5.

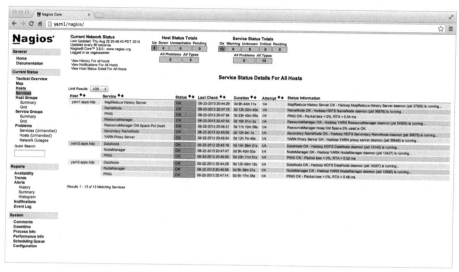

Figure 6.5 Nagios monitoring a Hadoop cluster

Real-time Monitoring: Ganglia

Nagios is great for monitoring and sending out alerts for events, but it does not provide real-time monitoring of the cluster. To get a real-time view of the cluster, the Ganglia monitoring system can be used. Ganglia's strength is that it ships with a large number of metrics for which it is able to generate real-time graphs. For the more visually inclined system administrator, this is the tool for you.

The Ganglia monitoring daemon is called gmond and must be installed on all servers you wish to monitor. On your main monitoring node, install the following packages:

```
# yum install ganglia ganglia-web ganglia-gmetad ganglia-gmond
```

All other nodes need only the monitoring daemon, which can be installed using pdsh.

```
# pdsh -w ^all_hosts yum install ganglia-gmond
```

You will need to add the multicast route to the monitoring node as follows:

```
# route add -host 239.2.11.71 dev eth0
```

Change eth0 to the cluster-wide Ethernet port (i.e., eth0, eth1, eth2, ...). This command can be made automatic on the next boot by adding it to the /etc/rc.local file on the monitoring node.

On the main monitoring node, edit the `/etc/ganglia/gmetad.conf` and make sure the following line is present in the file. This line tells the gmetad collection daemon to get all cluster data from the local gmond monitoring daemon.

```
data_source "my cluster" localhost
```

On all cluster nodes (including the monitoring node), edit the file `/etc/ganglia/gmond.conf` and enter a value for the cluster name by replacing the "unspecified" value in the cluster block shown in the following listing. Other values are optional but all values must be the same on all nodes in the cluster.

```
cluster {
  name = "unspecified"
  owner = "unspecified"
  latlong = "unspecified"
  url = "unspecified"
}
```

On the main monitoring node, start the data collection daemon and all monitoring daemons as follows:

```
# service gmetad start
# pdsh -w ^all_hosts service gmond start
```

Both gmond and gmetad can be set to start automatically by using chkconfig. The ganglia webpage can be viewed by opening a web browser on the monitoring node using the local Ganglia URL: http://localhost/ganglia. An example Ganglia page is shown in Figure 6.6.

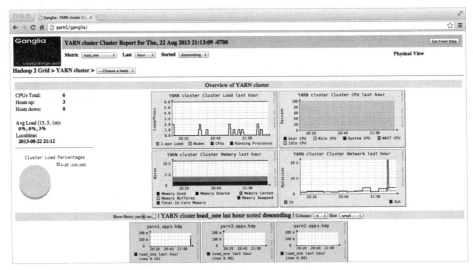

Figure 6.6   Ganglia monitoring a Hadoop cluster

Administration with Ambari

Apache Ambari was used in Chapter 5 to install Hadoop 2 and related packages across a cluster. In addition, Ambari can be used as a centralized point of administration for a Hadoop cluster. Using Ambari, administrators can configure cluster services, monitor the status of nodes or services, visualize hotspots using service metrics, start or stop services, and add new nodes to the cluster. All of these features provide a high level of agility to the processes of managing and monitoring your distributed environment.

After completing the initial installation and logging into Ambari, you will be presented with a dashboard. The dashboard provides a number of high-level metrics around HDFS, YARN, HBase, and the rest of the Hadoop stack components. The top navigation menu, shown in Figure 6.7, provides interfaces to access the Dashboard, Heatmaps, Services, Hosts, and Admin features. The status (up/down) of various Hadoop services is displayed on the left using green/red dots. Note that two of the services managed by Ambari are Nagios and Ganglia; these services are installed by Ambari and there is no need to reinstall them as described previously.

The Heatmaps section allows you to visualize all the nodes in the cluster. Visual indicators include Host metrics, YARN metrics, HDFS metrics, and HBase metrics. Host metrics show memory usage, CPU wait on I/O, and storage used. YARN metrics include JVM garbage collection times, JVM heap size, and percentage of container

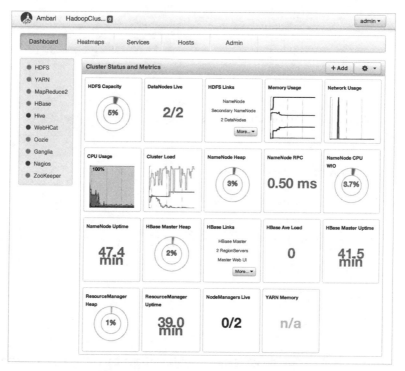

Figure 6.7 Ambari main control panel

node memory used. HDFS visuals show HDFS bytes read or written, JVM garbage collection, and JVM heap size. HBase metrics show read and write counts, compaction queue size, regions and memory store sizes. Figures 6.8 and 6.9 are examples of these types of heatmaps.

The Services page allows users to modify cluster-wide Hadoop configuration files and displays metrics for all the Hadoop services running on the cluster (e.g., HDFS, YARN, Hive, HBase). This window, shown in Figure 6.10, also provides the ability to start and stop some or all services on the cluster. A user can individually stop, start, or test a service, respectively, with the Stop, Start, and Maintenance buttons near the top right of the screen.

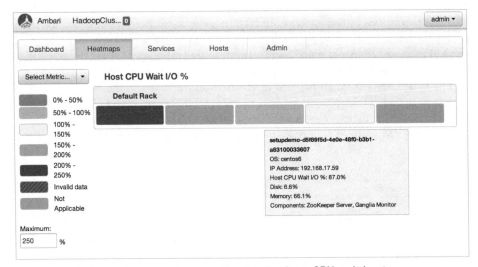

Figure 6.8   Ambari dashboard showing host CPU wait heatmap

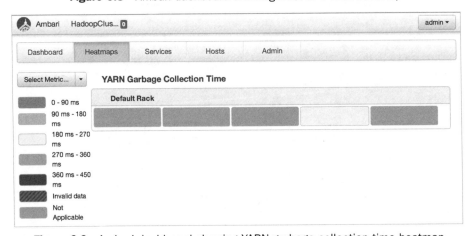

Figure 6.9   Ambari dashboard showing YARN garbage collection time heatmap

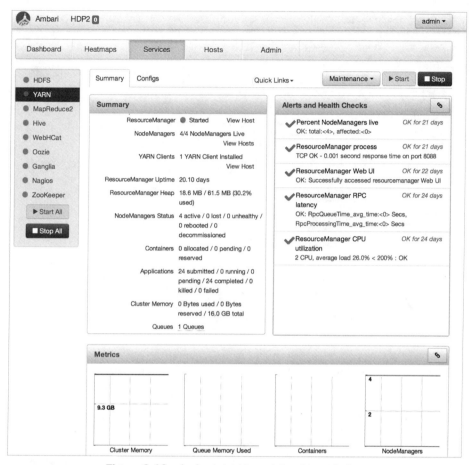

Figure 6.10   Ambari dashboard Services window

Figure 6.11 is an example of the MapReduce2 properties available in the Services window. Administrators can easily change these parameters without the need to change Hadoop configuration files by hand.

The Hosts tab provides the status for every node in the cluster. This window, shown in Figure 6.12, will warn users if a master or slave is down. It also shows when a node stops sending heartbeats, in addition to providing alerts about events such as the Hive Metastore MySQL database being down. Clicking the Add New Hosts button on the right allows you to grow your cluster and automatically install required services onto it, such as HDFS, YARN, and client tools. The light blue Components button produces a drop-down selection of installed service components (e.g., DataNodes, NodeManagers); by selecting a component here, you can filter out nodes lacking the selected component.

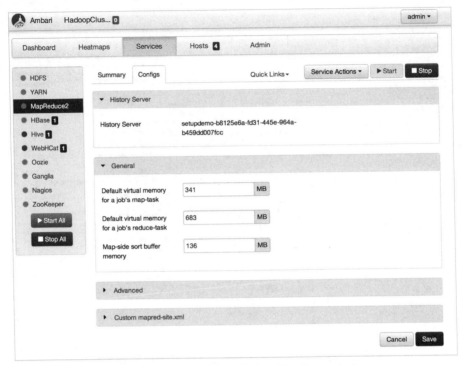

Figure 6.11   Ambari MapReduce2 options window

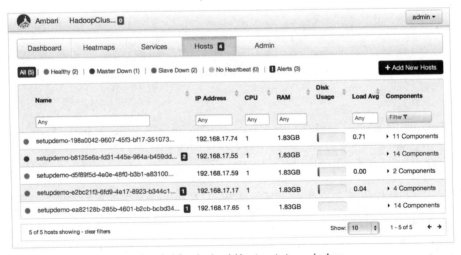

Figure 6.12   Ambari Hosts status window

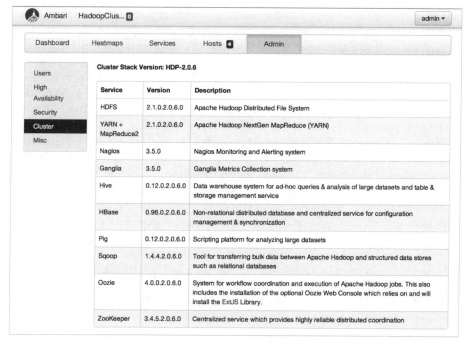

Figure 6.13   Ambari Admin window

The Admin tab provides information about users, HA, security, cluster stack versions, and other miscellaneous topics. The "User" section allows an administrator to create new users and grant them permissions ranging from complete control of the cluster to only viewing cluster metrics. NameNode High Availability can be enabled in the "High Availability" section, and Kerberos security can be enabled in the "Security" section. Details on the installed software stack versions can be found in the "Cluster" section, shown in Figure 6.13. Finally, the "Misc" section lists the usernames for specific services and their respective groups.

Ambari provides a single control panel for the entire Hadoop cluster. This control panel is a project with stable releases with more features planned for future versions. Currently, it is a highly usable and useful tool for installation and administration of Hadoop 2 clusters.

JVM Analysis

Because Hadoop is written almost entirely in Java, it may be helpful to understand some basic Java-related troubleshooting methods available to administrators.

A Java Virtual Machine (JVM) process is separated into three segments called generations—specifically, the young, old, and permanent generations. The young generation is sometimes referred to as the new generation, and the old generation is sometimes referred to as the tenured generation. The young and old generations can be given hints as to how big each is, but the exact size is calculated by the JVM. A young generation size can be initialized with the −XX:NewSize argument and a ratio given to calculate the old generation with −XX:NewRatio. If the −XX:NewRatio was given a value of 2, this means the old generation is twice as large as the new generation. Both the old and young generations are given an initial size by the JVM process with the −Xms option and can grow to the size specified by the −Xmx option.

The new generation is broken down into three subsegments: Eden, Survivor Space I, and Survivor Space II. When an object is created in the JVM, it's created first in Eden, then moved to Survivor Space I, then moved to Survivor Space II, and finally moved to the old generation. The JVM moves the objects to each subsegment in the young generation during minor garbage collection. When there is no more room in the old generation for objects during a garbage collection process, the JVM triggers a major garbage collection process that can have a negative performance impact on all Java applications, which, in our case, are the YARN applications.

One method to analyze memory usage on a running application is to use the jmap tool provided with most Java installations. The jmap tool can handle a number of different tasks, but one that is highly useful is attaching itself to a running Java process through the process ID. For example, a heap dump from a YARN container (like the container spawned in the Chapter 5 installation tests) can be obtained as follows. Here we tell jmap to dump the heap for process 21341 to file mr-container.hprof.

```
# jmap -dump:format=b,file=~/mr-container.hprof -F 21341
Attaching to process ID 21341, please wait...
Debugger attached successfully.
Server compiler detected.
JVM version is 20.6-b01
Dumping heap to /opt/rm.hprof ...
Finding object size using Printezis bits and skipping over...
Finding object size using Printezis bits and skipping over...
Heap dump file created
```

The heap dump can be read with the jhat utility, but a much better visual tool is the Eclipse Memory Analyzer (http://www.eclipse.org/mat/). Once installed, the mr-container.hprof generated with jmap can opened in the Eclipse Memory Analyzer, as shown in Figure 6.14.

From the main page, a number of reports can be run on the heap dump, showing things like the largest memory objects. For example, Figure 6.15 shows a histogram indicating which objects take up the most heap space in the JVM process.

When the Eclipse Memory Analyzer initially opens a heap dump file, it creates supplemental index files so that the dump file can be opened much more quickly during subsequent sessions. There is also an Object Query Language (OQL) window where we can query the heap dump for specific objects with specific values.

Analyzing JVM heap dumps is usually the last resort when you are trying to troubleshoot problematic Java processes; nevertheless, it's a valuable skill for the advanced

Hadoop and YARN administrator. It's likely that you will want to monitor YARN container processes through Nagios and Ganglia with advanced scripting or programming, but when those methods fail to find answers, the ability to sift through a JVM heap dump can prove to be an invaluable skill.

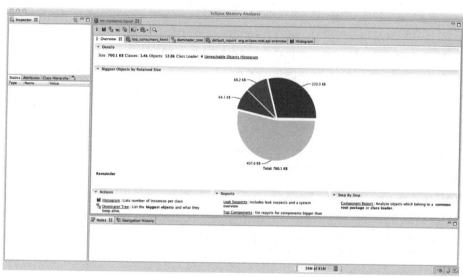

Figure 6.14   JVM heap dump displayed with Eclipse Memory Analyzer

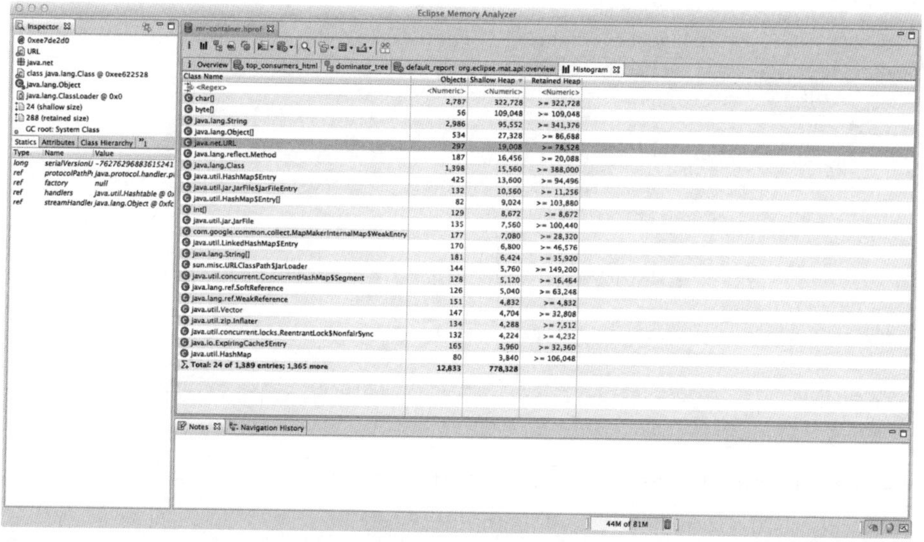

Figure 6.15   Eclipse Memory Analyzer histogram

Basic YARN Administration

As with Hadoop version 1, there are a multitude of configuration properties available to the administrators in Hadoop version 2. YARN has introduced and changed some configuration properties. The basic files are as follows:

- core-default.xml: System-wide properties
- hdfs-default.xml: Hadoop Distributed File System properties
- mapred-default.xml: Properties for the YARN MapReduce framework
- yarn-default.xml: YARN properties.

You can find a complete list of properties for all these files at http://hadoop.apache. org/docs/current/ (look at the lower-left side of the page under "Configuration"). A full discussion of all options is beyond the scope of this book, but you can find comments and defaults for each of the properties on the Apache Hadoop site. There are, however, some important administrative tasks worth mentioning.

YARN Administrative Tools

YARN has several built-in administrative features. These can be found by examining the yarn rmadmin command-line utility's description as shown in the following listing. Some of these options will be illustrated later.

```
# yarn rmadmin -help
rmadmin is the command to execute Map-Reduce administrative commands.
The full syntax is:

hadoop rmadmin [-refreshQueues] [-refreshNodes]
[-refreshSuperUserGroupsConfiguration] [-refreshUserToGroupsMappings]
[-refreshAdminAcls] [-refreshServiceAcl] [-getGroup [username]]
[-help [cmd]]

-refreshQueues: Reload the queues' acls, states, and scheduler-specific
                properties. ResourceManager will reload the mapred-queues
                configuration file.

-refreshNodes: Refresh the hosts information at the ResourceManager.

-refreshUserToGroupsMappings: Refresh user-to-groups mappings.

-refreshSuperUserGroupsConfiguration: Refresh superuser proxy groups
                                      mappings.

-refreshAdminAcls: Refresh acls for administration of ResourceManager.

-refreshServiceAcl: Reload the service-level authorization policy file.
                    ResourceManager will reload the authorization
                    policy file.
```

```
    -getGroups [username]: Get the groups which given user belongs to

    -help [cmd]:      Displays help for the given command or all commands
                      if none is specified.


Generic options supported are
-conf <configuration file>      specify an application configuration file
-D <property=value>             use value for given property
-fs <local|namenode:port>       specify a namenode
-jt <local|jobtracker:port>     specify a job tracker
-files <comma separated list of files>    specify comma separated files to
                                          be copied to the mapreduce
                                          cluster
-libjars <comma separated list of jars>   specify comma separated jar
                                           files to include in the
                                           class path.
-archives <comma separated list of archives>   specify comma separated
                                                archives to be unarchived
                                                on the compute machines.

The general commandline syntax is:
bin/hadoop command [genericOptions] [commandOptions]
```

Adding and Decommissioning YARN Nodes

In typical installations, nodes play the roles of both HDFS data node and YARN worker node. The procedures for adding and decommissioning HDFS nodes can be found in Appendix F. The following discussion is limited to YARN worker nodes, which can be managed by running the ResourceManager admin client.

Adding new nodes requires that all the necessary software and configuration be loaded on the new node. The following technique can be used for both adding and decommissioning nodes. Two files dictate which nodes are to be accepted and which are not to be used: yarn.resourcemanager.nodes.include-path and yarn.resourcemanager.exclude-path. The first property points to a file with a list of nodes that are accepted by the ResourceManager, and the second property points to a file with a list of nodes that are explicitly deemed as either not acceptable by the ResourceManager or possibly running but removed/decommissioned from Resource-Manager use. Both properties point to a local file system path on the Resource-Manager node. They can have hostnames or IP addresses separated by a newline, space, or tab. Lines that start with the "#" character are treated as comments. Once the files are modified by the administrator (only administrators should have write permission to these files on the ResourceManager local file system for security reasons), the administrator can then run the following command to inform ResourceManager about the change in the nodes list:

```
# yarn rmadmin -refreshNodes
```

Only administrators can perform this task. Administrators are defined as users restricted by the `admin-acl` that is dictated by the configuration property `yarn.admin.acl` on the ResourceManager.

Capacity Scheduler Configuration

Detailed information on configuration of the Capacity scheduler can be found in Chapter 8, "Capacity Scheduler in YARN." Queues can be reconfigured and added as described here.

Changing queue properties and adding new queues are very simple processes. You can use the `configure-hadoop2.sh` script, described previously, for this purpose, or you can directly edit `$HADOOP_CONF_DIR/etc/hadoop/capacity-scheduler.xml` file.

```
# yarn rmadmin -refreshQueues
```

Queues cannot be deleted at this point of time. Only addition of new queues is supported, and the updated queue configuration should be a valid one (i.e., the queue capacity at each level should be equal to 100%).

YARN WebProxy

The Web Application Proxy is a separate proxy server in YARN for managing security with the cluster web interface on ApplicationMasters. By default, the proxy is run as part of the Resource Manager itself, but it can be configured to run in a stand-alone mode by changing the configuration property `yarn.web-proxy.address`. Also by default, it is set to an empty string, which means it runs in the ResourceMaster. In a stand-alone mode, `yarn.web-proxy.principal` and `yarn.web-proxy.keytab` control the Kerberos principal name and the corresponding keytab for use in secure mode.

Using the JobHistoryServer

The removal of the JobTracker and migration of MapReduce from a system to an application-level framework necessitated creation of a place to store MapReduce job history. The JobHistoryServer allows all YARN MapReduce applications with a central location to aggregate completed jobs for historical reference and debugging. The settings for the JobHistoryServer can be found in the `mapred-default.xml` file.

Refreshing User-to-Groups Mappings

The `hadoop.security.group.mapping` property determines the user-to-group mappings that the ResourceManager uses. Such a class needs to implement the interface `org.apache.hadoop.security.GroupMappingServiceProvider`. The default value is `org.apache.hadoop.security.ShellBasedUnixGroupsMapping`. This refresh operation needs to happen whenever a user is added to the system and whenever a user's list of groups changes. Only cluster administrators can invoke this refresh:

```
# rmadmin -refreshUserToGroupsMapping
```

Refreshing Superuser Proxy Groups Mappings

The hadoop.proxyuser.<proxy-user-name>.groups property needs to be configured to allow the user $proxy-user-name to be treated as a special privi-
leged user who can impersonate any other users who are members of the value of
this property. The value can be a comma-separated list of groups. The value of
hadoop.proxyuser.<proxy-user-name>.hosts can be a comma-separated list of hosts
from which $proxy-user-name can be restricted to do the previously mentioned user
impersonation. Once either of these configurations is changed, administrators will
have to refresh the ResourceManager:

```
# yarn rmadmin -refreshSuperUserGroupsConfiguration
```

The $proxy-user-name noted previously can, therefore, perform the impersonation
only to specific users (who are members of the previous groups) and only from specific
hosts. This super-user itself also must be authenticated using Kerberos at the time of
such impersonation.

Refreshing ACLs for Administration of ResourceManager

The yarn.admin.acl property specifies the Access Control Lists (ACLs) indicating
who can be an administrator of the YARN cluster. A cluster administrator has special
privileges to refresh queues, node lists, user-group mappings, the admin list itself, and
service-level ACLs. This administrator can also view any user's applications, access all
web interfaces, invoke any web services, and kill any application in any queue. The
value of this configuration property is a comma-separated list of users and groups.
The user list comes first (comma separated) and is separated by a space, followed by
the list of groups—for example, "user1,user2 group1,group2". Whenever this property
changes, administrators must refresh the ResourceManager as follows:

```
# yarn rmadmin -refreshAdminAcls
```

Reloading the Service-level Authorization Policy File

The administrator may also have to reload the authorization policy file using the following command:

```
# yarn rmadmin -refreshServiceAcl
```

Managing YARN Jobs

YARN jobs can be managed using the "yarn application" command. The following options, including -kill, -list, and -status are available to the administrator
with this command. MapReduce jobs can also be controlled with the "mapred job"
command.

```
usage: application
 -appTypes <Comma-separated list of application types>   Works with
```

```
                              --list to filter applications based on
                              their type.
    -help                     Displays help for all commands.
    -kill <Application ID>    Kills the application.
    -list                     Lists applications from the RM. Supports optional
                              use of -appTypes to filter applications based
                              on application type.
    -status <Application ID>  Prints the status of the application.
```

Setting Container Memory

Controlling container memory takes place through three important values in the
`yarn-site.xml` file:

- `yarn.nodemanager.resource.memory-mb` is the amount of memory the Node-
  Manager can use for containers.
- `yarn.scheduler.minimum-allocation-mb` is the smallest container allowed by
  the ResourceManager. A requested container smaller than this value will result
  in an allocated container of this size (default 1024 MB).
- `yarn.scheduler.maximum-allocation-mb` is the largest container allowed by the
  ResourceManager (default 8192 MB).

Setting Container Cores

It is possible to set the number of cores for containers using the following properties in
the `yarn-stie.xml`:

- `yarn.scheduler.minimum-allocation-vcores` is the minimum number of cores
  a container can be requested to have.
- `yarn.scheduler.maximum-allocation-vcores` is the maximum number of
  cores a container can be requested to have.
- `yarn.nodemanager.resource.cpu-vcores` is the number of cores that containers
  can request from this node.

Setting MapReduce Properties

Since MapReduce now runs as a YARN application, it may be necessary to adjust
some of the `mapred-site.xml` properties as they relate to the map and reduce containers. The following properties are used to set some Java arguments and memory size for
both the map and reduce containers:

- `mapred.child.java.opts` provides a larger or smaller heap size for child JVMs
  of maps (e.g., `--Xmx2048m`).

- `mapreduce.map.memory.mb` provides a larger or smaller resource limit for maps (default = 1536 MB)

- `mapreduce.reduce.memory.mb` provides a resource-limit for child JVMs of maps (default = 3072 MB)

- `mapreduce.reduce.java.opts` provides a larger or smaller heap size for child reducers.

User Log Management

User logs of Hadoop jobs serve multiple purposes. First and foremost, they can be used to debug issues that occur while running a MapReduce application, including correctness problems with the application itself, race conditions when running on a cluster, and debugging task/job failures due to hardware or platform bugs. Second, one can do historical analyses of the logs to see how individual tasks in jobs or workflows perform over time. One can even analyze the Hadoop MapReduce user logs with Hadoop MapReduce to determine any performance issues.

Handling of user logs generated by applications has been one of the biggest pain points for Hadoop installations in the past. In Hadoop version 1, user logs are left on individual nodes by the TaskTracker, and the management of the log files on local nodes is both insufficient for longer-term analyses and non-deterministic for user access. YARN tackles this log management issue by having the NodeManagers provide the option of moving these logs securely onto HDFS after the application completes.

Log Aggregation in YARN

With YARN, logs for all the containers that belong to a single application and that ran on a given NodeManager are aggregated and written out to a single (possibly compressed) log file at a configured location in the designated file system. In the current implementation, once an application finishes, one will have an application-level log directory and a per-node log file that consists of logs for all the containers of the application that ran on this node.

With Hadoop version 2, users can gain access to these logs via YARN command-line tools, through the web UI, or directly from the file system. These logs potentially can be stored for much longer times than was possible in Hadoop version 1 because they reside within a large distributed file system. Hadoop version 2 does not need to truncate logs to very small lengths (as long as the log sizes are reasonable) and can afford to store the entire logs for longer periods of time. In addition, while the containers are running, the logs are written to multiple directories on each node for effective load balancing and improved fault tolerance. In addition, an AggregatedLog-DeletionService service periodically deletes aggregated logs; currently, it runs only inside the MapReduce JobHistoryServer.

Web User Interface

On the web interfaces, log aggregation is completely hidden from the user. While a MapReduce application is running, users can see the logs from the ApplicationMaster UI, which redirects the user to the NodeManager UI. Once an application finishes, the completed information is owned by the MapReduce JobHistoryServer, which again serves user logs transparently.

Command-Line Access

In addition to the web UI, a command-line utility can be used to interact with logs. The usage option can be listed by running the following:

```
$ yarn logs
Retrieve logs for completed YARN applications.
usage: yarn logs -applicationId <application ID> [OPTIONS]

general options are:
-appOwner <Application Owner>    AppOwner (assumed to be current user if
                                 not specified)
-containerId <Container ID>      ContainerId (must be specified if node
                                 address is specified)
-nodeAddress <Node Address>      NodeAddress in the format nodename:port
                                 (must be specified if container ID is specified)
```

For example, to print all the logs for a given application, one can simply enter the following line:

```
$ yarn logs -applicationId <application ID>
```

Logs of only one specific container can be printed using the following command:

```
yarn logs -applicationId <application ID> -containerId <Container ID> \
-nodeAddress <Node Address>
```

The obvious advantage with the command-line utility is that now you can use the regular shell utilities to help process files.

Log Administration and Configuration

The general log-related configuration properties are yarn.nodemanager.log-dirs and yarn.log-aggregation-enable. The function of each is described next.

The yarn.nodemanager.log-dirs property determines where the container logs are stored on the node when the containers are running. Its default value is ${yarn.log.dir}/userlogs. An application's localized log directory will be found in {yarn.nodemanager.log-dirs}/application_${appid}. Individual containers' log directories will be below this level, in subdirectories named container_{$containerId}.

For MapReduce applications, each container directory will contain the files stderr, stdin, and syslog generated by that container. Other frameworks can choose to write more or fewer files—YARN doesn't dictate the file names and number of files.

The `yarn.log-aggregation-enable` property specifies whether to enable or disable log aggregation. If this function is disabled, NodeManagers will keep the logs locally (as in Hadoop version 1) and not aggregate them.

The following properties are in force when log aggregation is enabled:

- `yarn.nodemanager.remote-app-log-dir`: This location is found on the default file system (usually HDFS) and indicates where the NodeManagers should aggregate logs. It *should not* be the local file system, because otherwise serving daemons such as the history server will not able to serve the aggregated logs. The default value is `/tmp/logs`.

- `yarn.nodemanager.remote-app-log-dir-suffix`: The remote log directory will be created at {`yarn.nodemanager.remote-app-log-dir`}/${user}/{suffix}. The default suffix value is "logs".

- `yarn.log-aggregation.retain-seconds`: This property defines how long to wait before deleting aggregated logs; −1 or another negative number disables the deletion of aggregated logs. Be careful not to set this property to a too-small value so as to not burden the distributed file system.

- `yarn.log-aggregation.retain-check-interval-seconds`: This property determines how long to wait between aggregated log retention checks. If its value is set to 0 or a negative value, then the value is computed as one-tenth of the aggregated log retention time. As with the previous configuration property, be careful not to set it to an inordinately low value. The default is −1.

- `yarn.log.server.url`: Once an application is done, NodeManagers redirect the web UI users to this URL, where aggregated logs are served. Today it points to the MapReduce-specific JobHistory.

The following properties are used when log aggregation is disabled:

- `yarn.nodemanager.log.retain-seconds`: The time in seconds to retain user logs on the individual nodes if log aggregation is disabled. The default is 10800.

- `yarn.nodemanager.log.deletion-threads-count`: The number of threads used by the NodeManagers to clean up logs once the log retention time is hit for local log files when aggregation is disabled.

Log Permissions

The remote root log directory is expected to have the permissions 1777 with ${NMUser} as owner and to be directory- and group-owned by ${NMGroup} (i.e., the group to which NMUser belongs).

Each application-level directory will be created with permission 770, but will be user-owned by the application submitter and group-owned by ${NMGroup}. This feature allows application submitters to access aggregated logs for their own use; ${NMUser} can access or modify the files for log management. Also, ${NMGroup}* should be a limited-access group so that there are no access leaks.

Wrap-up

Administering YARN is not that different from administering a Hadoop 1 installation where many of the parameters are set in the system-wide Hadoop XML files. Both bash scripts and the Ambari interface can be used to easily modify and (if necessary) restart the entire Hadoop system.

Cluster-wide monitoring is important, and Nagios alerts and Ganglia real-time metrics can be important tools for the Hadoop administrator. The fully integrated Ambari tool provides a single interface to manage the entire cluster. As it develops further, Ambari should become the standard method for Hadoop administration.

To truly understand YARN cluster administration, it's helpful to have not only a basic understanding of the configuration properties for YARN itself, but also an understanding of the JVM processes on your servers. Several open-source tools exist that can provide insights into Hadoop Java processes.

7

Apache Hadoop YARN Architecture Guide

Chapter 4 provided a functional overview of YARN components and a brief description of how a YARN application flows through the system. In this chapter, we will delve deeper into the inner workings of YARN and describe how the system is implemented from the ground up.

YARN separates all of its functionality into two layers: a *platform* layer responsible for resource management and what is called first-level scheduling, and a *framework* layer that coordinates application execution and second-level scheduling. Specifically, a per-cluster *ResourceManager* tracks usage of resources, monitors the health of various nodes in the cluster, enforces resource-allocation invariants, and arbitrates conflicts among users. By separating these multiple duties that were previously shouldered by a single daemon, the JobTracker, in Hadoop version 1, the ResourceManager can simply allocate resources centrally based on a specification of an application's requirements, but ignore how the application makes use of those resources. That responsibility is delegated to an *ApplicationMaster*, which coordinates the logical execution of a single application by requesting resources from the ResourceManager, generating a physical plan of its work, making use of the resources it receives, and coordinating the execution of such a physical plan.

Overview

The ResourceManager and NodeManagers running on individual nodes come together to form the core of YARN and constitute the **platform**. ApplicationMasters and the corresponding containers come together to form a YARN *application*. This separation of concerns is shown in Figure 7.1. From YARN's point of view, all users interact with it by submitting applications that then make use of the resources offered by the platform. From end-users' perspective, they may either (1) directly interact with YARN by running applications directly on the platform or (2) interact with a *framework*, which in turn runs as an application on top of YARN. Frameworks may expose a higher-level functionality to the end-users. As an example, the MapReduce code that comes bundled with Apache Hadoop can be looked at as a *framework* running on top of YARN. On the one hand, MapReduce gives to the users a map and reduce abstraction that they can code against, with the framework taking care of the gritty details of running smoothly on a distributed system—failure handling, reliability, resource allocation, and so. On the other hand, MapReduce uses the underlying platform's APIs to implement such functionality.

The overall architecture is described in Figure 7.2. The ResourceManager provides scheduling of applications. Each application is managed by an ApplicationMaster (per-task manager) that requests per-task computation resources in the form of containers. Containers are scheduled by the ResourceManager and locally managed by the per-node NodeManager.

A detailed description of the responsibilities and components of the Resource-Manager, NodeManager, and ApplicationMaster follows.

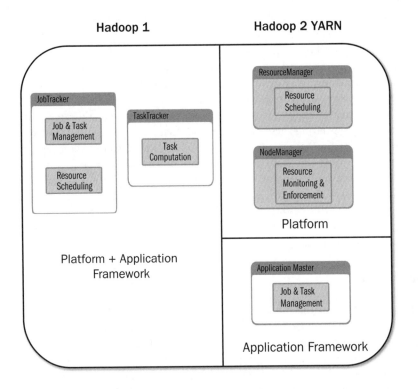

Figure 7.1   Hadoop version 1 with integrated platform and applications framework versus Hadoop version 2 with separate platform and application framework

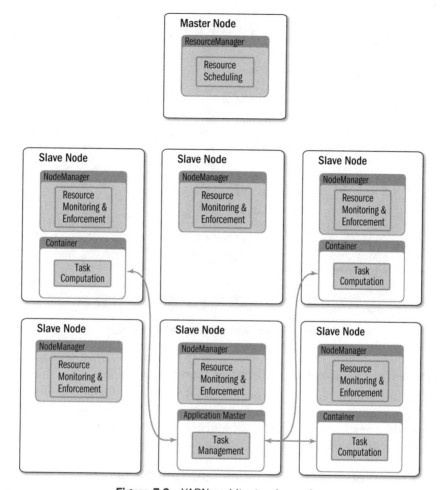

Figure 7.2   YARN architectural overview

ResourceManager

As previously described, the ResourceManager is the master that arbitrates all the available cluster resources, thereby helping manage the distributed applications running on the YARN platform. It works together with the following components:

- The per-node NodeManagers, which take instructions from the Resource-Manager, manage resources available on a single node, and accept container requests from ApplicationMasters

- The per-application ApplicationMasters, which are responsible for negotiating resources with the ResourceManager and for working with the NodeManagers to start, monitor, and stop the containers

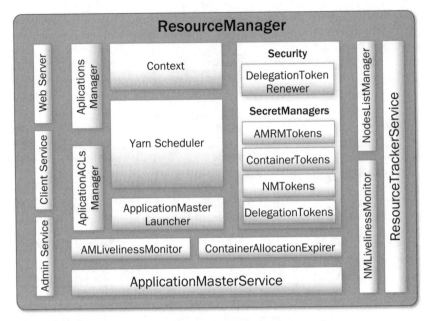

Figure 7.3   ResourceManager components

Overview of the ResourceManager Components

The ResourceManager components are illustrated in Figure 7.3. To better describe the workings of each component, they will be introduced separately by grouping them corresponding to each external entity for which they provide services: clients, the NodeManagers, the ApplicationMasters, or other internal core components.

Client Interaction with the ResourceManager

The first interaction point of a user with the platform comes in the form of a client to the ResourceManager. The following components in ResourceManager interact with the client.

Client Service

This service implements ApplicationClientProtocol, the basic client interface to the ResourceManager. This component handles all the remote procedure call (RPC) communications to the ResourceManager from the clients, including operations such as the following:

- Application submission
- Application termination
- Exposing information about applications, queues, cluster statistics, user ACLs, and more

Client Service provides additional protection to the ResourceManager depending on whether the administrator configured YARN to run in secure or nonsecure mode. In secure mode, the Client Service makes sure that all incoming requests from users are authenticated (for example, by Kerberos) and then authorizes each user by looking up application-level Access Control Lists (ACLs) and subsequently queue-level ALCs. For all clients that *cannot* be authenticated with Kerberos directly, this service also exposes APIs to obtain what are known as the ResourceManager delegation tokens. Delegation tokens are special objects that a Kerberos-authenticated client can first obtain by securely communicating with the ResourceManager and then pass along to its nonauthenticated processes. Any client process that has a handle to these delegation tokens can communicate with ResourceManager securely *without* separately authenticating with Kerberos first.

Administration Service

While Client Service is responsible for typical user invocations like application submission and termination, there is a list of activities that administrators of a YARN cluster have to perform from time to time. To make sure that administration requests don't get starved by the regular users' requests and to give the operators' commands a higher priority, all of the administrative operations are served via a separate interface called Administration Service. ResourceManagerAdministrationProtocol is the communication protocol that is implemented by this component. Some of the important administrative operations are highlighted here:

- Refreshing queues: for example, adding new queues, stopping existing queues, and reconfiguring queues to change some of their properties like capacities, limits, and more

- Refreshing the list of nodes handled by the ResourceManager: for example, adding newly installed nodes or decommissioning existing nodes for various reasons

- Adding new user-to-group mappings, adding/updating administrator ACLs, modifying the list of superusers, and so on

Both Client Service and Administration Service work closely with Application-Manager for ACL enforcement.

Application ACLs Manager

The ResourceManager needs to gate the user-facing APIs like the client and administrative requests so that they are accessible only to authorized users. This component maintains the ACLs per application and enforces them. Application ACLs are enabled on the ResourceManager by setting to true the configuration property `yarn.acl.enable`. There are two types of application accesses: (1) viewing and (2) modifying an application. ACLs against the view access determine who can "view" some or all of the application-related details on the RPC interfaces, web UI, and web services. The modify-application ACLs determine who can "modify" the application (e.g., kill the application).

An ACL is a list of users and groups who can perform a specific operation. Users can specify the ACLs for their submitted application as part of the ApplicationSubmissionContext. These ACLs are tracked per application by the ACLsManager and used for access control whenever a request comes in. Note that irrespective of the ACLs, all administrators (determined by the configuration property yarn.admin.acl) can perform any operation.

The same ACLs are transferred over to the ApplicationMaster so that the ApplicationMaster itself can use them for users accessing various services running inside the ApplicationMaster. The NodeManager also receives the same ACLs as part of ContainerLaunchContext (discussed later in this chapter) when a container is launched which then uses them for access control to serve requests about the applications/containers, mainly about their status, application logs, etc.

ResourceManager Web Application and Web Services

The ResourceManager has a web application that exposes information about the state of the cluster; metrics; lists of active, healthy, and unhealthy nodes; lists of applications, their state and status; hyper-references to the ApplicationMaster web interfaces; and a scheduler-specific interface.

Application Interaction with the ResourceManager

Once an application goes past the client-facing services in the ResourceManager and is accepted into the system, it travels through the internal machinery of the ResourceManager that is responsible for launching the ApplicationMaster. The following describes how the ApplicationMasters interact with the ResourceManager once they have started.

ApplicationMasters Service

This component responds to requests from all the ApplicationMasters. It implements ApplicationMasterProtocol, which is the one and only protocol that ApplicationMasters use to communicate with the ResourceManager. It is responsible for the following tasks:

- Registration of new ApplicationMasters
- Termination/unregistering of requests from any finishing ApplicationMasters
- Authorizing all requests from various ApplicationMasters to make sure that only valid ApplicationMasters are sending requests to the corresponding Application entity residing in the ResourceManager
- Obtaining container allocation and deallocation requests from all running ApplicationMasters and forwarding them asynchronously to the YarnScheduler

The ApplicationMasterService has additional logic to make sure that—at any point in time—only one thread in any ApplicationMaster can send requests to the ResourceManager. All the RPCs from ApplicationMasters are serialized on the ResourceManager, so it is expected that only one thread in the ApplicationMaster will make these requests.

This component works closely with ApplicationMaster liveliness monitor described next.

ApplicationMaster Liveliness Monitor

To help manage the list of live ApplicationMasters and dead/non-responding ApplicationMasters, this monitor keeps track of each ApplicationMaster and its last heartbeat time. Any ApplicationMaster that does not produce a heartbeat within a configured interval of time—by default, 10 minutes—is deemed dead and is expired by the ResourceManager. All containers currently running/allocated to an expired Application-Master are marked as dead. The ResourceManager reschedules the same application to run a new *Application Attempt* on a new container, allowing up to a maximum of two such attempts by default.

Interaction of Nodes with the ResourceManager

The following components in the ResourceManager interact with the NodeManagers running on cluster nodes.

Resource Tracker Service

NodeManagers periodically send heartbeats to the ResourceManager, and this component of the ResourceManager is responsible for responding to such RPCs from all the nodes. It implements the ResourceTracker interface to which all NodeManagers communicate. Specifically, it is responsible for the following tasks:

- Registering new nodes
- Accepting node heartbeats from previously registered nodes
- Ensuring that only "valid" nodes can interact with the ResourceManager and rejecting any other nodes

Before and during the registration of a new node to the system, lots of things happen. The administrators are supposed to install YARN on the node along with any other dependencies, and configure the node to communicate to its ResourceManager by setting up configuration similar to other existing nodes. If needed, this node should be removed from the excluded nodes list of the ResourceManager.

The ResourceManager will reject requests from any invalid or decommissioned nodes. Nodes that don't respect the ResourceManager's configuration for minimum resource requirements will also be rejected.

Following a successful registration, in its registration response the Resource-Manager will send security-related master keys needed by NodeManagers to authenticate container-related requests from the ApplicationMasters. NodeManagers need to be able to validate NodeManager tokens and container tokens that are submitted by ApplicationMasters as part of container-launch requests. The underlying master keys are rolled over every so often for security purposes; thus, on further heartbeats, Node-Managers will be notified of such updates whenever they happen.

The Resource Tracker Service forwards a valid node-heartbeat to the YarnScheduler, which then makes scheduling decisions based on freely available resources on that node and the resource requirements from various applications.

In addition, the Resource Tracker Service works closely with the NodeManager liveliness monitor and nodes-list manager, described next.

NodeManagers Liveliness Monitor

To keep track of live nodes and specifically identify any dead nodes, this component keeps track of each node's identifier (ID) and its last heartbeat time. Any node that doesn't send a heartbeat within a configured interval of time—by default, 10 minutes—is deemed dead and is expired by the ResourceManager. All the containers currently running on an expired node are marked as dead, and no new containers are scheduled on such node. Once such a node restarts (either automatically or by administrators' intervention) and reregisters, it will again be considered for scheduling.

Nodes-List Manager

The nodes-list manager is a collection in the ResourceManager's memory of both valid and excluded nodes. It is responsible for reading the host configuration files specified via the yarn.resourcemanager.nodes.include-path and yarn.resourcemanager.nodes.exclude-path configuration properties and seeding the initial list of nodes based on those files. It also keeps track of nodes that are explicitly decommissioned by administrators as time progresses.

Core ResourceManager Components

So far, we have described various components of the ResourceManager that interact with the outside world—namely, clients, ApplicationMasters, and NodeManagers. In this section, we'll present the core ResourceManager components that bind all of them together.

ApplicationsManager

The ApplicationsManager is responsible for maintaining a collection of submitted applications. After application submission, it first validates the application's specifications and rejects any application that requests unsatisfiable resources for its ApplicationMaster (i.e., there is no node in the cluster that has enough resources to run the ApplicationMaster itself). It then ensures that no other application was already submitted with the same application ID—a scenario that can be caused by an erroneous or a malicious client. Finally, it forwards the admitted application to the scheduler.

This component is also responsible for recording and managing finished applications for a while before they are completely evacuated from the ResourceManager's memory. When an application finishes, it places an *ApplicationSummary* in the daemon's log file. The *ApplicationSummary* is a compact representation of application information at the time of completion.

Finally, the ApplicationsManager keeps a cache of completed applications long after applications finish to support users' requests for application data (via web UI or command line). The configuration property `yarn.resourcemanager.max-completed-applications` controls the maximum number of such finished applications that the ResourceManager remembers at any point of time. The cache is a first-in, first-out list, with the oldest applications being moved out to accommodate freshly finished applications.

ApplicationMaster Launcher

In YARN, while every other container's launch is initiated by an ApplicationMaster, the ApplicationMaster itself is allocated and prepared for launch on a NodeManager by the ResourceManager itself. The ApplicationMaster Launcher is responsible for this job. This component maintains a thread pool to set up the environment and to communicate with NodeManagers so as to launch ApplicationMasters of newly submitted applications as well as applications for which previous ApplicationMaster attempts failed for some reason. It is also responsible for talking to NodeManagers about cleaning up the ApplicationMaster—mainly killing the process by signaling the corresponding NodeManager when an application finishes normally or is forcefully terminated.

YarnScheduler

The YarnScheduler is responsible for allocating resources to the various running applications subject to constraints of capacities, queues, and so on. It performs its scheduling function based on the resource requirements of the applications, such as memory, CPU, disk, and network needs. Currently, memory and CPU cores are supported resources. We already gave a brief coverage of various YARN scheduling options in Chapter 4, "Functional Overview of YARN Components." The default scheduler that is packaged with YARN, the Capacity scheduler, is discussed in Chapter 8.

ContainerAllocationExpirer

This component is in charge of ensuring that all allocated containers are eventually used by ApplicationMasters and subsequently launched on the corresponding NodeManagers. ApplicationMasters run as untrusted user code and may potentially hold on to allocations without using them; as such, they can lead to under-utilization and abuse of a cluster's resources. To address this, the ContainerAllocationExpirer maintains a list of containers that are allocated but still not used on the corresponding NodeManagers. For any container, if the corresponding NodeManager doesn't report to the ResourceManager that the container has started running within a configured interval of time (by default, 10 minutes), the container is deemed dead and is expired by the ResourceManager.

In addition, independently NodeManagers look at this expiry time, which is encoded in the ContainerToken tied to a container, and reject containers that are submitted for launch after the expiry time elapses. Obviously, this feature depends on the system clocks being synchronized across the ResourceManager and all NodeManagers in the system.

Security-related Components in the ResourceManager

The ResourceManager has a collection of components called SecretManagers that are charged with managing the tokens and secret keys that are used to authenticate/ authorize requests on various RPC interfaces. A brief summary of the tokens, secret keys, and the secret managers follows.

ContainerToken SecretManager

This SecretManager is responsible for managing ContainerTokens—a special set of tokens issued by the ResourceManager to an ApplicationMaster so that it can use an allocated container on a specific node. This ResourceManager-specific component keeps track of the underlying secret keys and rolls the keys over every so often.

ContainerTokens are a security tool used by the ResourceManager to send vital information related to starting a container to NodeManagers through the Application-Master. This information cannot be sent directly to a NodeManager without causing significant latencies. The ResourceManager can construct ContainerTokens only after a container is allocated, and the information to be encoded in a ContainerToken is available only after this allocation. Waiting for NodeManagers to acknowledge the token before ApplicationMasters can get the allocated container is a nonstarter. For this reason, they are routed to the NodeManagers through the ApplicationMasters.

From a security point of view, we cannot trust the ApplicationMaster to pass along correct information to the NodeManagers before starting a container. For example, it may just fabricate the amount of memory or cores before passing along this infor-mation to the NodeManager. To avoid this problem, the ResourceManager encrypts vital container-related information into a container token before sending it to the ApplicationMaster. A container token consists of the following fields:

- **Container ID**: This uniquely identifies a container. The NodeManager uses this information to bind it to a specific application or application attempt. This binding is important because any user may have multiple applications running concurrently and one ApplicationMaster should not start containers for another application.

- **NodeManager address**: The container token encodes the target Node-Manager's address so as to avoid abusive ApplicationMasters using container tokens corresponding to containers allocated on one NodeManager to start con-tainers on another unrelated NodeManager.

- **Application submitter**: This is the name of the user who submitted the applica-tion to the ResourceManager. It is important because the NodeManager needs to perform all container-related activities, such as localizing resources, starting a proc-ess for the container, and creating log directories, as the user for security reasons.

- **Resource**: This informs the NodeManager about the amount of each resource (e.g., memory, virtual cores) that the ResourceManager has authorized an ApplicationMaster to start. The NodeManager uses this information both to account for used resources and to monitor containers to not use resources beyond the corresponding limits.

- **Expiry timestamp**: NodeManagers look at this timestamp to determine if the container token passed is still valid. Any containers that are not used by the ApplicationMasters until after this expiry time is reached will be automatically cancelled by YARN.

  - For this feature to work, the clocks on the nodes running the ResourceManager and the NodeManagers must be in sync.

  - When the ResourceManager allocates a container, it also determines and sets its expiry time based on a cluster configuration, defaulting to 10 minutes.

  - When administrators set the expiry interval configuration, it should not be set (1) to a very low value, because ApplicationMasters may not have enough time to start containers before they are expired, or (2) to a very high value, because doing so permits rogue ApplicationMasters to allocate containers but not use them, which hurts cluster utilization.

  - If a container is not used before it expires, then the NodeManager will simply reject any start-container requests using this token. The NodeManager also has a cache of recently started containers to prevent ApplicationMasters from using the same token in a rapid manner on very short-lived containers.

- **Master key identifier**: This is used by NodeManagers to validate container tokens that are sent across them.

  - The ResourceManager generates a secret key and assigns a key ID to uniquely identify this key. This secret key, along with its ID, is shared with every NodeManager, first as a part of each node's registration and then during subsequent heartbeats whenever the ResourceManager rolls over the keys for security reasons. The key rollover period is a ResourceManager configurable value, but defaults to a day.

  - Whenever the ResourceManager rolls over the underlying keys, they aren't immediately used to generate new tokens; thus there is enough time for all the NodeManagers in the cluster to learn about the rollover. As NodeManagers emit heartbeats and learn about the new key, or once the activation period expires, the ResourceManager replaces its older key with a newly created key. Thereafter, it uses the new key only for generating container tokens. This activation period is set to be 1.5 times the node-expiry interval.

  - As you can see, there will be times before key activation when NodeManagers may receive tokens generated using different keys. In such a case, even when the ResourceManager instructs NodeManagers that a key has rolled over, NodeManagers continue to remember both the current (new) key and the previous (old) key, and use the correct key based on the master key ID present in the token.

- **ResourceManager identifier**: It is possible that the ResourceManager might restart after allocating a container but before the ApplicationMaster can reach the NodeManager to start the container. To ensure both the new ResourceManager and the NodeManagers are able to recognize containers from the old instance of

ResourceManager separately from the ones allocated by the new instance, the ResourceManager identifier is encoded into the container token. At the time of this writing, the ResourceManager on restart will kill all of the previously running containers; in a similar vein, NodeManagers simply reject containers issued by the older ResourceManager.

AMRMToken SecretManager

Only ApplicationMasters can initiate requests for resources in the form of containers. To avoid the possibility of arbitrary processes maliciously imitating a real Application-Master and sending scheduling requests to the ResourceManager, the Resource-Manager uses per-ApplicationAttempt tokens called AMRMTokens. This secret manager saves each token locally in memory until an ApplicationMaster finishes and uses it to authenticate any request coming from a valid ApplicationMaster process.

ApplicationMasters can obtain this token by loading a credentials file localized by YARN. The location of this file is determined by the public constant `ApplicationConstants.CONTAINER_TOKEN_FILE_ENV_NAME`.

Unlike the container tokens, the underlying master key for AMRMTokens doesn't need to be shared with any other entity in the system. Like the container tokens, the keys are rolled every so often for security reasons, but there are no corresponding activation periods.

NMToken SecretManager

Container tokens are in a way used for **authorization** of start-container requests from the ApplicationMasters. They are valid only during the connection to the NodeManager that is created for starting the container. Further, if there is no other **authentication** mechanism, a connection created using a container token cannot be used to start other containers. The whole point of a container token is to prevent resource abuse, which would be possible with shared connections.

Besides starting a container, NodeManagers allow ApplicationMasters to stop a container or get the status of a container. These requests can be submitted long after containers are allocated, so mandating the ApplicationMasters to create a persistent but separate connection per container with each NodeManager is not practical.

NMTokens serve this purpose. ApplicationMasters use NMTokens to manage one connection per NodeManager and use it to send all requests to that node.

- The ResourceManager generates one NMToken per application attempt per NodeManager.
- Whenever a new container is created, ResourceManager issues the Application-Master an NMToken corresponding to that node. ApplicationMasters will get NMTokens only for those NodeManagers on which they started containers.
- As a network optimization, NMTokens are not sent to the ApplicationMasters for each and every allocated container, but only for the first time or if NMTokens have to be invalidated due to the rollover of the underlying master key.

- Whenever an ApplicationMaster receives a new NMToken, it should replace the existing token, if present, for that NodeManager with the newer token. A library, NMTokenCache, is available for the token management.

- ApplicationMasters are always expected to use the latest NMToken, and each NodeManager accepts only one NMToken from any ApplicationMaster. If a new NMToken is received from the ResourceManager, then older connections for corresponding NodeManagers should be closed and a new connection should be created with the latest NMToken. If connections created with older NMTokens are then used for launching newly assigned containers, the NodeManagers simply reject them.

- As with container tokens, NMTokens issued for one ApplicationMaster cannot be used by another. To make this happen, the application attempt ID is encoded into the NMTokens.

RMDelegationToken SecretManager

This component is a ResourceManager-specific delegation token secret manager. It is responsible for generating delegation tokens to clients, which can be passed on to processes that wish to be able to talk to the ResourceManager but are not Kerberos authenticated.

DelegationToken Renewer

In secure mode, the ResourceManager is Kerberos authenticated and so provides the service of renewing file system tokens on behalf of the applications. This component renews tokens of submitted applications as long as the application runs and until the tokens can no longer be renewed.

NodeManager

A NodeManager is YARN's per-node agent that takes care of the individual compute nodes in a Hadoop YARN cluster and uses the physical resources on the nodes to run containers as requested by YARN applications. It is essentially the "worker" daemon in YARN. Its responsibilities include the following tasks:

- Keeping up-to-date with the ResourceManager
- Tracking node health
- Overseeing containers' life-cycle management; monitoring resource usage (e.g., memory, CPU) of individual containers
- Managing the distributed cache (a local file system cache of files such as jars and libraries that are used by containers)
- Managing the logs generated by containers
- Auxiliary services that may be exploited by different YARN applications

We'll now give a brief overview of NodeManagers' functionality before describing the components in more detail.

Overview of the NodeManager Components

Among the previously listed responsibilities, container management is the core responsibility of a NodeManager. From this point of view, the NodeManager accepts requests from ApplicationMasters to start and stop containers, authenticates container tokens (a security mechanism to make sure applications can appropriately use resources as given out by the ResourceManager), manages libraries that containers depend on for execution, and monitors containers' execution. Operators configure each NodeManager with a certain amount of memory, number of CPUs, and other resources available at the node by way of configuration files (`yarn-default.xml` and/or `yarn-site.xml`). After registering with the ResourceManager, the NodeManager periodically sends a heartbeat with its current status and receives instructions, if any, from the Resource-Manager. When the scheduler gets to process the node's heartbeat (which can happen after a delay follows a node's heartbeat), containers are allocated against that NodeManager and then are subsequently returned to the ApplicationMasters when the ApplicationMasters themselves send a heartbeat to the ResourceManager.

All containers in YARN—including ApplicationMasters—are described by a *Container Launch Context* (CLC). This request object includes environment variables, library dependencies (which may be present on remotely accessible storage), security tokens that are needed both for downloading libraries required to start a container and for usage by the container itself, container-specific payloads for NodeManager auxiliary services, and the command necessary to create the process. After validating the authenticity of a start-container request, the NodeManager configures the environment for the container, forcing any administrator-provided settings that may be configured.

Before actually launching a container, the NodeManager copies all the necessary libraries—data files, executables, tarballs, jar files, shell scripts, and so on—to the local file system. The downloaded libraries may be shared between containers of a specific application via a local application-level cache, between containers launched by the same user via a local user-level cache, and even between users via a public cache, as can be specified in the CLC. The NodeManager eventually garbage-collects libraries that are not in use by any running containers.

The NodeManager may also kill containers as directed by the ResourceManager. Containers may be killed in the following situations:

- The ResourceManager sends a signal that an application has completed.
- The scheduler decides to preempt it for another application or user.
- The NodeManager detects that the container exceeded the resource limits as specified by its ContainerToken.

Whenever a container exits, the NodeManager will clean up its working directory in local storage. When an application completes, all resources owned by its containers are cleaned up.

In addition to starting and stopping containers, cleaning up after exited containers, and managing local resources, the NodeManager offers other local services to containers running on the node. For example, the *log aggregation* service uploads all the logs written by the application's containers to stdout and stderr to a file system once the application completes.

As described in the ResourceManager section, when any NodeManager fails (which may occur for various reasons), the ResourceManager detects this failure using a timeout, and reports the failure to all running applications. If the fault or condition causing the timeout is transient, the NodeManager will resynchronize with the ResourceManager, clean up its local state, and continue. Similarly, when a new NodeManager joins the cluster, the ResourceManager notifies all ApplicationMasters about the availability of new resources for spawning containers.

NodeManager Components

Similar to the ResourceManager, the NodeManager is divided internally into a host of nested components, each of which has a clear responsibility. Figure 7.4 gives an overview of the NodeManager components.

NodeStatusUpdater

On start-up, this component registers with the ResourceManager, sends information about the resources available on this node, and identifies the ports at which the

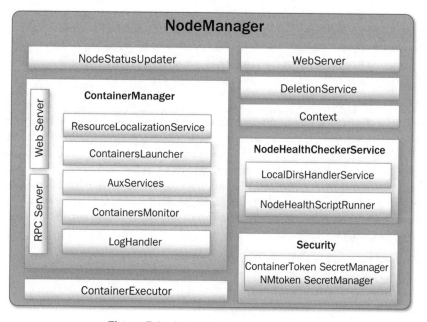

Figure 7.4 NodeManager components

NodeManager's web server and the RPC server are listening. As part of the registration, the ResourceManager sends the NodeManager security-related keys needed by the NodeManager to authenticate future container requests from the ApplicationMasters. Subsequent NodeManager–ResourceManager communication provides the Resource-Manager with any updates on existing containers' status, new containers started on the node by the ApplicationMasters, containers that have completed, and so on.

In addition, the ResourceManager may signal the NodeManager via this component to potentially kill currently running containers because of, say, a scheduling policy that shuts down the NodeManager in situations such as explicit decommissioning by the operator or resynchronizing of the NodeManager in case of network issues. Finally, when any application finishes on the ResourceManager, the ResourceManager signals the NodeManager to clean up various application-specific entities on the NodeManager—for example, internal per-application data structures and application-level local resources—and then initiate and finish the per-application logs' aggregation onto a file system.

ContainerManager

This component is the core of the NodeManager. It is composed of the following subcomponents, each of which performs a subset of the functionality that is needed to manage the containers running on the node.

RPC Server

ContainerManager accepts requests from ApplicationMasters to start new containers, or to stop running ones. It works with NMToken SecretManager and ContainerToken SecretManager (described later) to authenticate and authorize all requests. All the operations performed on containers running on this node are recorded in an audit log, which can be postprocessed by security tools.

Resource Localization Service

Resource localization is one of the important services offered by NodeManagers to user applications. Overall, the resource localization service is responsible for securely downloading and organizing various file resources needed by containers. It tries its best to distribute the files across all the available disks. It also enforces access control restrictions on the downloaded files and puts appropriate usage limits on them. To understand how localization happens inside NodeManager, a brief recap of some definitions related to resource localization from Chapter 4, "Functional Overview of YARN Components," follows.

- **Localization**: Localization is the process of copying/downloading remote resources onto the local file system. Instead of always accessing a resource remotely, that resource is copied to the local machine, which can then be accessed locally.

- **LocalResource**: LocalResource represents a file/library required to run a container. The localization service is responsible for localizing the resource prior to launching the container. For each LocalResource, applications can specify the following information:
    - **URL**: Remote location from where a LocalResource has to be downloaded.
    - **Size**: Size in bytes of the LocalResource.
    - **Creation timestamp**: Resource creation time on the remote file system.
    - **LocalResourceType**: The type of a resource localized by the NodeManager —FILE, ARCHIVE, or PATTERN.
    - **Pattern**: The pattern that should be used to extract entries from the archive (used only when the type is PATTERN).
    - **LocalResourceVisibility**: Specifies the visibility of a resource localized by the NodeManager. The visibility can be either PUBLIC, PRIVATE, or APPLICATION.
- **DeletionService**: A service that runs inside the NodeManager and deletes local paths as and when instructed to do so.
- **Localizer**: The actual thread or process that does localization. There are two types of localizers: PublicLocalizer for PUBLIC resources and ContainerLocalizers for PRIVATE and APPLICATION resources.
- **LocalCache**: NodeManager maintains and manages several local caches of all the files downloaded. The resources are uniquely identified based on the remote URL originally used while copying that file.

The Localization Process

As you will recall from Chapter 4, "Functional Overview of YARN Components," there are three types of LocalResources: PUBLIC, PRIVATE, and APPLICATION. For security reasons, the NodeManager localizes PRIVATE/APPLICATION Local-Resources in a completely different manner than PUBLIC LocalResources. Figure 7.5 gives an overview of where and how resource localization happens.

Localization of PUBLIC Resources

Localization of PUBLIC resources is taken care of by a pool of threads called Public-Localizers. PublicLocalizers run inside the address space of the NodeManager itself. The number of PublicLocalizer threads is controlled by the configuration property `yarn.nodemanager.localizer.fetch.thread-count`, which sets the maximum parallelism during downloading of PUBLIC resources to this thread count. While localizing PUBLIC resources, the localizer validates that all the requested resources are, indeed, PUBLIC by checking their permissions on the remote file system. Any LocalResource that doesn't match that condition is rejected for localization. Each

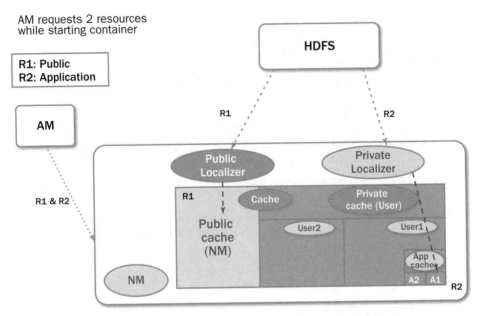

Figure 7.5   Resource-localization process inside the NodeManager

PublicLocalizer uses credentials passed as part of ContainerLaunchContext (discussed later) to securely copy the resources from the remote file system.

Localization of PRIVATE/APPLICATON Resources

Localization of PRIVATE/APPLICATION resources is not done inside the Node-Manager and, therefore, is not centralized. The process is a little involved and is outlined here.

- Localization of these resources happen in a separate process called ContainerLocalizer.
- Every ContainerLocalizer process is managed by a single thread in Node-Manager called LocalizerRunner. Every container will trigger one Localizer-Runner if it has any resources that are not yet downloaded.
- LocalResourcesTracker is a per-user or per-application object that tracks all the LocalResources for a given user or an application.
- When a container first requests a PRIVATE/APPLICATION LocalResource, if it is not found in LocalResourcesTracker (or is found but is in the INITIAL-IZED state), it is added to pending resources list.
- A LocalizerRunner may (or may not) be created depending on the need for downloading something new.

- The LocalResource is added to its LocalizerRunner's pending resources list.
- One requirement for the NodeManager in secure mode is to download/copy these resources as the application submitter, rather than as a yarn-user (privileged user). Therefore, the LocalizerRunner starts a LinuxContainerExecutor (LCE). The LCE is a process running as application submitter, which then executes a ContainerLocalizer. The ContainerLocalizer works as follows:
  - Once started, the ContainerLocalizer starts a heartbeat with the Node-Manager process.
  - On each heartbeat, the LocalizerRunner either assigns one resource at a time to a ContainerLocalizer or asks it to die. The ContainerLocalizer informs the LocalizerRunner about the status of the download.
  - If it fails to download a resource, then that particular resource is removed from LocalResourcesTracker and the container eventually is marked as failed. When this happens, the LocalizerRunner stops the running ContainerLocalizers and exits.
  - If it is a successful download, then the LocalizerRunner gives a Container-Localizer another resource again and again, continuing to do so until all pending resources are successfully downloaded.
- As of this writing, each ContainerLocalizer doesn't support parallel downloading of multiple PRIVATE/APPLICATION resources. In addition, the maximum parallelism is the number of containers requested for the same user on the same NodeManager at that point of time. The worst case for this process occurs when an ApplicationMaster itself is starting. If the ApplicationMaster needs any resources to be localized then, they will be downloaded serially before its container starts.

Target Locations of LocalResources

On each of the NodeManager machines, LocalResources are ultimately localized in the following target directories, under each local directory:

- PUBLIC: `<local-dir>/filecache`
- PRIVATE: `<local-dir>/usercache/<username>/filecache`
- APPLICATION: `<local-dir>/usercache/<username>/appcache/<app-id>/`

Irrespective of the application type, once the resources are downloaded and the containers are running, the containers can access these resources locally by making use of the symbolic links created by the NodeManager in each container's working directory.

Resource Localization Configuration

Administrators can control various aspects of resource localization by setting or changing certain configuration parameters in `yarn-site.xml` when starting a NodeManager:

- `yarn.nodemanager.local-dirs`: A comma-separated list of local directories that one can configure to be used for copying files during localization. The idea behind allowing multiple directories is to use multiple disks for localization so as to provide both fail-over (one or a few disks going bad doesn't affect all containers) and load balancing (no single disk is bottlenecked with writes) capabilities. Thus, individual directories should be configured if possible on different local disks.

- `yarn.nodemanager.local-cache.max-files-per-directory`: Limits the maximum number of files that will be localized in each of the localization directories (separately for PUBLIC, PRIVATE, and APPLICATION resources). The default value is 8192 and this parameter should, in general, not be assigned a large value (configure a value that is sufficiently less than the per-directory maximum file limit of the underlying file system, such as ext3).

- `yarn.nodemanager.localizer.address`: The network address where Resource-LocalizationService listens for requests from various localizers.

- `yarn.nodemanager.localizer.client.thread-count`: Limits the number of RPC threads in ResourceLocalizationService that are used for handling localization requests from localizers. The default is 5, which means that at any point of time, only five localizers will be processed while others wait in the RPC queues.

- `yarn.nodemanager.localizer.fetch.thread-count`: Configures the number of threads used for localizing PUBLIC resources. Recall that localization of PUBLIC resources happens inside the NodeManager address space; thus this property limits how many threads will be spawned inside the NodeManager for localization of PUBLIC resources. The default is 4.

- `yarn.nodemanager.delete.thread-count`: Controls the number of threads used by DeletionService for deleting files. This DeletionService is used all over the NodeManager for deleting log files as well as local cache files. The default is 4.

- `yarn.nodemanager.localizer.cache.target-size-mb`: This property decides the maximum disk space to be used for localizing resources. (As of this book's writing, there was no individual limit for PRIVATE, APPLICATION, or PUBLIC caches.) Once the total disk size of the cache exceeds this value, the DeletionService will try to remove files that are not used by any running containers. This limit is applicable to all the disks and is not used on a per-disk basis.

- `yarn.nodemanager.localizer.cache.cleanup.interval-ms`: After the interval specified by this configuration property elapses, ResourceLocalizationService will try to delete any unused resources if the total cache size exceeds the configured maximum cache size. Unused resources are those resources that are not referred to by any running container. Every time a container requests a resource, that container is added to the resource's reference list. It will remain there until the container finishes, thereby preventing accidental deletion of this resource. As a part of container resource cleanup (when the container finishes), the container will be removed from the resource's reference list. When the reference count drops to zero, it is an ideal candidate for deletion. The resources will be deleted on a least recently used (LRU) basis until the current cache size drops below the target size.

Containers Launcher

The Containers Launcher maintains a pool of threads to prepare and launch containers as quickly as possible. It also cleans up the containers' processes when the Resource-Manager sends such a request through the NodeStatusUpdater or when the Application-Masters send requests via the RPC server. The launch or cleanup of a container happens in one thread of the thread pool, which will return only when the corresponding operation finishes. Consequently, launch or cleanup of one container doesn't affect any other operations and all container operations are isolated inside the NodeManager process.

Auxiliary Services

An administrator may configure the NodeManager with a set of pluggable, *auxiliary services*. The NodeManager provides a framework for extending its functionality by configuring these services. This feature allows per-node custom services that specific frameworks may require, yet places them in a local "sandbox" separate from the rest of the Node-Manager. These services must be configured before the NodeManager starts. Auxiliary services are notified when an application's first container starts on the node, whenever a container starts or finishes, and finally when the application is considered to be complete.

While a container's local storage will be cleaned up after it exits, it can promote some output so that it will be preserved until the application finishes. In this way, a container may produce data that persists beyond the life of the container, to be managed by the node. This property of output persistence, together with auxiliary services, enables a powerful feature. One important use-case that takes advantage of this feature is Hadoop MapReduce. For Hadoop MapReduce applications, the intermediate data are transferred between the map and reduce tasks using an auxiliary service called ShuffleHandler. As mentioned earlier, the CLC allows ApplicationMasters to address a payload to auxiliary services. MapReduce applications use this channel to pass tokens that authenticate reduce tasks to the shuffle service.

When a container starts, the service information for auxiliary services is returned to the ApplicationMaster so that the ApplicationMaster can use this information to take advantage of any available auxiliary services. As an example, the MapReduce framework gets the ShuffleHandler's port information, which it then passes on to the reduce tasks for shuffling map outputs.

Containers Monitor

After a container is launched, this component starts observing its resource utilization while the container is running. To enforce isolation and fair sharing of resources like memory, each container is allocated some amount of such a resource by the Resource-Manager. The ContainersMonitor monitors each container's usage continuously. If a container exceeds its allocation, this component signals the container to be killed. This check is done to prevent any runaway container from adversely affecting other well-behaved containers running on the same node.

Log Handler

The LogHandler is a pluggable component that offers the option of either keeping the containers' logs on the local disks or zipping them together and uploading them onto a file system. We describe this feature in Chapter 6 under the heading "User Log Management."

Container Executor

This NodeManager component interacts with the underlying operating system to securely place files and directories needed by containers and subsequently to launch and clean up processes corresponding to containers in a secure manner.

Node Health Checker Service

The NodeHealthCheckerService provides for checking the health of a node by running a configured script frequently. It also monitors the health of the disks by creating temporary files on the disks every so often. Any changes in the health of the system are sent to NodeStatusUpdater (described earlier), which in turn passes the information to the ResourceManager.

NodeManager Security Components

This section outlines the NodeManager security components.

Application ACLs Manager in the NodeManager

The NodeManager needs to gate the user-facing APIs to allow specific users to access them. For instance, container logs can be displayed on the web interface. This component maintains the ACL for each application and enforces the access permissions whenever such a request is received.

ContainerToken SecretManager in the NodeManager

In the NodeManager, this component mirrors the corresponding functionality in the ResourceManager. It verifies various incoming requests to ensure that all of the start-container requests are properly authorized by the ResourceManager.

NMToken SecretManager in the NodeManager

This component also mirrors the corresponding functionality in the Resource-Manager. It verifies all incoming API calls to ensure that the requests are properly authenticated using NMTokens.

Web Server

This component exposes the list of applications, containers running on the node at a given point of time, node-health-related information, and the logs produced by the containers.

Important NodeManager Functions

The flow of a few important NodeManager functions with respect to running a YARN application are summarized next.

Container Launch

To facilitate container launch, the NodeManager expects to receive detailed information about a container's run time, as part of the total container specification. This includes the container's command line, environment variables, a list of (file) resources required by the container, and any security tokens.

On receiving a container-launch request, the NodeManager first verifies this request and determines if security is enabled, so as to authorize the user, correct resources assignment, and other aspects of the request. The NodeManager then performs the following set of steps to launch the container.

1. A local copy of all the specified resources is created (distributed cache).
2. Isolated work directories are created for the container, and the local resources are made available in these directories by way of symbolic links to the downloaded resources.
3. The launch environment and command line are used to start the actual container.

User Log Management and Aggregation

Hadoop version 2 has much improved user log management, including log aggregation in HDFS. A full discussion of user log management can be found in Chapter 6, "Apache Hadoop YARN Administration."

MapReduce Shuffle Auxiliary Service

The shuffle functionality required to run a MapReduce application is implemented as an auxiliary service. This service starts up a Netty web server, and knows how to handle MapReduce-specific shuffle requests from reduce tasks. The MapReduce ApplicationMaster specifies the service ID for the shuffle service, along with security tokens that may be required. The NodeManager provides the ApplicationMaster with the port on which the shuffle service is running; this information is then passed to the reduce tasks.

In YARN, the NodeManager is primarily limited to managing abstract containers (i.e., only processes corresponding to a container) and does not concern itself with per-application state management like MapReduce tasks. It also does away with the notion of named slots, such as map and reduce slots. Because of this clear separation of responsibilities coupled with the modular architecture described previously, the NodeManager can scale much more easily and its code is much more maintainable.

ApplicationMaster

The per-application ApplicationMaster is the bootstrap process that kicks off every-thing for a YARN application once it gets past the application submission and achieves its own launch. If one compares this approach to the Hadoop 1 architecture, the ApplicationMaster is in essence the per-application JobTracker. We start with a brief overview of the ApplicationMaster and then describe each of its chief responsibilities in detail.

Overview

Once an application is submitted, the application's representation in the Resource-Manager negotiates for a container to spawn this bootstrap process. Once such a container is allocated, as described in the ResourceManager section, the Appli-cationMaster's launcher directly communicates with the ApplicationMaster con-tainer's NodeManager to set up and launch the container. Thus begins the life of an ApplicationMaster. A brief overview of its overall interaction with the rest of YARN is shown in Figure 7.6.

The process starts when (1) an application submits a request to the ResourceManager. Next, the ApplicationMaster is started and registers with the ResourceManager (2). The

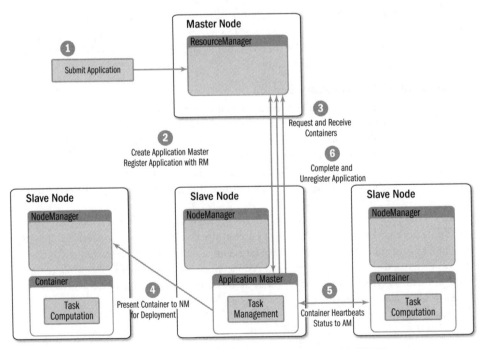

Figure 7.6 Application Master interactions with YARN

ApplicationMaster then requests containers (3) from the ResourceManager to perform actual work. The assigned containers are presented to the NodeManager for use by the ApplicationMaster (4). Computation takes place in the containers, which keep in contact (5) with the ApplicationMaster (not the ResourceManager) as the job progresses. When the application is complete, containers are stopped and the ApplicationMaster is unregistered (6) from the ResourceManager.

Once successfully launched, the ApplicationMaster is responsible for the following tasks:

- Initializing the process of reporting liveliness to the ResourceManager
- Computing the resource requirements of the application
- Translating the requirements into ResourceRequests that are understood by the YARN scheduler
- Negotiating those resource requests with the scheduler
- Using allocated containers by working with the NodeManagers
- Tracking the status of running containers and monitoring their progress
- Reacting to container or node failures by requesting alternative resources from the scheduler if needed

In the remainder of this section, we'll describe these individual responsibilities in greater detail.

Liveliness

The first operation that any ApplicationMaster has to perform is to register with the ResourceManager. As part of the registration, ApplicationMasters can inform the ResourceManager about an IPC address and/or a web URL. The IPC address refers to a client-facing service address—a location that the application's client can visit to obtain nongeneric information about the running application. The communication on the IPC server is application specific: It can be RPC, a simple socket connection, or something else. ApplicationMasters can also report an HTTP tracking URL that points to either an embedded web application running inside the ApplicationMaster's address space or an external web server. This feature enables the clients to obtain application status and information via HTTP.

In the registration response, the ResourceManager returns information that the ApplicationMaster can use, such as the minimum and maximum sizes of resources that YARN accepts, and the ACLs associated with the application that are set by the user during application submission. The ApplicationMaster can use these ACLs for authorizing user requests on its own client-facing service.

Once registered, an ApplicationMaster periodically needs to send heartbeats to the ResourceManager to affirm its liveliness and health. Any ApplicationMaster that fails to report the status for the `yarn.am.liveliness-monitor.expiry-interval-ms` property (a configuration property of the ResourceManager, whose default is

10 minutes) will be deemed to be a dead ApplicationMaster and will be killed by the platform. This configuration is controlled by administrators and should always be less than the value of the nodes' expiry interval governed by the `yarn.nm.liveness-monitor.expiry-interval-ms` property. Otherwise, in situations involving network partitions, nodes may be marked as dead long before ApplicationMasters are marked as such, which may lead to correctness issues on the ResourceManager.

Resource Requirements

Once the liveliness reports with the ResourceManager are taken care of, the application/framework needs to figure out its own resource requirements. It may need either a **static** definition of resources or a **dynamic** one.

Resource requirements are referred to as static when they are decided at the time of application submission (in most cases, by the client) and when, once the Application-Master starts running, there is no change in that specification. For example, in the case of Hadoop MapReduce, the number of maps is based on the input splits for MapReduce applications and the number of reducers on user input; thus this number depends on a static set of resources selected before the application's submission.

Even if the requirements are static, there is another differentiating characteristic in terms of how the scheduling of those resources happens:

- All of the allocated containers may be required to run together—a kind of gang scheduling where resource usage follows a static all-or-nothing model.
- Alternatively, resource usage may change elastically, such that containers can proceed with their work as they are allocated independently of the availability of resources for the remaining containers.

When dynamic resource requirements are applied, the ApplicationMaster may choose how many resources to request at run time based on criteria such as user hints, availability of cluster resources, and business logic.

In either case, once a set of resource requirements is clearly defined, the ApplicationMaster can begin sending the requests across to the scheduler and then schedule the allocated containers to do the desired work.

Scheduling

When an ApplicationMaster accumulates enough resource requests or a timer expires, it can send the requests in a heartbeat message, via the *allocate* API, to the ResourceManager. The **allocate** call is the single most important API between the ApplicationMaster and the scheduler. It is used by the ApplicationMaster to inform the ResourceManager about its requests; it is also used as the liveliness signal. At any point in time, only one thread in the ApplicationMaster can invoke the *allocate* API; all such calls are *serialized* on the ResourceManager per ApplicationAttempt. Because of this, if multiple threads ask for resources via the *allocate* API, each thread may get an inconsistent view of the overall resource requests.

The ApplicationMaster asks for specific resources via a list of ResourceRequests of resourceAsks, and a list of container IDs or containersToBeReleased. The containersToBeReleased are any containers that were allocated by the scheduler in earlier cycles but are no longer needed. The response contains a list of newly allocated containers, the statuses of application-specific containers that completed since the previous interaction between the ApplicationMaster and the ResourceManager, and an indicator (availResources) to the application about available headroom for cluster resources. The ApplicationMaster can use the container statuses to glean information about completed containers and, for example, react to failure. The headroom can be used by the ApplicationMaster to tune its future requests for resources. For example, the MapReduce ApplicationMaster can use this information to schedule map and reduce tasks appropriately so as to avoid deadlocks (e.g., to prevent using up all its headroom for reduce tasks).

After the initial request, in response to subsequent heartbeats, the ApplicationMaster will receive allocated resources at a particular node in the cluster in the form of a container. Based on the containers it receives from the ResourceManager, the ApplicationMaster can do a second level of scheduling and assign its container to whichever task that is part of its execution plan. Note that, depending on the availability of resources, the timing of node heartbeats, and the scheduling algorithm, some of the subsequent calls may not return any containers even though there are outstanding requests. ApplicationMasters are supposed to keep making more *allocate* calls with unchanged requests until they get the containers that they need. If the requests set needs to change, the next *allocate* API can send the modified set of requests, and can potentially get containers for previous requests that were already submitted. The ApplicationMaster will also need to update its resource requests to the ResourceManager as the containers it receives start fulfilling requirements.

In contrast to other resource management systems, resource allocations in YARN to an application are late binding; that is, the ApplicationMaster is obligated only to use resources as provided by the container; it does not have to apply them to the logical task for which it originally requested the resources. There are two ways the ApplicationMaster can request and schedule resources:

- Inform ResourceManager of all the resource requests upfront and let the global scheduler make all the decisions.
- Interact dynamically with ResourceManager to let the scheduler take care of the global scheduling and, depending on the availability of resources and the application's business logic, do a second scheduling pass on the allocated containers.

As an example, the MapReduce ApplicationMaster takes advantage of the dynamic two-level scheduling. When the MapReduce ApplicationMaster receives a container, it matches that container against the set of pending map tasks, selecting a task with input data closest to the container, first trying data local tasks, and then falling back to rack locality. If the ApplicationMaster decides to run a map task in the container, the ApplicationMaster will update its request so that the requests on other nodes where this map task was originally needed are adjusted accordingly.

Scheduling Protocol and Locality

In YARN, an application (via the ApplicationMaster) can ask for containers of varying sizes, ranging from a minimum size all the way to the maximum size stipulated by the scheduler. It can also ask for different numbers of container types.

Resource Requests

The ResourceRequest object is used by the ApplicationMaster for resource requests. As use-cases evolve, this API is expected to change. At this time, it includes the following elements:

- **Priority** of the request.
- The name of the **resource location** on which the allocation is desired. It currently accepts a machine or a rack name. A special value of "*" (asterisk) signifies that any host/rack is acceptable to the application.
- **Resource capability**, which is the amount or size of each container required for that request.
- **Number of containers**, with respect to the specifications of priority and resource location, that are required by the application.
- A Boolean **relaxLocality** flag (defaults to true), which tells the Resource-Manager if the application wants locality to be loose (i.e., allow fall-through to rack or "*" in case of no local containers) or strict (i.e., specify hard constraints on container placement).

The ApplicationMaster is responsible for computing the resource requirements of the application (e.g., input splits for MapReduce applications) and translating them into the ResourceRequest objects understood by the scheduler.

The main advantage of such a specification for the ResourceRequest is that it is extremely compact in terms of the amount of state necessary per application. It is also not stressful on the ResourceManager in terms of scheduling demands, and it lessens the amount of information exchanged between the ApplicationMaster and the Resource-Manager. This design is crucial for scaling the ResourceManager. The size of the requests per application in this model is bounded by the cluster size (number of nodes + number of racks) and by the number of priorities and resource capabilities that are acceptable.

There is an apparent limitation to this model because there is a **loss of information** in the translation from the application's affinity to the hosts/racks. This translation is one-way and irreversible; hence the ResourceManager has no concept of relationships in between the resource requests. For example, an application might need only one container on a specific rack, but specify that it wants one container each on the two hosts on the rack. The moment a container is allocated on one of the nodes, the request on the other node can be automatically cancelled. Currently, the existing grammar doesn't let applications specify such complex relationships. YARN stipulates that the second-level scheduling pass that happens in the ApplicationMaster handles such relationships, which may be very specific to the application in question.

Scheduling Example

Assume there are four racks—rackA, rackB, rackC, and rackD—in the cluster. Also assume that each rack has only four machines each, named host-*rackName*-12[3-6].domain.com. Imagine an application whose data consists of a total of four files, which are physically located on host-A-123.domain.com, host-A-124.domain.com, host-B-123.domain.com, and host-B-124.domain.com, respectively. For efficient operation, this application expects YARN to allocate containers of 1 GB memory, one container each on each node. But depending on the cluster status and other users' applications, YARN may or may not be able to allocate containers exactly in that manner. The application decides that it can live with rack-local containers in case node-local resources are not available, so it specifies a requirement of two containers each on the racks rackA and rackB. It doesn't care about containers being allocated on the remaining hosts or racks, so it doesn't specify anything for them. Overall, it has a requirement of getting four containers, so it specifies that "*" matches to a total of four containers. The entire ResourceRequest can be expressed as shown in Table 7.1.

Note that the number of required containers at a rack doesn't necessarily need to be the aggregate across all nodes on that rack. For example, if the application definitely prefers one container each on host-A-123 and host-A-124 for doing a specific piece of computation and needs one more container on rackA in addition to do some kind of rack-level aggregation, it can make the request shown in Table 7.2.

Similarly, the sum total of requirements across all racks doesn't necessarily need to match the value against "*". Unlike the host- and rack-level specifications, the number of containers specified against "*" denotes the total number of containers absolutely required by the application.

Table 7.1   **Example ResourceRequest**

Priority	Resource Location	Resource Capability (Memory)	Number of Containers
1	host-A-123.domain.com	1 GB	1
1	host-A-124.domain.com	1 GB	1
1	host-B-123.domain.com	1 GB	1
1	host-B-124.domain.com	1 GB	1
1	rackA	1 GB	2
1	rackB	1 GB	2
1	*	1 GB	4
2	*	2 GB	3

Table 7.2   **Example Resource Request for Two Specific Hosts and Rack**

Priority	Resource Location	Resource Capability (Memory)	Number of Containers
1	host-A-123.domain.com	1 GB	1
1	host-A-124.domain.com	1 GB	1
1	rackA	1 GB	3
1	*	1 GB	3

Table 7.3   **Example Change in Resource Request**

Priority	Resource Location	Resource Capability (Memory)	Number of Containers
1	host-A-123.domain.com	1 GB	1
1	rackA	1 GB	2 (was 3)
1	*	1 GB	2 (was 3)

Now assume that the application no longer needs the container on host–A–124 anymore. It then needs to update the ResourceRequest as shown in Table 7.3.

By the time this newly updated request is sent out, the ResourceManager may have already allocated a container on host–A–124. When such conditions arise, the ApplicationMaster is responsible for resolving any allocations in flight, with the local changes taking place in its resource requirements.

Locality Constraints

All the locality constraints for the application can be specified using the resource locations as described in the preceding example. In addition, the application can specify whether locality should be loose or strict using the `relaxLocality` flag against each request. If it is set to true, which is the default, the ResourceManager will wait for a while to allocate local containers; if this effort fails, it will fall through to the next level of resource location, from node to rack or from rack to "*". In the case where the `relaxLocality` flag is set to false, the ResourceManager will not serve such request until such a resource-location has enough free capacity to satisfy the request.

Priorities

Priorities are used for ordering the importance of resource requests. Higher-priority requests of an application are served first by the ResourceManager before the lower-priority requests of the same application are handled. There is no cross-application implication of priorities. Potentially, resources of different capabilities can be requested at the same priority, in which case the ResourceManager may order them arbitrarily.

Launching Containers

Once the ApplicationMaster obtains containers from the ResourceManager, it can then proceed to actual launch of the containers. Before launching a container, it first has to construct the ContainerLaunchContext object according to its needs, which can include allocated resource capability, security tokens (if enabled), the command to be executed to start the container, an environment for the process, necessary binaries/jar/shared objects, and more. It can either launch containers one by one by communicating to a NodeManager, or it can batch all containers on a single node together and launch them in a single call by providing a list of StartContainerRequests to the NodeManager.

The NodeManager sends a response via StartContainerResponse that includes a list of successfully launched containers, a container ID-to-exception map for each failed StartContainerRequest in which the exception indicates errors per container, and an allServicesMetaData map from the names of auxiliary services and their corresponding metadata.

The ApplicationMaster can also get updated statuses for submitted but still to be launched containers as well as already launched containers.

Figure 7.7 illustrates the interaction of the ApplicationMaster with the NodeManagers to start/stop containers and get container status. Note that the ApplicationMaster does not communicate with the ResourceManager at this point.

The ApplicationMaster can also request a NodeManager to stop a list of containers running on that node by sending a StopContainersRequest that includes the container IDs of the containers that should be stopped. The NodeManager sends a response via StopContainersResponse, which includes a list of container IDs of successfully stopped containers as well as a container ID-to-exception map for each failed request in which the exception indicates errors from the particular container.

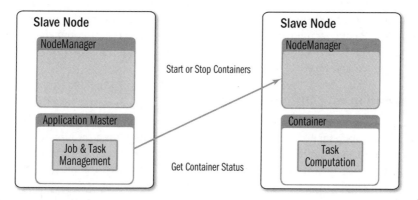

Figure 7.7   ApplicationMaster interacting with NodeManager

When an ApplicationMaster exits, depending on its submission context, the ResourceManager may choose to kill all the running containers that are not explicitly terminated by the ApplicationMaster itself.

Completed Containers

As previously described, when containers finish, the ApplicationMasters are informed by the ResourceManager about the event. Because the ResourceManager does not interpret (or care about) the container status, the ApplicationMaster determines the semantics of the success or failure of the container exit status reported through the ResourceManager.

Handling of container failures is the responsibility of the applications/frameworks. YARN is responsible only for providing information to the applications/framework. The ResourceManager collects information about all the finished containers as part of the *allocate* API's response, and it returns this information to the corresponding ApplicationMaster. It is up to the ApplicationMaster to look at information such as the container status, exit code, and diagnostics information and act on it appropriately. For example, when the MapReduce ApplicationMaster learns about container failures, it retries map or reduce tasks by requesting new containers from the ResourceManager until a configured number of attempts fail for a single task.

ApplicationMaster Failures and Recovery

The ApplicationMaster is also tasked with recovering the application after a restart that was due to the ApplicationMaster's own failure. When an ApplicationMaster fails, the ResourceManager simply restarts an application by launching a new Application-Master (or, more precisely, the container running the ApplicationMaster) for a new ApplicationAttempt; it is the responsibility of the new ApplicationMaster to recover the application's previous state This goal can be achieved by having the current ApplicationAttempts persist their current state to external storage for use by future attempts. Any ApplicationMaster can obviously just run the application from scratch all over again instead of recovering the past state. For example, as of this book's writing, the Hadoop MapReduce framework's ApplicationMaster recovered its completed tasks, but running tasks as well as the tasks that completed during ApplicationMaster recovery would be killed and rerun.

Coordination and Output Commit

The ApplicationMaster is also tasked with any coordination needed by containers. If a framework supports multiple containers contending for a resource or an output commit, ApplicationMaster should provide synchronization primitives for them, so that only one of those containers can access the shared resource, or it should promote the output of one while the other is ordered to wait or abort. The Map-Reduce ApplicationMaster defines the number of multiple attempts per task that can potentially run concurrently; it also provides APIs for tasks so that the output-commit operation demonstrates consistency.

There is another dimension of application-level coordination or output commit with YARN. Even though one can control the number of application attempts, for any given application the platform will try its best to make sure that there is only one valid ApplicationMaster running in the cluster at any point in time. However, YARN cannot guarantee this. Thus there may be a presently running valid ApplicationMaster and another ApplicationMaster from a previous attempt that is marked as either failed or killed but is actually still running. There are several situations where this can happen. One of the most common cases involves a network partition: The node running the ApplicationMaster may be cut off from ResourceManager, so YARN cannot really enforce the one-ApplicationMaster-at-a-time restriction. Application writers must be aware of this possibility, and should code their applications and frameworks to handle the potential multiple-writer problems. Such a multiple-writer problem has the biggest impact on the application-level commit, when two ApplicationAttempts of the same application race to a shared resource, and the output commit, where one may run into issues like data corruption.

Information for Clients

Some services previously offered by the Hadoop JobTracker—such as returning job progress over RPC, a web interface to find job status, and tracking finished jobs via JobHistory—are no longer part of YARN. They are provided either by the ApplicationMasters or by custom-built framework daemons. At the time of this writing, a generic solution to server framework-specific data with reasonable abstractions was a work in progress.

Security

If the application exposes a web service or an HTTP/socket/RPC interface, it is also responsible for all aspects of its secure operation. YARN merely secures its deployment.

Cleanup on ApplicationMaster Exit

When an ApplicationMaster is done with all its work, it should explicitly unregister with the ResourceManager by sending a FinishApplicationRequest. Similar to registration, as part of this request ApplicationMasters can report IPC and web URLs where clients can go once the application finishes and the ApplicationMaster is no longer running.

Once an ApplicationMaster's *finish* API causes the application to finish, the ApplicationMaster (i.e., the ApplicationMaster's container) will not immediately be killed until either the ApplicationMaster exits on its own or the ApplicationMaster liveliness interval is reached. This is done so as to enable ApplicationMasters to do some cleanup *after* the *finish* API is successfully recorded on the ResourceManager.

YARN Containers

As described earlier, a container in YARN represents a unit of work in an application. A container runs on a node, managed by a NodeManager; makes use of some resources on a node (e.g., memory, disk, CPU); depends on some libraries that are represented as local resources; and performs the needed work. While we have discussed most of how a container comes into existence, we have not talked about what constitutes the running responsibilities of a container. Note that because containers in YARN are directly mapped to a process in the underlying operation system, we may be using these terms interchangeably.

Container Environment

Once a container starts, for it to be able to perform its duties, it may depend on the availability of various pieces of information. Some of this information may be static, and some may be dynamic—that is, resolvable only at run time.

Static information may include libraries, input and output paths, and specifications of external systems like database or file system URLs. The following list highlights some of this information and explains how a container can obtain it:

- The ApplicationMaster should describe all libraries and other dependencies needed by a container for its start-up as part of its ContainerLaunchContext. That way, at the time of the container launch, such dependencies will already be downloaded by the localization in the NodeManager and be ready for linking directly.
- Input/output paths and file-system URLs are a part of the configuration that is beyond the control of YARN. Applications are required to propagate this information themselves. There are multiple ways one can do this:
  - Environment variables
  - Command-line parameters
  - Separate configuration files that are themselves passed as local resources
- Local directories where containers can write some outputs are determined by the environment variable `ApplicationConstants.Environment.LOCAL_DIRS`.
- Containers that need to log output or error statements to files need to make use of the log directory functionality. The NodeManager decide the location of log directories at run time. Because of this, a container's command line or its environment variables should point to the log directory by using a specialized marker defined by `ApplicationConstants.LOG_DIR_EXPANSION_VAR` (i.e., `<LOG_DIR>`). This marker will be automatically replaced with the correct log directory on the local file system when a container is launched.
- The user name, home directory, container ID, and some other environment-specific information are exposed as environment variables by the NodeManager;

containers can simply look them up in their environment. All such environment variables are documented by the *ApplicationConstants.Environment* API.

- Security-related tokens are all available on the local file system in a file whose name is provided in the container's environment, keyed by the name `ApplicationConstants.CONTAINER_TOKEN_FILE_ENV_NAME`. Containers can simply read this file and load all the credentials into memory.

Dynamic information includes settings that can potentially change during the lifetime of a container. It is composed of things like the location of the parent ApplicationMaster and the location of map outputs for a reduce task. Most of this information is the responsibility of the application-specific implementation. Some of the options include the following:

- The ApplicationMaster's URL can be passed to the container via environment variables, a command-line argument, or the configuration, but any dynamic changes to it during fail-over can be found by directly communicating to the ResourceManager as a client.

- The ApplicationMaster can coordinate the locations of the container's output and the corresponding auxiliary services, making this information available to other containers.

- The location of the HDFS NameNode (in case of a fail-over scenario) may be obtained from a dynamic plug-in that performs a configuration-based lookup of where an active NameNode is running.

Communication with the ApplicationMaster

Unlike with Hadoop version 1 MapReduce, there is no communication from a container to the parent NodeManager in YARN. Once a container starts, it is not required to report anything to the NodeManager. The code that runs the container is completely user written and, as such, all the NodeManager really enforces is the proper utilization of resources so that container runs within its limits.

It is also not required that containers report to their parent ApplicationMasters. In many cases, containers may just run in isolation, perform their work, and go away. On their exit, ApplicationMasters will eventually learn about their completion status, either directly from the NodeManager or via the NodeManager–ResourceManager–ApplicationMaster channel for status of completed containers. If an application needs its container to be in communication with its ApplicationMaster, however, it is entirely up to the application/framework to implement such a protocol. YARN neither enforces this type of communication nor supports it. Consequently, an application that needs to monitor the application-specific progress, counters, or status should have its container configured to report such status directly to the ApplicationMaster via some interprocess communication. Figure 7.8 shows an overview of the interaction of containers with the NodeManager and the ApplicationMaster.

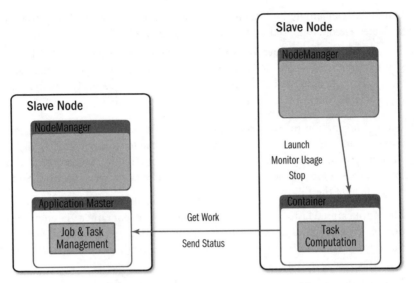

Figure 7.8   Container's interaction with
ApplicationMaster and NodeManager

Summary for Application-writers

The following is a quick summary of the responsibilities for application writers. Consult Chapter 10, "Apache Hadoop YARN Application Example," and Chapter 11, "Using Apache Hadoop YARN Distributed-Shell," for actual application examples.

- Submit the application by passing a ContainerLaunchContext for the ApplicationMaster to the ResourceManager.

- After the ResourceManager starts the ApplicationMaster, the ApplicationMaster should register with the ResourceManager and periodically report its liveliness and resource requirements over the wire.

- Once the ResourceManager allocates a container, the ApplicationMaster can construct a ContainerLaunchContext to launch the container on the corresponding NodeManager. It may also monitor the status of the running container and stop it when the work is done. Monitoring the progress of work done inside the container is strictly the ApplicationMaster's responsibility.

- Once the ApplicationMaster is done with its overall work, it should unregister from the ResourceManager and exit cleanly.

- Optionally, frameworks may add control flow between their containers and the ApplicationMaster as well as between their own clients and the Application-Master to report status information.

In general, an ApplicationMaster that is hardened against faults, including its own, is nontrivial. The client libraries that ship with YARN—YarnClient, NMClient, and AMRMClient—expose a higher-level API and are strongly recommended over using low-level protocols.

Wrap-up

In YARN, the ResourceManager is fundamentally limited to scheduling and does not manage user applications. This design addresses the issues of better scalability and support for alternative (non-MapReduce) programming paradigms.

The YARN NodeManager has more responsibility than the Hadoop version 1 TaskTracker and is designed to tightly manage node resources in the form of application containers. It also supports better log management and provides a flexible method for multiple-container interaction by providing the auxiliary services capability.

Finally, some of the responsibility for managing resources has been pushed to the user with the introduction of the ApplicationMaster. This responsibility also offers great flexibility, such that applications can now manage their containers and application resources requirements dynamically at run time.

8

Capacity Scheduler in YARN

Typically organizations start Apache Hadoop deployments as single-user environments and/or just for a single team. As organizations start deriving more value from data processing and move toward mature cluster deployments, there are significant drivers to consolidate Hadoop clusters into a small number of scaled, shared clusters. This need is driven by the desire to minimize data fragmentation on multiple systems. Such concentration of data on a few HDFS clusters liberates data for organization-wide access, avoids data silos, and allows all-accommodating data-processing workflows. In addition, the operational costs and complexity of managing multiple small clusters are reduced.

Once the deployment architecture in an organization evolves toward centralized data repositories, shared compute clusters should follow suit for the same reasons. A successful model for this is for multiple teams, suborganizations, or business units within a single parent organization to come together to pool compute resources and share resources for efficiency. Apache Hadoop started supporting such shared clusters beginning with Hadoop version 0.20 (the version predated, and eventually evolved into, Apache Hadoop version 1.x). Initially, Hadoop supported a simple first-in, first-out (FIFO) job scheduler that allowed scheduling for shared clusters but was insufficient to address various emerging use-cases. This situation eventually led to the implementation of the Capacity scheduler. YARN and Hadoop version 2 inherit most of the same Capacity scheduler functionality, along with lots of improvements and enhancements required to take full advantage of the new capabilities unlocked in YARN.

Introduction to the Capacity Scheduler

As we discussed in Chapter 1, "Apache Hadoop YARN: A Brief History and Rationale," the Capacity scheduler originally came about in Hadoop version 1 to address some of the issues with Hadoop on Demand (HOD)–based architecture. It is designed to run applications in a shared cluster supporting multitenancy, while maximizing application throughput and enabling high utilization of the cluster. Given the new support in YARN for applications of arbitrary frameworks and workload characteristics, the Capacity scheduler in Hadoop version 2 with YARN has been enhanced with other features to support these new use-cases.

In the HOD architecture, each user or team would have its own private compute cluster allocated dynamically but with constricted elasticity. This would lead to poor cluster utilization and poor locality of data. Sharing clusters between organizations is a cost-effective way to run multitenant Hadoop installations that leads to improvements in utilization, better performance, and the potential for more intelligent scheduling. However, resource sharing also brings up concerns about application isolation, security, and the issue of resource contention.

The Capacity scheduler is built to address all these concerns. It is designed around the following ideas.

Elasticity with Multitenancy

Organizations prefer to share resources between individuals, teams, and suborganizations in an elastic fashion. Free resources should be allocated to any entity as long as those resources remain underutilized otherwise. When there is an emergent demand for these resources, they should be pulled back with minimal impact to service level agreements (SLAs) of the originally entitled entities.

The Capacity scheduler supports these features with queue capacities, minimum user percentages, and limits. It is designed to enable sharing of a single YARN cluster while simultaneously giving each organization guarantees on the allocated capacities. To improve utilization, organizations can make use of idle capacities "belonging" to other organizations. The Capacity scheduler also enforces stringent limits to avoid a single application, user, or queue from overwhelming the cluster and impacting co-tenants.

Security

Multitenant clusters also raise concerns about security even within an umbrella organization. The Capacity scheduler provides tools like queue-level Access Control Lists (ACLs) for the administrators so that there are enough safeguards to address cross-organization security-related compliance.

Resource Awareness

Organizations should be able to use YARN to orchestrate applications with differing resource requirements and to arbitrate resources of all kinds, including memory, CPU, disks, or other cluster-wide shared resources. The current version of the Capacity scheduler supports CPU and memory resources, and support for other resources is expected. Scheduling policies exist to take into account the memory and CPU requirements of submitted applications and support the dynamic needs of ApplicationMasters.

Granular Scheduling

Organizations should be able to share individual nodes in a fine-grained manner as opposed to loaning full nodes to tenants. Assigning complete nodes hurts utilization and should be avoided.

Compared to the other traditional resource managers with which HOD worked, YARN deals with resources in a different manner—namely, by not partitioning nodes in a static way and assigning them to queues. The unit of scheduling in YARN is much more granular and dynamic. Queues in YARN are simply a logical view of resources on physical nodes. This design enables finer-grained sharing of individual nodes by various applications, users, and organizations and, therefore, facilitates high utilization.

Locality

Following one of YARN's core goals, the Capacity scheduler supports specifying the locality of computation as well as node or rack affinity by applications. Furthermore, the Capacity scheduler itself is locality aware, and is very good at automatically allocating resources on not only preferred nodes/racks, but also nodes/racks that are close to the preferred ones. In doing so, it ensures that the framework developer does not have to worry about locality. This feature is one of the key differences between YARN and other, traditional, resource managers.

Scheduling Policies

Organizations may need to control various aspects of scheduling depending on their anticipated workloads. For example, there may be a need to balance data processing through batch workflows with applications driving interactive analysis. In addition, there may be requirements for support of an all-or-nothing kind of gang scheduling, or there may be a need for executing long-running services alongside applications vying for sustained throughput.

The Capacity scheduler offers support for churning through applications to attain high throughput. Given its historical roots of scheduling MapReduce applications in Hadoop version 1, the Capacity scheduler understands that even though containers may not be running, they can still consume resources in the cluster. Consider the output of MapReduce map tasks: Even after a map task completes, it still consumes resources to store its map outputs. The first-in, first-out (FIFO) scheduling policy of the Capacity scheduler strives for maximum throughput, thereby enabling efficient use of cluster resources.

At the time of this book's writing, the YARN community was working on several innovations to support emerging use-cases like long-running services and special needs of interactive data analysis.

Capacity Scheduler Configuration

The Capacity scheduler is the default scheduler that ships with Hadoop YARN. In the event that it becomes necessary to explicitly set the scheduler in the configuration, one should set the following values in the configuration file `yarn-site.xml` on the ResourceManager node:

- **Property**: `yarn.resourcemanager.scheduler.class`

- **Value**: org.apache.hadoop.yarn.server.resourcemanager.scheduler.
  capacity.CapacityScheduler

The Capacity scheduler itself depends on a special configuration file called
capacity-scheduler.xml to be present in the ResourceManager's class path for its
settings. This location is typically in a conf directory. The scheduler reads this file
both when it is starting and when an administrator modifies it and issues a special signal for reloading it.

Changing various configuration settings in the Capacity scheduler (e.g., queue
properties, application limits) is very straightforward and can be done at run time.
This task can be accomplished by editing capacity-scheduler.xml with the desired
modifications and then running the following admin command:

```
$ yarn rmadmin -refreshQueues
```

This command can be run only by cluster administrators, and is configured using a
list at the ResourceManager via the yarn.admin.acl property.

Queues

The fundamental unit of scheduling in YARN is a **queue**. A queue is either a logical
collection of applications submitted by various users or a composition of more queues.
Every queue in the Capacity scheduler has the following properties:

- A short queue **name**
- A full queue **path** name
- A list of child queues and applications associated with them
- Guaranteed capacity of the queue
- Maximum capacity to which a queue can grow
- A list of active users and the corresponding limits of sharing between users.
- State of the queue
- ACLs governing the access to the queue

The following discussion describes what these properties are, how the Capacity
scheduler uses them for making various scheduling decisions, and how they can be
configured to meet specific needs.

Hierarchical Queues

In the Capacity scheduler, each queue typically represents an organization, while the
capacity of the queue represents the capacity (of the cluster) that the organization is
entitled to use. In Hadoop version 1, the Capacity scheduler supported only a flat list

of queues, which was eventually found to be limiting. Most organizations are large and need to further share their queues among users from different suborganizations in a fine-grained manner. This desire to divide capacity further and share it among suborganizations is also accentuated by the existence of various categories of users within a given queue. For example, within an organization, some applications may belong to different categories, such as interactive and batch workloads, production and ad hoc research applications, and so on. The Capacity scheduler in YARN supports hierarchical queues to address this gap.

Key Characteristics

Some important characteristics of hierarchical queues are highlighted here:

- Queues are of two types: **parent queues** and **leaf queues**.
  - Parent queues enable the management of resources across organizations and suborganizations. They can contain more parent queues or leaf queues. They do not themselves accept any application submissions directly.
  - Leaf queues denote the queues that live under a parent queue and accept applications. Leaf queues do not have any more child queues.
- The top-level parent queue called ROOT queue doesn't belong to any organization and denotes the cluster itself.
- Using parent and leaf queues, administrators can do capacity allocations to various organizations and suborganizations.

Scheduling Among Queues

Hierarchical queues ensure that guaranteed resources are first shared among the subqueues of an organization before queues belonging to other organizations are allowed to use free resources from this queue. This design enables each organization to have more control over how resources guaranteed to them are predictably utilized. The scheduling algorithm works as follows:

- At every level in the hierarchy, every parent queue keeps the list of its child queues in a sorted manner based on demand. The sorting of the queues is determined by the currently used fraction of each queue's capacity (or the queue names [i.e., full path names] if the utilization of any two queues is equal) at any point in time.
- The ROOT queue understands how the cluster capacity has to be distributed among the first level of parent queues and invokes scheduling on each of its child queues.
- Every parent queue also tries to follow the same capacity constraints for all of its child queues and schedules them accordingly.

- Leaf queues hold the list of active applications, potentially from multiple users, and schedule resources in a FIFO manner while simultaneously respecting the limits on how much a single user can take within that queue.

Defining Hierarchical Queues

Queues have evolved from a flat list to a hierarchy, and as a result their naming has also needed to change. The Capacity scheduler uses **queue paths** to refer to any queue in the hierarchy. The queue path names each queue in its ancestral hierarchy starting with the ROOT queue, with each name separated by a dot ("."). As of this book's writing, the configuration of hierarchical queues was still driven by a flat list of configuration properties. The Capacity scheduler uses the same queue paths to specify its configuration in `capacity-scheduler.xml`, as described earlier.

Let's look at an example that will be used in the rest of the chapter to explain the concepts associated with the Capacity scheduler. Assume that in a company named YARNRollers, there are three organizations called grumpy-engineers, finance-wizards, and marketing-moguls. In addition, assume the grumpy-engineers organization has two subteams: infinite-monkeys and pesky-testers. The finance-wizards organization has two suborganizations: meticulous-accountants and thrifty-treasurers. Finally, the marketing-moguls are divided into brand-exploders and social-savants. The overall hierarchy of queues in this example is shown in Figure 8.1.

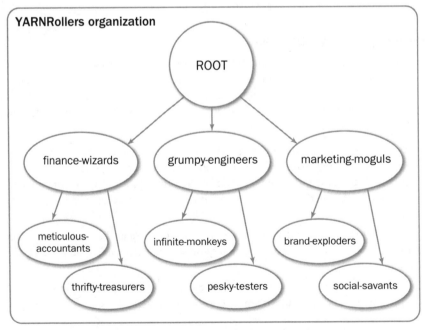

Figure 8.1 Example hierarchies for use by Capacity scheduler

Child queues are tied to their parent queue by defining the configuration property `yarn.scheduler.capacity.<queue-path>.queues`. For example, the top-level queues (grumpy-engineers, finance-wizards, and marketing-moguls) should be tied to the ROOT queue. Thus the queue hierarchy is configured as follows:

- **Property**: `yarn.scheduler.capacity.root.queues`
- **Value**: `grumpy-engineers,finance-wizards,marketing-moguls`

Similarly, the children of the parent queue finance-wizards are defined as follows:

- **Property**: `yarn.scheduler.capacity.finance-wizards.queues`
- **Value**: `meticulous-accountants,thrifty-treasurers`

Leaf queues have no further children, so they should *not* have any corresponding configuration property that ends with the `.queues` suffix.

There are limitations on how one can name the queues. To avoid confusion, the Capacity scheduler doesn't allow two leaf queues to have the same name across the whole hierarchy.

As of this book's writing, queues could not be deleted completely at run time, but they could be stopped (as will be described later in this chapter). New queues can be added dynamically at run time by simply defining a new queue, attaching it to its parent, and refreshing the configuration using the `yarn rmadmin` utility mentioned earlier. Note that newly added queues cannot invalidate constraints, such as the constraint that queue capacity at each level be no more than 100%. Further, one cannot (for obvious reasons) change what was previously a leaf-level queue to be a parent queue by adding a new child queue to it.

Queue Access Control

The point of having queues is to enable sharing and at the same time to give control back to the organization, limiting who can submit applications to any given queue and who can administer a queue.

Queues can be configured to restrict submission to queues at various levels. Although application submission can really happen only at the leaf queue level, an ACL on a parent queue can be set to control admittance to all the descendant queues.

Access Control Lists in Hadoop are configured by specifying the list of users and/ or groups as a string property. For specifying a list of users and groups, the format is "user1,user2 group1,group" (a comma-separated list of users, followed by a space separator, followed by a comma-separated list of groups). If it is set to "*" (asterisk), all users and groups are allowed to perform the operation guarded by the ACL in question. If it is set to " " (i.e., space), no users or groups are allowed to perform the operation. With that specification of ACLs, for example, to restrict access to *any* queue originating under the finance-wizards queue to only sherlock, pacioli, and a special group called cfo-group, one can make the following assignments:

- **Property**: `yarn.scheduler.capacity.root.finance-wizards.acl_submit_applications`
- **Value**: `sherlock,pacioli cfo-group`

A separate ACL can be used to control administration of queues at various levels. Queue administrators have permission to submit applications without an explicit submit ACL, kill any application in the queue, and obtain information about any application in the queue; by comparison, regular users are restricted from viewing all the details of other users' applications. Administrators' ACLs can be configured similar to submit ACLs, for example, to make the special group cfo-group the sole administrators of the finance-wizards queues:

- **Property**: `yarn.scheduler.capacity.root.finance-wizards.acl_administer_queue`
- **Value**: `" cfo-group"`
- **Description**: A space character followed by `cfo-group`, unquoted

With YARN's Capacity scheduler supporting a hierarchy of queues, delegation of the administration is possible. Queue administrators of a suborganization can take control of monitoring queues for irregularities. Ideally, administrators of suborganizations should be able to add new queues, stop queues, and perform other queue-related tasks; these abilities are expected to be available in future versions of YARN.

Capacity Management with Queues

The Capacity scheduler is designed to allow organizations to share compute clusters using the very familiar notion of first-in, first-out queues. YARN doesn't assign whole nodes to queues. Instead, queues own a fraction of the capacity of the cluster, which can be fulfilled from any number of nodes in a dynamic fashion. Scheduling is the process of matching the resource requirements of multiple applications from various users, each submitted to different queues at multiple levels in the queue hierarchy, with free capacity available at any point in time on the nodes in the cluster.

Queues are configured by the administrators to be allocated as a fraction of the capacity of the whole cluster. In our example, assuming that the administrators decide to share the cluster resources between the grumpy-engineers, finance-wizards, and marketing-moguls in a 6:1:3 ratio, the corresponding queue configuration will be as follows:

- **Property**: `yarn.scheduler.capacity.root.grumpy-engineers.capacity`
- **Value**: 60
- **Property**: `yarn.scheduler.capacity.root.finance-wizards.capacity`
- **Value**: 10

- **Property**: yarn.scheduler.capacity.root.marketing-moguls.capacity
- **Value**: 30

YARN is built around the fundamental requirements of fault tolerance and elasticity. In a YARN cluster built out of commodity hardware, subcomponents of a node like disks or even whole nodes can go down for any of several reasons. In addition, depending on workloads and historical cluster usage, administrators may choose to either add new physical machines or take away existing nodes to account for under-utilization. Any of these changes will cause corresponding variations in cluster capacity, as seen by the Capacity scheduler for the sake of scheduling. Queue capacity configuration is indicated in terms of percentages for this reason; this scheme ensures that organizations and suborganizations can reason well about their shares and guarantees irrespective of small variations in the total cluster capacity.

As discussed in the section dealing with hierarchical queues, there is a capacity planning problem at a suborganization level. Continuing with our example, let's assume the grumpy-engineers decide to share their capacity between the infinite-monkeys and the pesky-testers in a 1:4 ratio (so that testing of YARN gets as much resources as possible). The corresponding configuration should be as follows, again given in terms of percentages:

- **Property**: yarn.scheduler.capacity.root.grumpy-engineers.infinite-monkeys.capacity
- **Value**: 20
- **Property**: yarn.scheduler.capacity.root.grumpy-engineers.pesky-testers.capacity
- **Value**: 80

Note that the sum of capacities at any level in the hierarchy should be no more than 100% (for obvious reasons).

As described earlier, during scheduling, queues at any level in the hierarchy are sorted in the order of their current used capacity and available resources are distributed among them, starting with those queues that are the most under-served at that point in time. With respect to just capacities, the resource scheduling has the following flow:

- The more under-served the queues, the higher the priority that is given to them during resource allocation. The most under-served queue is the queue with the smallest ratio of used capacity to the total cluster capacity.
  - The used capacity of any parent queue is defined as the aggregate sum of used capacity of all the descendant queues recursively.
  - The used capacity of a leaf queue is the amount of resources that is used by allocated containers of all applications running in that queue.

- Once it is decided to give a parent queue the freely available resources, further similar scheduling is done to decide recursively as to which child queue gets to use the resources based on the same concept of used capacities.

- Scheduling inside a leaf queue further happens to allocate resources to applications arriving in a FIFO order.

  - Such scheduling also depends on locality, user level limits, and application limits (to be described soon).

  - Once an application within a leaf queue is chosen, scheduling happens within an application, too. Applications may have different resource requests at different priorities.

- To ensure elasticity, capacity that is configured but not utilized by any queue due to lack of demand is automatically assigned to the queues that are in need of resources.

To get a better understanding of how the cluster is divided and how scheduling happens, consider how available memory in the cluster is scheduled. Assuming a cluster of 100 nodes, each with 10 GB of memory allocated for YARN containers, we have a total cluster capacity of 1000 GB (one 1 TB). Now according to the previously described configuration, the grumpy-engineers organization is assigned a capacity of 60% of cluster capacity (i.e., an absolute capacity of 600 GB). Similarly, the finance-wizards are assigned 100 GB and the marketing-moguls suborganization gets 300 GB.

Under the grumpy-engineers organization, capacity needs to be distributed between the infinite-monkeys team and the pesky-testers in the ratio 1:4. Thus the infinite-monkeys get 120 GB, and 480 GB is assigned to the pesky-testers.

Consider the following timeline of events happening in the cluster:

- In the beginning, the entire grumpy-engineers queue is free, with no application in any queues or from any users in a running state. Other queues at that level used by the finance-wizards and the marketing-moguls are completely utilizing their capacities.

- The users sid and hitesh first submit applications to the leaf queue infinite-monkeys. Their applications are elastic and can run with either all the resources available in the cluster or a subset depending on the state of the resource usage.

  - As the first set of users in the system, even though each of them may be controlled to be within the queue (120 GB, because of user-limit factor described later), together they can occupy 240 GB (two users controlled to queue capacity each).

  - This situation can occur despite the fact that infinite-monkeys are configured to be run with only 120 GB. The Capacity scheduler lets this happen to ensure elastic sharing of cluster resources and for high utilization.

- Assume the users jian, zhijie, and xuan submit more applications to the leaf queue infinite-monkeys, such that even though each leaf queue is restricted to

120 GB, the overall used capacity in the queue becomes 600 GB—essentially taking over all the capacity to which the pesky-testers are entitled.

- Next the user gupta submits his own application to the queue pesky-testers, so as to start running an analysis of historical testing of his software project. With no free resources in the cluster, his application will wait.
  - Given that the infinite-monkeys queue has now taken over the whole cluster, the user gupta may or may not be able to get back the guaranteed capacity of his queue immediately depending on whether preemption is enabled.
- As resources start being freed up from the applications of sid, hitesh, jian, zhijie, and xuan in the infinite-monkeys queue, the freed-up containers will start being allocated to gupta's applications. This will continue until the cluster stabilizes at the intended 1:4 ratio of resource allocation between the two queues.

As one can see, this setup leaves the door open for abusive users to submit applications continuously and lock out other queues from resource allocation until the abusive users' containers finish or get preempted. To avoid this problem, the Capacity scheduler supports limits on the elastic growth of any queue. For example, to restrict the infinite-monkeys from monopolizing the queue capacity and to box them into their capacity, administrators can set the following limit:

- **Property**: `yarn.scheduler.capacity.root.grumpy-engineers.infinite-monkeys.maximum-capacity`
- **Value**: `40`

Once this limit is set, the infinite-monkeys can still go beyond their capacity of 120 GB, but they cannot get resources allocated to them that exceed 40% of the parent queue grumpy-engineers' capacity (i.e., 40% of 600 GB = 240 GB).

The capacity and maximum capacity configuration come together to provide the basic control over sharing and elasticity across organizations or suborganizations on a YARN cluster. Administrators need to balance the elasticity with the limits so that there isn't a loss of utilization due to too-strict limits and, conversely, there isn't any cross-organization impact due to excessive sharing.

Capacities and maximum capacities can be dynamically changed at run time using the `rmadmin` "refresh queues" functionality. It is a good practice for administrators to audit queue usage and grow or shrink user limits at various levels to find the desired balance.

User Limits

Leaf queues have the additional responsibility of ensuring fairness with regard to scheduling applications submitted by various users in *that* queue. The Capacity scheduler places various limits on users to enforce this fairness. Recall that applications can only be submitted to leaf queues in the Capacity scheduler; thus, parent queues do not have any role in enforcing user limits.

When configuring the user limits of a queue, administrators have to decide upfront the amount of user sharing that they would like to enable at run time. Let's start with an example of an administrator who decides to configure user limits for the finance-wizards suborganization. As mentioned, user limits need to be set for every leaf queue. Let's focus on the leaf queue called `root.finance-wizards.thrifty-treasurers`.

All user limits are based on the queue's capacity. As mentioned earlier, queue capacity is a dynamically changing entity, so user limits are also dynamically adjusted in every scheduling cycle based on capacity changes.

Assume the queue capacity needs to be shared among not more than five users in the thrifty-treasurers queue. When you account for fairness, this results in each of those five users being given an equal share (20%) of the capacity of the `root.finance-wizards.thrifty-treasurers` queue. The following configuration for the finance-wizards queue applies this limit:

- **Property**: `yarn.scheduler.capacity.root.finance-wizards.thrifty-treasurers.minimum-user-limit-percent`
- Value: 20

This configuration property is named **minimum-user-limit-percent** to reflect the fact that it determines only the minimum to which any user's share of the queue capacity can shrink. In other words, irrespective of this limit, any user can come into the queue and take more than his or her fair share if there are idle resources. Let's look at an example to see how this situation can occur.

- Assume the queue started out being empty. Only user hillegas submits an application, which occupies the entire queue's capacity.
- Now when another user meredith submits an application, hillegas and meredith are both "assigned" 50% of the capacity of the queue. By "assigned," we mean that from that point onward, all scheduling decisions are based on the assumption that each of those users deserves a 50% share of the queue.
  - Whether the containers of user hillegas are immediately killed to satisfy the requests from user meredith is a function of whether preemption is enabled in the Capacity scheduler. If hillegas's containers are preempted in due time, meredith's application will start getting those containers until the 50% balance is reached. Otherwise, as containers from hillegas gradually finish in their usual manner after completing their work, they will be assigned to meredith.
  - Once the balance of 50% share for each user is reached, any freshly freed-up capacity is alternately allocated to the applications of each user.

- If either of the users doesn't require the entire queue capacity to run his or her application(s), the Capacity scheduler will automatically assign the extra idle capacity to the other user who needs it, all in an elastic manner—even if the current capacity assignments are 50% each. Thus, the sharing is based on both the number of existing users and the outstanding demands of a specific user. If a user has a 50% share but doesn't have enough resource requirements to make use of that share, the idle capacity is automatically allocated to the other user, even if the other user is already meeting his or her 50% minimum requirement.

- As long as there are outstanding resource requests from existing as well as newly submitted applications from the same set of users, the capacity assignments to these users will not change.

- Now if user tucker begins to submit applications to the same queue, the share of each and every user currently present in the queue—that is, hillegas, meredith, and tucker—becomes 33.3% of the queue capacity (again, assuming there is sufficient demand from each user's applications). The same rules of allocation and reassignment apply as before.

- This trend continues until five users are admitted into the queue and each of them is assigned a 20% share as dictated by the minimum-user-limit-percent configuration property for this queue.

- If a sixth user selden now enters the queue, the behavior changes to respect the administrator's desire set via the configuration. Instead of continuing to further divide the capacity among six users, the Capacity scheduler halts the sharing to satisfy the minimum user limit percentage for each of the existing five users (i.e., 20%). User selden will be put on a wait list until the applications of one or more of the existing users finish.

- Just as a growing number of users is managed, so a shrinking number of users is also handled. As any users' applications finish, other existing users with outstanding requirements begin to reclaim the share. For example, in an alternative scenario, if hillegas, meredith, and tucker are each using 33% of the queue capacity and user meredith's applications complete, hillegas and tucker can now each get 50% of the queue capacity, reflecting the fact that there are only two users in the queue now.

- Despite this sharing among users, the fundamental nature of the Capacity scheduler to schedule applications based on a FIFO order doesn't change! This guarantees that users cannot monopolize queues by submitting new applications continuously: Applications (and thus the corresponding users) that are submitted earlier always get a higher priority than applications that are submitted later.

Overall, user limits are put in place to enable fair sharing of queue resources, but only up to a certain amount. A balance is sought between not spreading resources too thin among users and avoiding the case in which one or a few users overwhelm the queue with a continuous barrage of resource requests.

In addition to being governed by the configuration that controls sharing among users, the Capacity scheduler's leaf queues have the ability to restrict or expand a user's share within and beyond the queue's capacity through the per-leaf-queue **user-limit-factor** configuration. It denotes the fraction of queue capacity that any single user can grow, up to a maximum, irrespective of whether there are idle resources in the cluster. This same configuration also dictates various other application limits, as we will see later.

- **Property**: `yarn.scheduler.capacity.root.finance-wizards.user-limit-factor`
- **Value**: 1

The default value of 1 means that any single user in that queue can, at a maximum, occupy only the queue's configured capacity. This value avoids the case in which users in a single queue monopolize resources across all queues in a cluster. By extension, setting the value to 2 allows the queue to grow to a maximum of twice the size of the queue's configured capacity. Similarly, setting it to 0.5 restricts any user from growing his or her share beyond half of the queue capacity.

Note that, like everything else, these limits can be dynamically changed at run time using the refresh-queues functionality.

Reservations

The Capacity scheduler's responsibility is to match free resources in the cluster with the resource requirements of an application. Many times, however, a scheduling cycle occurs in such a way that even though there are free resources on a node, they are not large enough in size to satisfy the application that is at the head of the queue. This situation typically happens with large-memory applications whose resource demand for each of their containers is much larger than the typical application running in the cluster. When such applications run in the cluster, anytime a regular application's containers finish, thereby releasing previously used resources for new cycles of scheduling, nodes will have freely available resources but the large-memory applications cannot take advantage of them because the resources are still too small. If left unchecked, this mismatch can cause starving of resource-intensive applications.

The Capacity scheduler solves this problem with a feature called reservations. The scheduling flow for reservations resembles the following:

- When a node reports in with a finished container and thus a certain amount of freely available resources, the scheduler chooses the right queue based on capacities and maximum capacities.
- Within that queue, the scheduler looks at the application in a FIFO order together with the user limits. Once a needy application is found, it tries to see if the requirements of that application can be met by this node's free capacity.

- If there is a size mismatch, the Capacity scheduler immediately creates a reservation for this application's container on this node.

- Once a reservation is made for an application on a node, those resources are not used by the scheduler for any other queue, application, or container until the original application for which the reservation was made is served.

- The node on which a reservation was made can eventually report back that enough containers have finished such that the total free capacity on the node now matches the reservation size. When that happens, the Capacity scheduler marks the reservation as fulfilled, removes it, and allocates a container on that node.

- Meanwhile, some other node may fulfill the resource needs of the application such that the application no longer needs the reserved capacity. In such a situation, when the reserved node eventually comes back, the reservation is simply cancelled.

To limit the number of reservations from growing in an unbounded manner, and to prevent any potential scheduling deadlocks, the Capacity scheduler simplifies the problem drastically by maintaining only one active reservation per node.

State of the Queues

Queues in YARN can be in one of two states: RUNNING and STOPPED. These states are not specific to the Capacity scheduler. As should already be obvious, the RUNNING state indicates that a queue can accept application submissions, while a STOPPED queue doesn't accept any such requests. The default state of any configured queue is RUNNING.

In the Capacity scheduler, both leaf queues and parent queues can be stopped. This state includes the root queue as well. For an application to be accepted at any leaf queue, all of the queues in the ancestry—all the way to the root queue—need to be running. This requirement means that once a parent queue is stopped, all the descendant queues in that hierarchy are inactive even if their own state is RUNNING.

In our example, the following configuration dictates the state of the finance-wizards queue:

- **Property**: `yarn.scheduler.capacity.root.finance-wizards.state`
- **Value**: `RUNNING`

The rationale for enabling the ability to stop queues is that in various scenarios, administrators wish to drain applications in a queue for many reasons. Decommissioning a queue to migrate users to other queues is one such example. Administrators can stop queues at run time so that while currently present applications run to completion, no new applications are admitted. Existing applications can continue until they complete, allowing the queue to be drained gracefully without any end-user impact.

Administrators can also restart the stopped queues by modifying the same configuration property and refreshing the queue using the `rmadmin` utility as described earlier.

Limits on Applications

To avoid system thrash due to an unmanageable load, created either by accident or by malicious users, the Capacity scheduler puts a static configurable limit on the total number of concurrently active (both running and pending) applications at any single point in time. The default is 10,000. The following configuration property controls this value.

- **Property**: `yarn.scheduler.capacity.maximum-applications`
- **Value**: `10000`

The limit on any specific queue is a fraction of this total limit proportional to its capacity. This setting is a hard limit, which means that once this limit is reached for a queue, any new applications to that queue will be rejected and clients will have to retry their requests after a while.

This limit can be explicitly overridden on a per-queue basis by the following configuration property:

- **Property**: `yarn.scheduler.capacity.<queue-path>.maximum-applications`
- **Value**: `absolute-capacity * yarn.scheduler.capacity.maximum-applications`

There is also a limit on the maximum percentage of resources in the cluster that can be used by the ApplicationMasters. This limit defaults to 10%. It exists to avoid cross-application deadlocks where significant resources in the cluster are occupied entirely by the containers running ApplicationMasters that are waiting for other applications to release containers to proceed with their own work. This configuration indirectly controls the number of concurrent running applications in the cluster, with each queue limited to a number of applications proportional to its capacity.

- **Property**: `yarn.scheduler.capacity.maximum-am-resource-percent`
- **Value**: `0.1`

Similar to the maximum number of applications, this limit can be overridden on a per-queue basis as follows.

- **Property**: `yarn.scheduler.capacity.<queue-path>.maximum-am-resource-percent`
- **Value**: `0.1`

All of these limits ensure that a single application, user, or queue cannot cause catastrophic failures or monopolize the cluster and cause unreasonable degradation of cluster performance or utilization.

User Interface

When the ResourceManager is started with Capacity scheduler, a scheduler webpage is available on the main YARN web interface (http://localhost:8080). The scheduler webpage is available by clicking the scheduler link in the left-hand column. As shown in Figure 8.2, the interface shows the queue hierarchy and information about individual queues.

Wrap-up

The Capacity scheduler has been successfully managing large-scale systems for several years. Many of its concepts are directly inherited from the incarnation of CapacityTask-Scheduler in Hadoop version 1. Thanks to knowledge garnered from the YARN community's experience of running the Capacity scheduler on very large, shared clusters, it

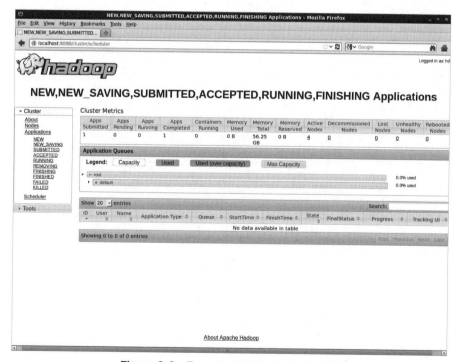

Figure 8.2 Example YARN scheduler GUI

has been continuously enhanced to improve upon its original design goals of providing elasticity in computing, a flexible resource model, isolation using appropriate limits, support for multitenancy, and the ability to manage new scheduling policies.

The continuous growth of Hadoop clusters and new users has helped refine the Capacity scheduler to its present form. It has become a useful tool to help manage the operational complexity (at run time) of hierarchical queues, Access Control Lists, and user and application limits; to set reservations; and to manage queue states.

## 9

MapReduce with Apache Hadoop YARN

The introduction of Hadoop version 2 has changed much of how MapReduce applications run on a cluster. Unlike the monolithic MapReduce–Schedule in Hadoop Version 1, Hadoop YARN has generalized the cluster resources available to users. To keep compatibility with Hadoop version 1, the YARN team has written a MapReduce framework that works on top of YARN. The framework is highly compatible with Hadoop version 1, with only a small number of issues to consider. As with Hadoop version 1, Hadoop YARN comes with virtually the same MapReduce examples and benchmarks that help demonstrate how Hadoop YARN functions.

Running Hadoop YARN MapReduce Examples

Running the existing MapReduce examples is a straightforward process. The examples are located in `hadoop-[VERSION]/share/hadoop/mapreduce`. Depending on where you installed Hadoop, this path may vary. For the purposes of this example, let's define this path:

```
export YARN_EXAMPLES=$YARN_HOME/share/hadoop/mapreduce
```

$YARN_HOME should be defined as part of your installation. Also, the examples given in this section have a version tag—in this case, "2.2.0." Your installation may have a different version tag. The following discussion provides some examples of Hadoop YARN-based MapReduce programs and benchmarks.

Listing Available Examples

Using our $YARN_HOME environment variable, we can get a list of possible examples by running

```
$ yarn jar $YARN_EXAMPLES/hadoop-mapreduce-examples-2.2.0.jar
```

The possible examples are as follows:

```
An example program must be given as the first argument.
Valid program names are:
  aggregatewordcount: An Aggregate based map/reduce program that counts
  the words in the input files.
  aggregatewordhist: An Aggregate based map/reduce program that computes
  the histogram of the words in the input files.
  bbp: A map/reduce program that uses Bailey-Borwein-Plouffe to compute
  exact digits of Pi.
  dbcount: An example job that counts the pageview counts from a database.
  distbbp: A map/reduce program that uses a BBP-type formula to compute
  exact bits of Pi.
  grep: A map/reduce program that counts the matches of a regex in the
  input.
  join: A job that effects a join over sorted, equally partitioned
  data sets
  multifilewc: A job that counts words from several files.
  pentomino: A map/reduce tile laying program to find solutions to
  pentomino problems.
  pi: A map/reduce program that estimates Pi using a quasi-Monte Carlo
  method.
  randomtextwriter: A map/reduce program that writes 10GB of random
  textual data per node.
  randomwriter: A map/reduce program that writes 10GB of random data per
  node.
  secondarysort: An example defining a secondary sort to the reduce.
  sort: A map/reduce program that sorts the data written by the random
  writer.
  sudoku: A sudoku solver.
  teragen: Generate data for the terasort.
  terasort: Run the terasort.
  teravalidate: Checking results of terasort
  wordcount: A map/reduce program that counts the words in the input
  files.
  wordmean: A map/reduce program that counts the average length of the
  words in the input files.
  wordmedian: A map/reduce program that counts the median length of the
  words in the input files.
  wordstandarddeviation: A map/reduce program that counts the standard
  deviation of the length of the words in the input files.
```

To illustrate several capabilities of Hadoop YARN, we will show how to run the pi benchmark, the terasort examples, and the TestDFSIO benchmark.

Running the Pi Example

To run the pi example with 16 maps and 100,000 samples, enter the following:

```
$ yarn jar $YARN_EXAMPLES/hadoop-mapreduce-examples-2.2.0.jar pi 16 100000
```

If the program runs correctly, you should see the following (after the log messages):

```
13/10/14 20:10:01 INFO mapreduce.Job: map 0% reduce 0%
13/10/14 20:10:08 INFO mapreduce.Job: map 25% reduce 0%
13/10/14 20:10:16 INFO mapreduce.Job: map 56% reduce 0%
13/10/14 20:10:17 INFO mapreduce.Job: map 100% reduce 0%
13/10/14 20:10:17 INFO mapreduce.Job: map 100% reduce 100%
13/10/14 20:10:17 INFO mapreduce.Job: Job job_1381790835497_0003 completed
successfully
13/10/14 20:10:17 INFO mapreduce.Job: Counters: 44
        File System Counters
                FILE: Number of bytes read=358
                FILE: Number of bytes written=1365080
                FILE: Number of read operations=0
                FILE: Number of large read operations=0
                FILE: Number of write operations=0
                HDFS: Number of bytes read=4214
                HDFS: Number of bytes written=215
                HDFS: Number of read operations=67
                HDFS: Number of large read operations=0
                HDFS: Number of write operations=3
        Job Counters
                Launched map tasks=16
                Launched reduce tasks=1
                Data-local map tasks=14
                Rack-local map tasks=2
                Total time spent by all maps in occupied slots (ms)=174725
                Total time spent by all reduces in occupied slots
                (ms)=7294
        Map-Reduce Framework
                Map input records=16
                Map output records=32
                Map output bytes=288
                Map output materialized bytes=448
                Input split bytes=2326
                Combine input records=0
                Combine output records=0
                Reduce input groups=2
                Reduce shuffle bytes=448
                Reduce input records=32
                Reduce output records=0
                Spilled Records=64
                Shuffled Maps =16
                Failed Shuffles=0
                Merged Map outputs=16
                GC time elapsed (ms)=195
                CPU time spent (ms)=7740
                Physical memory (bytes) snapshot=6143696896
                Virtual memory (bytes) snapshot=23140454400
                Total committed heap usage (bytes)=4240769024
```

```
      Shuffle Errors
              BAD_ID=0
              CONNECTION=0
              IO_ERROR=0
              WRONG_LENGTH=0
              WRONG_MAP=0
              WRONG_REDUCE=0
      File Input Format Counters
              Bytes Read=1888
      File Output Format Counters
              Bytes Written=97
Job Finished in 20.854 seconds
Estimated value of Pi is 3.14127500000000000000
```

Notice that the MapReduce progress is shown in the same way as in MapReduce version 1, but the application statistics are different. Most of the statistics are self-explanatory. The one important item to note is that the YARN "Map-Reduce Framework" is used to run the program. The use of this framework, which is designed to be compatible with Hadoop version 1, will be discussed further later in this chapter.

Using the Web GUI to Monitor Examples

The Hadoop YARN web GUI differs from the web GUI found in Hadoop version 1. This section provides an illustration of how to use the web GUI to monitor and find information about YARN jobs. Figure 9.1 shows the main YARN web interface (http://hostname:8088). For this example, we use the pi application, which can run quickly and finish before you have explored the GUI. A longer-running application, like terasort, may be helpful when exploring all the various links in the GUI.

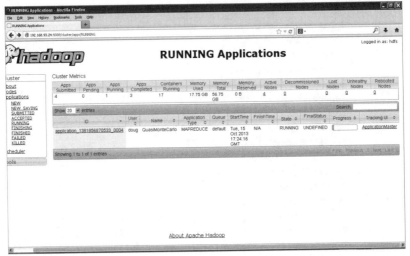

Figure 9.1   Hadoop YARN running applications web GUI for pi example

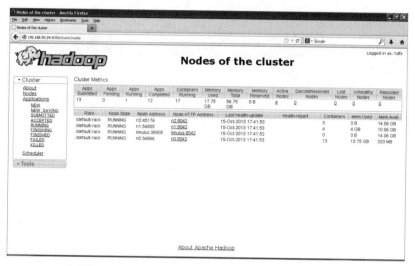

Figure 9.2   Hadoop YARN nodes status window

If you look at the Cluster Metrics table, you will see some new information. First, you will notice that rather than Hadoop version 1 "Map/Reduce Task Capacity," there is now information on the number of running containers. If YARN is running a MapReduce job, these containers will be used for both map and reduce tasks. Unlike in Hadoop version 1, the number of mappers and reducers is not fixed. There are also memory metrics and links to node status. If you click on the nodes link, you can get a summary of the node activity. For example, Figure 9.2 is a snapshot of the node activity while the pi application is running. Note again the number of containers, which are used by the MapReduce framework as either mappers or reducers.

Going back to the main Applications/Running window, if you click on the `application_138...` link, the Application status window in Figure 9.3 will be presented. This window provides similar information as the Running Applications window, but only for the selected job.

Clicking on the ApplicationMaster link in Figure 9.3 takes us to the window shown in Figure 9.4. Note that the link to the application's ApplicationMaster is also found on the main Running Applications screen in the last column.

In the MapReduce Application window, the details of the MapReduce job can be observed. Clicking on the `job_138...` brings up the window shown in Figure 9.5. (Your job number will be different.)

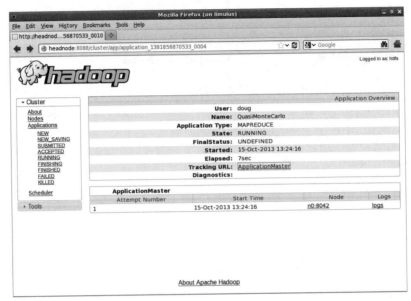

Figure 9.3   Hadoop YARN application status for pi example

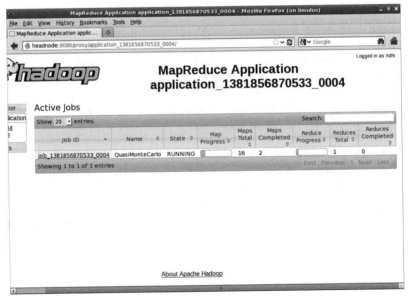

Figure 9.4   Hadoop YARN ApplicationMaster for MapReduce application

The status of the job is now presented in more detail. When the job is finished, the window is updated to that shown in Figure 9.6.

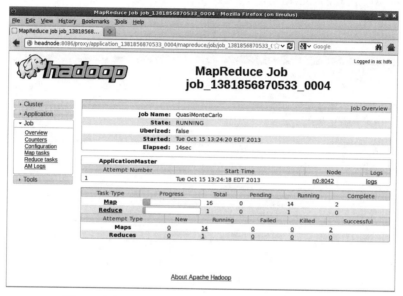

Figure 9.5   Hadoop YARN MapReduce job progress

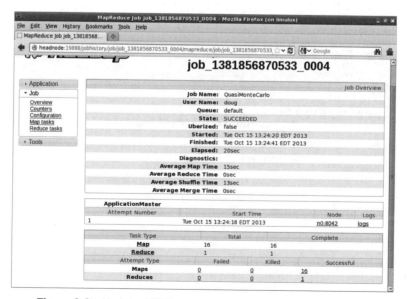

Figure 9.6   Hadoop YARN completed MapReduce job summary

If you click on the node used to run the ApplicationMaster (n0:8042 in our example), the window in Figure 9.7 opens and provides a summary from the Node-Manager. Again, the NodeManager tracks only containers; the actual tasks that the containers run are determined by the ApplicationMaster.

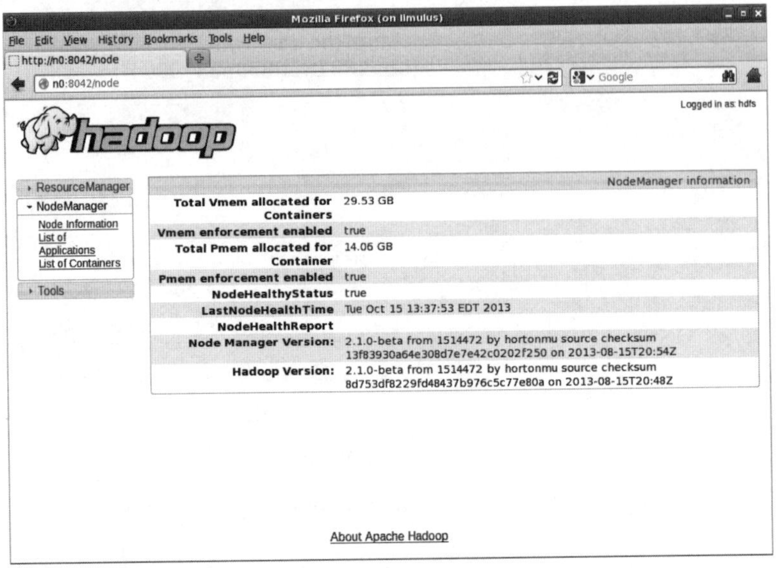

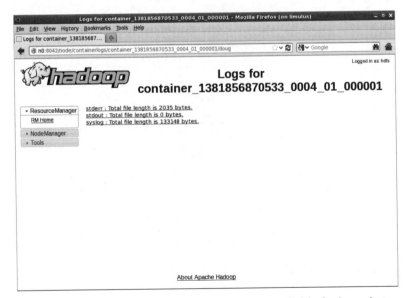

Figure 9.7   Hadoop YARN NodeManager job summary

Figure 9.8   Hadoop YARN NodeManager logs available for browsing

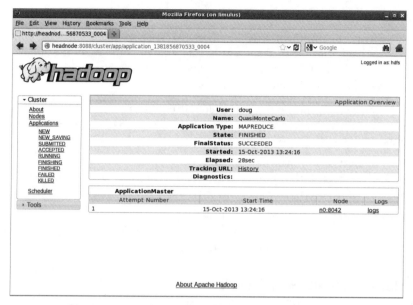

Figure 9.9   Hadoop YARN application summary page

Going back to the job summary page, you can also examine the logs for the ApplicationMaster by clicking the "logs" link. In the resulting window, shown in Figure 9.8, stdout, stderr, and the syslog can all be browsed.

If we return to the main cluster window, choose Applications/Finished, and then select our job, we will see the summary page shown in Figure 9.9.

There are a few things to notice as we moved through the windows as described previously. First, because YARN manages applications, all input from YARN refers to an application. YARN has no data about the actual application. Data from the Map-Reduce job are provided by the MapReduce framework. Thus there are two clearly different data streams that are combined in the web GUI: YARN *applications* and MapReduce framework *jobs*. If the framework does not provide job information, then certain parts of the web GUI will have nothing to display.

Another interesting aspect to note is the dynamic nature of the mapper and reducer tasks. These are executed as YARN containers, and their number will change as the application runs. This feature provides much better cluster utilization due to the absence of static slots.

Finally, other links in the windows can be explored (e.g., the History link in Figure 9.9). With the MapReduce framework, it is possible to drill down to the individual map and reduce tasks. If log aggregation is enabled (see Chapter 6, "Apache Hadoop YARN Administration"), then the individual logs for each map and reduce task can be viewed.

Running the Terasort Test

To run the terasort benchmark, three separate steps are required. In general, the rows are 100 bytes long; thus the total amount of data written is 100 times the number of rows (i.e., to write 100 GB of data, use 1,000,000,000 rows). You will also need to specify input and output directories in HDFS.

1. Run teragen to generate rows of random data to sort.

   ```
   $ yarn jar $YARN_EXAMPLES/hadoop-mapreduce-examples-2.2.0.jar teragen
   ➥<number of 100-byte rows> <output dir>
   ```

2. Run terasort to sort the database.

   ```
   $ yarn jar $YARN_EXAMPLES/hadoop-mapreduce-examples-2.2.0.jar terasort
   ➥<input dir> <output dir>
   ```

3. Run teravalidate to validate the sort teragen.

   ```
   $ yarn jar $YARN_EXAMPLES/hadoop-mapreduce-examples-2.2.0.jar teravalidate
   ➥<terasort output dir> <teravalidate output dir>
   ```

Run the TestDFSIO Benchmark

YARN also includes an HDFS benchmark application called TestDFSIO. Similar to terasort, it has several steps. We will write and read ten 1 GB files.

1. Run TestDFSIO in write mode and create data.

   ```
   $ yarn jar $YARN_EXAMPLES/hadoop-mapreduce-client-jobclient-2.2.0-tests.jar
   ➥TestDFSIO -write  -nrFiles 10 -fileSize 1000
   ```

   Example results are as follows (date and time removed):

   ```
   fs.TestDFSIO: ----- TestDFSIO ----- : write
   fs.TestDFSIO:            Date & time: Wed Oct 16 10:58:20 EDT 2013
   fs.TestDFSIO:        Number of files: 10
   fs.TestDFSIO: Total MBytes processed: 10000.0
   fs.TestDFSIO:      Throughput mb/sec: 10.124306231915458
   fs.TestDFSIO: Average IO rate mb/sec: 10.125661849975586
   fs.TestDFSIO:  IO rate std deviation: 0.11729341192174683
   fs.TestDFSIO:     Test exec time sec: 120.45
   fs.TestDFSIO:
   ```

2. Run TestDFSIO in read mode.

   ```
   $ yarn jar  $YARN_EXAMPLES/hadoop-mapreduce-client-jobclient-2.2.0-tests.jar
   ➥TestDFSIO -read  -nrFiles 10 -fileSize 1000
   ```

   Example results are as follows (date and time removed):

   ```
   fs.TestDFSIO: ----- TestDFSIO ----- : read
   fs.TestDFSIO:            Date & time: Wed Oct 16 11:09:00 EDT 2013
   fs.TestDFSIO:        Number of files: 10
   ```

```
fs.TestDFSIO: Total MBytes processed: 10000.0
fs.TestDFSIO:      Throughput mb/sec: 40.946519750553804
fs.TestDFSIO: Average IO rate mb/sec: 45.240928649902344
fs.TestDFSIO:  IO rate std deviation: 18.27387874605978
fs.TestDFSIO:     Test exec time sec: 47.937
fs.TestDFSIO:
```

3. Clean up the TestDFSIO data.

```
$ yarn jar  $YARN_EXAMPLES/hadoop-mapreduce-client-jobclient-2.2.0-tests.jar
➥TestDFSIO -clean
```

MapReduce Compatibility

MapReduce was the original use-case for which Hadoop was developed. To graph the
World Wide Web and illustrate how it changes over time, MapReduce was developed
to process this graph and its billions of nodes and trillions of edges. Moving this technology to YARN made it a complex application to build due to the requirements for
data locality, fault tolerance, and application priorities.

To provide data locality, the MapReduce ApplicationMaster is required to locate
blocks for processing and then request containers on these blocks. To implement fault
tolerance, the ability to handle failed map or reduce tasks and request them again on
other nodes was needed. Fault tolerance moved hand-in-hand with the complex intra-
application priorities.

The logic to handle complex intra-application priorities for map and reduce tasks
had to be built into the ApplicationMaster. There is no need to start idle reducers
before mappers finish processing enough data. Reducers are now under control of the
ApplicationMaster and are not fixed, as they had been in Hadoop version 1.

One rather unique failure mode occurs when a node fails after all the maps have
finished. When this happens, the map task must be repeated because the results are
unavailable. In many cases, all available containers are being used by the reducer tasks,
preventing the spawning of another mapper task to process the missing data. Logically, this would create a deadlock with reducers waiting for missing mapper data. The
MapReduce ApplicationMaster has been designed to detect this situation and, while
the solution is not ideal, will kill enough reducers to free up sufficient resources for
mappers to finish processing the missing data. The killed reducer will then start again,
allowing the job to complete.

The MapReduce ApplicationMaster

The MapReduce ApplicationMaster is implemented as a composition of loosely
coupled services. The services interact with one another via events. Each component
acts on the received events and sends out any required events to other components.
This design keeps it highly concurrent, with no or minimal synchronization needs.

The events are dispatched by a central Dispatch mechanism. All components register with the Dispatcher, and this information is shared across different components using AppContext.

In Hadoop version 1, the death of the JobTracker would result in the loss of all jobs, both running and queued. With YARN, the ApplicationMaster is a MapReduce job that serves as the equivalent to the JobTracker. The ApplicationMaster will now run on compute nodes, which can lead to an increase in failure scenarios. To combat the threat of MapReduce ApplicationMaster failures, YARN has the capability to restart the ApplicationMaster a specified number of times and the capability to recover completed tasks. Additionally, much like the JobTracker, the ApplicationMaster keeps metrics for jobs that are currently running. Typically, the ApplicationMaster tracking URL makes these metrics available and can be found as part of the YARN web GUI (discussed in the earlier pi example). The following setting can enable MapReduce recovery in YARN.

Enabling Application Master Restarts

To enable ApplicationMaster restarts, do the following:

1. Inside `yarn-site.xml`, you can tune the property `yarn.resourcemanager.am.max-retries`. The default is 2.

2. Inside `mapred-site.xml`, you can more directly tune how many times a MapReduce ApplicationMaster should restart with the property `mapreduce.am.max-attempts`. The default is 2.

Enabling Recovery of Completed Tasks

To enable recovery of completed tasks, look inside the `mapred-site.xml` file. The property `yarn.app.mapreduce.am.job.recovery.enable` enables the recovery of tasks. By default, it is true.

The JobHistory Server

With the ApplicationMaster now taking the place of the JobTracker, a centralized location for the history of all MapReduce jobs was required. The JobHistory server helps fill the void left by the transitory ApplicationMaster by hosting these completed job metrics and logs. This new history daemon is unrelated to the services provided by YARN and is directly tied to the MapReduce application framework.

Calculating the Capacity of a Node

Since YARN has now removed the hard-partitioned mapper and reducer slots of Hadoop version 1, new capacity calculations are required. There are eight important parameters for calculating a node's capacity; they are found in the `mapred-site.xml` and `yarn-site.xml` files.

- `mapred-site.xml`
  - `mapreduce.map.memory.mb`
    `mapreduce.reduce.memory.mb`

    The hard limit enforced by Hadoop on the mapper or reducer task.
  - `mapreduce.map.java.opts`
    `mapreduce.reduce.java.opts`

    The heap size of the `jvm -Xmx` for the mapper or reducer task. Remember to leave room for the JVM Perm Gen and Native Libs used. This value should always be smaller than `mapreduce.[map|reduce].memory.mb`.
- `yarn-site.xml`
  - `yarn.scheduler.minimum-allocation-mb`

    The smallest container YARN will allow.
  - `yarn.scheduler.maximum-allocation-mb`

    The largest container YARN will allow.
  - `yarn.nodemanager.resource.memory-mb`

    The amount of physical memory (RAM) on the compute node for containers. It is important that this value isn't the total RAM on the node, as other Hadoop services also require RAM.
  - `yarn.nodemanager.vmem-pmem-ratio`

    The amount of virtual memory each container is allowed. This is calculated by the following formula: `containerMemoryRequest*vmem-pmem-ratio`.

As an example, consider a configuration with the settings in Table 9.1. Using these settings, we have given each map and reduce task a generous 512 MB of overhead for the container, as seen with the difference between the `mapreduce.[map|reduce].memory.mb` and the `mapreduce.[map|reduce].java.opts`.

Table 9.1   **Example YARN MapReduce Settings**

Property	Value
`mapreduce.map.memory.mb`	1536
`mapreduce.reduce.memory.mb`	2560
`mapreduce.map.java.opts`	-Xmx1024m
`mapreduce.reduce.java.opts`	-Xmx2048m
`yarn.scheduler.minimum-allocation-mb`	512
`yarn.scheduler.maximum-allocation-mb`	4096
`yarn.nodemanager.resource.memory-mb`	36864
`yarn.nodemanager.vmem-pmem-ratio`	2.1

Next YARN has been configured to allow a container no smaller than 512 MB and no larger than 4 GB; the compute nodes have 36 GB of RAM available for containers. With a virtual memory ratio of 2.1 (the default value), each map can have as much as 3225.6 MB and a reducer can have 5376 MB of virtual memory. Thus our compute node configured for 36 GB of container space can support up to 24 maps or 14 reducers, or any combination of mappers and reducers allowed by the available resources on the node.

Changes to the Shuffle Service

As in Hadoop version 1, the shuffle functionality is required for parallel MapReduce job operation. Reducers fetch the outputs from all the maps by "shuffling" map output data from the corresponding nodes where map tasks have run. The MapReduce shuffle functionality is implemented as an auxiliary service in the NodeManager. This service starts up a Netty web server in the NodeManager address space and knows how to handle MapReduce-specific shuffle requests from reduce tasks. The MapReduce ApplicationMaster specifies the service ID for the shuffle service, along with security tokens that may be required when the ApplicationMaster starts any container. In the returning response, the NodeManager provides the ApplicationMaster with the port on which the shuffle service is running, which is then passed on to the reduce tasks.

Hadoop version 2 also provides the option for encrypted shuffle. With encrypted shuffle functionality, the ability to use HTTPS with optional client authentication is possible. The feature is implemented with a toggle for HTTP or HTTPS, keystore/truststore properties, and the distribution of these stores to new and existing nodes. For details of the multistep configuration of encrypted shuffle, it is recommended that users read the most current documentation for this feature on the Apache Hadoop website.

Running Existing Hadoop Version 1 Applications

To ease the transition from Hadoop version 1 to YARN, a major goal of YARN and the MapReduce framework implementation on top of YARN is to ensure that existing MapReduce applications that were programmed and compiled against previous MapReduce APIs (we'll call these MRv1 applications) can continue to run with little work on top of YARN (we'll call these MRv2 applications).

Binary Compatibility of org.apache.hadoop.mapred APIs

For the vast majority of users who use the `org.apache.hadoop.mapred` APIs, MapReduce on YARN ensures full binary compatibility. These existing applications can run on YARN directly without recompilation. You can use jar files of your existing application that code against MapReduce APIs, and use `bin/hadoop` to submit them directly to YARN.

Source Compatibility of org.apache.hadoop.mapreduce APIs

Unfortunately, it has proved difficult to ensure full binary compatibility of applications that were originally compiled against MRv1 org.apache.hadoop.mapreduce APIs. These APIs have gone through lots of changes. For example, a bunch of classes stopped being abstract classes and changed to interfaces. The YARN community eventually reached a compromise on this issue, supporting source compatibility only for org.apache.hadoop.mapreduce APIs. Existing applications using MapReduce APIs are source compatible and can run on YARN either with no changes, with simple recompilation against MRv2 jar files that are shipped with Hadoop version 2, or with minor updates.

Compatibility of Command-line Scripts

Most of the command-line scripts from Hadoop 1.x should just work, without any tweaking. The only exception is MRAdmin, whose functionality was removed from MRv2 because JobTracker and TaskTracker no longer exist. The MRAdmin functionality has been replaced with RMAdmin. The suggested method to invoke MRAdmin (as well as RMAdmin) is through the command line, even though one can directly invoke the APIs. In YARN, when mradmin commands are executed, warning messages will appear, reminding users to use YARN commands (i.e., rmadmin commands). Conversely, if the user's applications programmatically invoke MRAdmin, those applications will break when running on top of YARN. There is no support for either binary or source compatibility under YARN.

Compatibility Tradeoff Between MRv1 and Early MRv2 (0.23.x) Applications

Unfortunately, there are some APIs that may be compatible either with MRv1 applications or with early MRv2 applications (in particular, the applications compiled against Hadoop 0.23), but not both. Some of these APIs were exactly the same in both MRv1 and MRv2, except for the return type change in their method signatures. Therefore, we were forced to trade off the compatibility between the two.

- We decided to make MapReduce APIs be compatible with MRv1 applications, which have a larger user base.
- If MapReduce APIs don't significantly break Hadoop 0.23 applications, we made the same decision of making them compatible with version 0.23 but only source compatible with 1.x versions.

Table 9.2 lists the APIs that are incompatible with Hadoop 0.23. If early Hadoop 2 adopters using 0.23.x versions included the following methods in their custom routines, they must modify the code accordingly. For some problematic methods, we provided an alternative method with the same functionality and similar method signature to MRv2 applications.

Table 9.2 MRv2 Incompatible APIs

Problematic Method: org.apache.hadoop	Incompatible Return Type Change	Alternative Method
util.ProgramDriver#drive	void -> int	run
mapred.jobcontrol.Job#getMapredJobID	String -> JobID	getMapredJobId
mapred.TaskReport#getTaskId	String -> TaskID	getTaskID
mapred.ClusterStatus	long -> int	N/A
➤ #UNINITIALIZED_MEMORY_VALUE		
mapreduce.filecache.DistributedCache	long[] -> String[]	N/A
➤ #getArchiveTimestamps		
mapreduce.filecache.DistributedCache	long[] -> String[]	N/A
➤ #getFileTimestamps		
mapreduce.Job#failTask	void -> boolean	killTask(TaskAttemptID, boolean)
mapreduce.Job#killTask	void -> boolean	killTask(TaskAttemptID, boolean)
mapreduce.Job#getTaskCompletionEvents	mapred.TaskCompletionEvent[]	N/A
	➤ -> mapreduce.TaskCompletionEvent[]	

Running MapReduce Version 1 Existing Code

Most of the MRv1 examples continue to work on YARN, except that they are now present in a newly versioned jar file. One exception worth mentioning is that the sleep example, which was originally found in `hadoop-examples-1.x.x.jar`, is no longer in `hadoop-mapreduce-examples-2.x.x.jar` but rather was moved into the test jar `hadoop-mapreduce-client-jobclient-2.x.x-tests.jar`.

That exception aside, users may want to directly try `hadoop-examples-1.x.x.jar` on YARN. Running `hadoop -jar hadoop-examples-1.x.x.jar` will still pick the classes in `hadoop-mapreduce-examples-2.x.x.jar`. This behavior is due to Java first searching the desired class in the system jar files; if the class is not found there, it will go on to search in the user jar files in `classpath.hadoop-mapreduce-examples-2.x.x.jar`, which is installed together with other MRv2 jar files in the Hadoop class path. Thus the desired class (e.g., `WordCount`) will be picked from this 2.x.x jar file instead of the 1.x.x jar file. However, it is possible to let Java pick the classes from the jar file that is specified after `-jar` option. Users have two options:

- Add `HADOOP\_USER\_CLASSPATH\_FIRST=true` and `HADOOP\_CLASSPATH=...:hadoop-examples-1.x.x.jar` as environment variables, and add `mapreduce.job.user.classpath.first = true` in `mapred-site.xml`.

- Remove the 2.x.x jar from the class path. If it is a multiple-node cluster, the jar file needs to be removed from the class path on all the nodes.

Running Apache Pig Scripts on YARN

Pig is one of the two major data process applications in the Hadoop ecosystem, with the other being Hive. Because of significant efforts from the Pig community, Pig scripts of existing users don't need any modifications. Pig on YARN in Hadoop 0.23 has been supported since version 0.10.0 and Pig working with Hadoop 2.x has been supported since version 0.10.1.

Existing Pig scripts that work with Pig 0.10.1 and beyond will work just fine on top of YARN. In contrast, versions earlier than Pig 0.10.x may not run directly on YARN due to some of the incompatible MapReduce APIs and configuration.

Running Apache Hive Queries on YARN

Hive queries of existing users don't need any change to work on top of YARN, starting with Hive 0.10.0, thanks to the work done by Hive community. Support for Hive to work on YARN in the Hadoop 0.23 and 2.x releases has been in place since version 0.10.0. Queries that work in Hive 0.10.0 and beyond will work without changes on top of YARN. However, as with Pig, earlier versions of Hive may not run directly on YARN, as those Hive releases don't support Hadoop 0.23 and 2.x.

Running Apache Oozie Workflows on YARN

Like the Pig and Hive communities, the Apache Oozie community worked to make sure existing Oozie workflows would run in a completely backward-compatible manner on Hadoop version 2. Support for Hadoop 0.23 and 2.x is available starting with Oozie release 3.2.0. Existing Oozie workflows can start taking advantage of YARN in versions 0.23 and 2.x with Oozie 3.2.0 and above.

Advanced Features

The following features are included in Hadoop version 2 but have not been extensively tested. The user community is encouraged to play with these features and provide feedback to the Apache Hadoop community.

Uber Jobs

An Uber Job occurs when multiple mapper and reducers are combined to use a single container. There are four core settings around the configuration of Uber Jobs found in the `mapred-site.xml` options presented in Table 9.3.

Pluggable Shuffle and Sort

This plug-in allows users to replace built-in shuffle and sort logic with alternative paradigms but is currently considered unstable. These properties can be set on a per-job basis, as shown in Table 9.4, or as a site-wide property, as shown in Table 9.5. The properties identified in Table 9.4 can also be set in `mapred-site.xml` to change the default values for all jobs. Use-cases include protocol changes between mappers and reducers as well as the use of custom algorithms enabling new types of sorting. While the NodeManagers handle all shuffle services for the default shuffle, any pluggable shuffle and sort configurations will run in the job tasks themselves.

> **Important**
>
> If you are setting an auxiliary service in addition to the default `mapreduce_shuffle` service, then you should add a new service key to the `yarn.nodemanager.aux-services` property—for example, `mapreduce_shufflex`. Then the property defining the corresponding class must be `yarn.nodemanager.aux-services.mapreduce_shufflex.class`.

Table 9.3   **Configuration Options for Uber Jobs**

Property	Explanation
`mapreduce.job.ubertask.enable`	Whether to enable the small-jobs "ubertask" optimization, which runs "sufficiently small" jobs sequentially within a single JVM. "Small" is defined by the `maxmaps`, `maxreduces`, and `maxbytes` settings. Users may override this value. Default = false.
`mapreduce.job.ubertask.maxmaps`	Threshold for the number of maps beyond which the job is considered too big for the ubertasking optimization. Users may override this value, but only downward. Default = 9.
`mapreduce.job.ubertask.maxreduces`	Threshold for the number of reduces beyond which the job is considered too big for the ubertasking optimization. *Currently the code cannot support more than one reduce* and will ignore larger values. (Zero is a valid maximum, however.) Users may override this value, but only downward. Default = 1.
`mapreduce.job.ubertask.maxbytes`	Threshold for the number of input bytes beyond which the job is considered too big for the ubertasking optimization. If no value is specified, `dfs.block.size` is used as a default. Be sure to specify a default value in `mapred-site.xml` if the underlying file system is not HDFS. Users may override this value, but only downward. Default = HDFS block size.

Table 9.4   **Job Configuration Properties (on a Per-Job Basis)**

Property	Default Value
`mapreduce.job.reduce.shuffle` `➥.consumer.plugin.class`	`org.apache.hadoop.mapreduce.task.reduce.Shuffle`
`mapreduce.job.map.output.collector` `➥.class`	`org.apache.hadoop.mapred.MapTask$MapOutputBuffer`

Table 9.5   **NodeManager Configuration Properties (yarn-site.xml on All Nodes)**

Property	Default Value
`yarn.nodemanager.aux-services`	`mapreduce.shuffle`
`yarn.nodemanager.aux-services.mapreduce` `➥.shuffle.class`	`org.apache.hadoop.mapred.ShuffleHandler`

Wrap-up

Running Hadoop version 1 MapReduce applications on Hadoop YARN has been made as simple and as compatible as possible. Because MapReduce is now a YARN framework, the execution life cycle is different than that found in Hadoop version 1. The results are the same, however.

The shift from discrete mappers and reducers to containers can be seen by running and monitoring the example MapReduce programs with the web GUI. The distinction between YARN containers and MapReduce mappers and reducers is clearly evident in these examples.

In most cases, Hadoop YARN version 2 provides source code compatibility with all Hadoop version 1 MapReduce code. There is also a fair amount of binary compatibility with many applications, such as Pig and Hive.

10

Apache Hadoop YARN
Application Example

In describing how to write a YARN application, it can be helpful to review a bit of YARN's architecture. YARN is a platform for allowing distributed applications to take full advantage of the resources that YARN has deployed. Currently, resources can be things like CPU, memory, and data. Many developers coming from a server-side application development background or from a classic MapReduce developer background may be accustomed to a certain flow in the development and deployment cycle. In this chapter, the application development life cycle in YARN will be described and the unique requirements of a YARN application will be demonstrated. YARN applications can launch containers encapsulating virtually any application written in any language; however, for the initial releases of YARN, application clients and ApplicationMasters are only demonstrated in Java. Toward this end, we assume familiarity with basic Java programming methods.

To illustrate writing a working YARN application, we'll walk through the process of writing an application that creates a cluster of JBoss Application Servers (JBoss AS). JBoss AS is an open-source Java EE server that is itself a Java application. It can operate in what it calls "domain mode," meaning there is a defined cluster of JBoss AS instances. To run in this mode, we not only need to deploy and run JBoss AS, but we also need to configure each JBoss AS instance. In YARN terminology, a JBoss AS instance is under the control of a single YARN container.

As depicted in Figure 10.1, the JBoss client requests resources from the Resource-Manager, by providing a container request in the form of an ApplicationSubmission-Context, starting the application on the cluster.

The YARN Client

We'll also need to write a YARN client. First, however, let's discuss what a YARN client actually does. The YARN client is a plain Java object that does not extend any class or implement any interface. It is a main-method runnable class that learns about the YARN

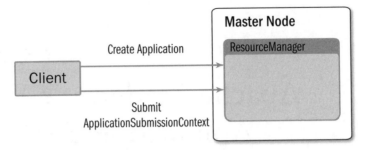

Figure 10.1   Communication pathways between the client submitting the application and the ResourceManager

environment by instantiating an org.apache.hadoop.yarn.conf.YarnConfiguration object. The YarnConfiguration object depends on finding the yarn-default.xml and yarn-site.xml files in its class path. If these requirements are met, there should be no problems with running your YARN client.

Once a YarnConfiguration object is created in your client, you'll use that object to create an org.apache.hadoop.client.api.YarnClient. This YarnClient object will do much of the heavy lifting in your YARN application's client, as suggested by some of its tasks:

- Instantiate a YarnClient object
- Initialize itself with the YarnConfiguration object
- Start a YarnClient
- Get YARN cluster metrics
- Get YARN node reports
- Get queue information
- Get ACL information for the user running the client
- Create the client application
- Submit the application to the YARN ResourceManager
- Get application reports after submitting the application

In addition to providing this core functionality, a YARN client will prepare your application for the YARN cluster by propagating environment variables and whatever resources your application needs—resources like dependent libraries and archive files that can be automatically unarchived by YARN. The YARN client will also create contexts for application submission and for AM container's launch.

As a runnable Java object, the YARN client generally takes command-line arguments or, at the very least, parse a configuration file that the client users can supply. A number of options are available for parsing command-line options with Java, ranging from using the java.util.Scanner class as a foundation to build your own parser to using a library specifically built for this use-case. In this chapter's example, we'll use the Apache Commons CLI library.

Let's start to see what a client looks like by examining the first part of the code example, shown in Listing 10.1.

Listing 10.1 YARN client main method

```java
public class JBossClient {
    private static final Logger LOG =
        Logger.getLogger(JBossClient.class.getName());

    private Configuration conf;
    private YarnClient yarnClient;
    private String appName;
    private int amPriority;
    private String amQueue = "";
    private int amMemory;

    private String appJar = "";
    private final String appMasterMainClass =
        JBossApplicationMaster.class
        .getName();

    private int priority;

    private int containerMemory;
    private int numContainers;

    private String adminUser;
    private String adminPassword;
    private String jbossAppUri;

    private String log4jPropFile = "";
    boolean debugFlag = false;

    private Options opts;

    public static void main(String[] args) {
        boolean result = false;
        try {
            JBossClient client = new JBossClient();

            try {
                boolean doRun = client.init(args);
                    if (!doRun) {
                        System.exit(0);
                    }
            } catch (IllegalArgumentException e) {
```

```
        client.printUsage();
        System.exit(-1);
    }
    result = client.run();
    } catch (Throwable t) {
        System.exit(1);
    }
    if (result) {
        System.exit(0);
    }
    System.exit(2);
    }
. . . .
}
```

The package and import statements are omitted for brevity, as are the logging statements. We'll focus on building key pieces of the application, with the entire example available in the book repository (see Appendix A). In Listing 10.1, we see a standard main-method class structure with global variables, most of which will be assigned values from command-line arguments. The conf variable is the object that will have its values populated from the YarnConfiguration object instantiation mentioned earlier. The yarnClient variable is, as its name suggests, the variable that references the YarnClient object also discussed earlier. The opts variable references an org.apache.commons.cli.Options object, which is the object we will use to hold the command-line argument names and their values.

After creating the client object that will represent our JBossClient, we initialize the object with the command-line arguments and then run the client with the method named run(). Let's take a look at each of these steps in greater detail by adding to the class we're building. When we create the JBossClient object, we're using the default constructor. In the constructor, we instantiate a YarnClient, as shown in Listing 10.2.

Listing 10.2   **YARN client constructor**

```
public JBossClient() throws Exception {

    this.conf = new YarnConfiguration();
    yarnClient = YarnClient.createYarnClient();
    yarnClient.init(conf);
    opts = new Options();

    opts.addOption("appname", true,
        "Application Name. Default value - JBoss on YARN");

    opts.addOption("priority", true, "Application Priority. Default 0");

    opts.addOption("queue", true,
        "RM Queue in which this application is to be submitted");
```

```
opts.addOption("timeout", true, "Application timeout in milliseconds");

opts.addOption("master_memory", true,
    "Amount of memory in MB to be requested to run the application master");

opts.addOption("jar", true,
    "JAR file containing the applicationmaster");

opts.addOption("container_memory", true,
    "Amount of memory in MB to be requested to run the shell command");

opts.addOption("num_containers", true,
    "No. of containers on which the shell command needs to be executed");

opts.addOption("admin_user", true,
    "User id for initial administrator user");

opts.addOption("admin_password", true,
    "Password for initial administrator user");

opts.addOption("debug", false, "Dump out debug information");

opts.addOption("help", false, "Print usage");
}
```

In the constructor, the first step is to make sure that the environment for YARN is available to our client. The YarnConfiguration class is a subclass of the org.apache.hadoop.conf.Configuration class. The Configuration class should be familiar to MapReduce programmers: It is the class used in MapReduce version 1 as an argument in creating the org.apache.hadoop.mapreduce.Job object. Similarly, the YarnConfiguration object is used during the creation of the YarnClient object. Creating a YarnConfiguration object successfully and without unexpected results requires you to ensure the appropriate XML configuration files are correctly configured and in the client's class path, particularly yarn-site.xml and yarn-default.xml. You can avoid a lot of wasted time by making sure duplicate and conflicting configuration files aren't in your class path. The yarn-site.xml file is typically found in the standard configuration directory for Hadoop installations: ~/etc/hadoop. The yarn-default.xml file will provide default values for any property not explicitly configured in yarn-site.xml. The yarn-default.xml file is found in the hadoop-yarn-common-<version>.jar file, which normally resides in a directory that is in the default Hadoop class path.

Once a YarnConfiguration object is successfully created, it's a simple process to create a YarnClient object. The YarnClient object is created through a factory method of the YarnClient class itself. Once the YarnClient is instantiated, it's initialized with the

YarnConfiguration object. The YarnClient needs the configuration because a YarnClient is one of many so-called YARN services. YARN has built into its core architecture the notion of services. For instance, the log aggregation service, node status and health services, and the MapReduce version 2 shuffle handler are all examples of services shipped with YARN. Services have as their functionality life-cycle methods like init, start, and stop, as well as methods to determine the service state and, in the case of a service failure, to determine the cause of the failure. Services also have the capability of registering listeners that will receive callbacks from YARN on certain events.

The initialization of the YarnClient first determines the ResourceManager's IP address and port. These values are taken from the yarn-site.xml or yarn-default.xml file mentioned earlier. They are specified by the yarn.resourcemanager.address property. Next, the YarnClient looks for the interval in which it should poll for the application's state. The property yarn.client.app-submission.poll-interval is used to determine this value in milliseconds; the default value is 1000.

Once the YarnClient is initialized, it creates a ResourceManager client proxy that is internal to the YarnClient object. This proxy is intended to be abstracted from the YARN application developer. A YarnClient method is the preferred means for the developer to code YARN client operations.

After the YARN client objects have been properly created, we use the Options class to add command-line options. For each option, we must add has three arguments that are passed to the Options.addOption method: (1) the argument name, (2) an indicator whether the argument is required, and (3) a description of the argument that we can have as console output when the user requests help or when we want to display the usage of the command after detecting bad command-line input.

The command-line options we will create for our sample application are basic in nature. We can specify the application's name, a priority, the queue in the scheduler, and the memory we'll request for the ApplicationMaster as well as the containers. Most of the arguments are specific to the YARN environment. A few options we specify are specific to the JBoss AS instances we set up—namely, the user ID and password of the initial JBoss AS admin user.

Next, we will create the initialization process by adding a method to our class, as shown in Listing 10.3. This init method is where we'll parse the command-line arguments entered by the user.

Listing 10.3 **YARN client initialization**

```
public boolean init(String[] args) throws ParseException {

    CommandLine cliParser =
        new GnuParser().parse(opts, args);

    if (args.length == 0) {
        throw new IllegalArgumentException(
            "No args specified for client to initialize");
    }
```

```
if (cliParser.hasOption("help")) {
    printUsage();
    return false;
}

if (cliParser.hasOption("debug")) {
    debugFlag = true;
}

appName = cliParser.getOptionValue(
    "appname", "JBoss on YARN");

amPriority = Integer
        .parseInt(cliParser.getOptionValue("priority",
    "0"));

amQueue = cliParser.getOptionValue(
    "queue", "default");

amMemory = Integer.parseInt(
    cliParser.getOptionValue("master_memory",
    "1024"));

if (amMemory < 0) {
    throw new IllegalArgumentException(
        "Invalid memory specified for application
        master exiting." + " Specified memory=" +
        amMemory);
}

if (!cliParser.hasOption("jar")) {
    throw new IllegalArgumentException(
    "No jar file specified for application master");
}
appJar = cliParser.getOptionValue("jar");

containerMemory = Integer.parseInt(
    cliParser.getOptionValue(
    "container_memory", "1024"));

numContainers = Integer.parseInt(
    cliParser.getOptionValue("num_containers", "2"));

adminUser = cliParser.getOptionValue(
    "admin_user", "yarn");

adminPassword = cliParser.getOptionValue(
```

```
          "admin_password", "yarn");

     if (containerMemory < 0 || numContainers < 1) {
         throw new IllegalArgumentException(
         "Invalid no. of containers or container memory
         specified, exiting." + " Specified
         containerMemory=" + containerMemory
         + ", numContainer=" + numContainers);
     }
     return true;
}
```

The creation of an `org.apache.commons.cli.CommandLine` object is fairly simple and a good reason to use this library to handle command-line input. It takes the options we created in our constructor and the entire input from the command line and does the parsing for us. To assign values to the global variables we created in Listing 10.1, we get the values from the CommandLine object; in the event the user forgot or didn't specify a required argument, we can identify a default value. As with any command-line application, here is where we'll do our validation to make sure that the user has not entered any values that would cause problems (e.g., problems like specifying the number of containers to run on as 0 or less). After the initialization, we need to actually submit the application to YARN (Listing 10.4).

Listing 10.4 Submit an application to YARN

```
public boolean run() throws IOException, YarnException {

   yarnClient.start();

   YarnClientApplication app =
       yarnClient.createApplication();

   GetNewApplicationResponse appResponse =
       app.getNewApplicationResponse();

   int maxMem =
       appResponse.getMaximumResourceCapability()
       .getMemory();

   if (amMemory > maxMem) {
       amMemory = maxMem;
   }

   ApplicationSubmissionContext appContext =
       app.getApplicationSubmissionContext();

   ApplicationId appId =
```

```
    appContext.getApplicationId();

appContext.setApplicationName(appName);

ContainerLaunchContext amContainer =
    Records.newRecord(ContainerLaunchContext.class);

Map<String, LocalResource> localResources =
    new HashMap<String, LocalResource>();

FileSystem fs = FileSystem.get(conf);
Path src = new Path(appJar);
String pathSuffix = appName + File.separator +
    appId.getId() + File.separator + "JBossApp.jar";

Path dst = new Path(fs.getHomeDirectory(),
    pathSuffix);

jbossAppUri = dst.toUri().toString();
fs.copyFromLocalFile(false, true, src, dst);
FileStatus destStatus = fs.getFileStatus(dst);

LocalResource amJarRsrc =
Records.newRecord(LocalResource.class);

amJarRsrc.setType(LocalResourceType.FILE);
amJarRsrc.setVisibility(
    LocalResourceVisibility.APPLICATION);

amJarRsrc.setResource(
    ConverterUtils.getYarnUrlFromPath(dst));

amJarRsrc.setTimestamp(
    destStatus.getModificationTime());

amJarRsrc.setSize(destStatus.getLen());

localResources.put("JBossApp.jar", amJarRsrc);

amContainer.setLocalResources(localResources);

Map<String, String> env =
    new HashMap<String, String>();

StringBuilder classPathEnv = new StringBuilder(
    Environment.CLASSPATH.$()).append(
    File.pathSeparatorChar).append("./*");
```

```java
for (String c : conf.getStrings(
    YarnConfiguration.YARN_APPLICATION_CLASSPATH,
YarnConfiguration.DEFAULT_YARN_APPLICATION_CLASSPATH))
{
    classPathEnv.append(File.pathSeparatorChar);
    classPathEnv.append(c.trim());
}

env.put("CLASSPATH", classPathEnv.toString());

amContainer.setEnvironment(env);

Vector<CharSequence> vargs = new
    Vector<CharSequence>(30);

vargs.add(Environment.JAVA_HOME.$() + "/bin/java");
vargs.add("-Xmx" + amMemory + "m");
vargs.add(appMasterMainClass);
vargs.add("--container_memory " +
    String.valueOf(containerMemory));

vargs.add("--num_containers " +
    String.valueOf(numContainers));

vargs.add("--priority " + String.valueOf(priority));
vargs.add("--admin_user " + adminUser);
vargs.add("--admin_password " + adminPassword);
vargs.add("--jar " + jbossAppUri);

if (debugFlag) {
    vargs.add("--debug");
}

vargs.add("1>" +
    JBossConstants.JBOSS_CONTAINER_LOG_DIR
    + "/JBossApplicationMaster.stdout");

vargs.add("2>" +
    JBossConstants.JBOSS_CONTAINER_LOG_DIR
    + "/JBossApplicationMaster.stderr");

StringBuilder command = new StringBuilder();
for (CharSequence str : vargs) {
    command.append(str).append(" ");
}

List<String> commands = new ArrayList<String>();
```

```
    commands.add(command.toString());
    amContainer.setCommands(commands);

    Resource capability =
        Records.newRecord(Resource.class);
    capability.setMemory(amMemory);
    appContext.setResource(capability);

    appContext.setAMContainerSpec(amContainer);

    Priority pri = Records.newRecord(Priority.class);
    pri.setPriority(amPriority);
    appContext.setPriority(pri);

    appContext.setQueue(amQueue);

    yarnClient.submitApplication(appContext);

    return monitorApplication(appId);
}
```

The run method shown in Listing 10.4 is rather long, but we show the functionality in a single method to keep the example client's steps of client creation, initialization, and execution easy to follow. Let's take the code in Listing 10.4 and break it down. As we described earlier, a YarnClient is a YARN service that has life-cycle methods. We called the init method in our client's constructor, so now we'll call the start method in the run method.

Once the YarnClient is started, we use the object to create an org.apache.hadoop .yarn.client.api.YarnClientApplication. This YarnClientApplication object will be populated for us with a couple of key objects—namely, org.apache.hadoop.yarn .api.protocolrecords.GetNewApplicationResponse and org.apache.hadoop.yarn .api.records.ApplicationSubmissionContext. The GetNewApplicationResponse will let us get the maximum resources available, such as the maximum memory and maximum virtual cores. The ApplicationSubmissionContext will give us a unique application ID for the YARN cluster; in addition, it will be the object where we will define the specification for the application's ApplicationMaster. The code that follows illustrates the beginning of this flow in our run method.

```
yarnClient.start();

YarnClientApplication app =
    yarnClient.createApplication();

GetNewApplicationResponse appResponse =
    app.getNewApplicationResponse();
```

The first thing we'll use from the YarnClientApplication is the GetNewApplication-Response object, which we'll use to determine the maximum memory available on any given node in the cluster. One of the command-line options we gave the user was to specify how much memory to give the ApplicationMaster through the `master_memory` option. If the user specifies more memory than the amount available, we simply give the ApplicationMaster the maximum amount available instead of the requested amount.

Next, we'll use the ApplicationSubmissionContext to get the application ID that we'll use a little later. The first value we give the ApplicationSubmissionContext is the application's name. This name is used in a few places, including in the built-in YARN web application, where we can see it displayed. The following snippet from the run method shows what we've described.

```
int maxMem =
      appResponse.getMaximumResourceCapability()
      .getMemory();

if (amMemory > maxMem) {
    amMemory = maxMem;
}

ApplicationSubmissionContext appContext =
    app.getApplicationSubmissionContext();

ApplicationId appId =
    appContext.getApplicationId();

appContext.setApplicationName(appName);
```

The next value we give to the ApplicationSubmissionContext is the Container-LaunchContext. The ApplicationMaster is itself a YARN container, albeit a special kind of container, often referred to as "container 0." So that the ApplicationMaster container can launch, we create an object of type `org.apache.hadoop.yarn.api .records.ContainerLaunchContext`. The ContainerLaunchContext for an ApplicationMaster typically has resources it needs for its run time, with the most obvious one being the jar file with the ApplicationMaster class. The ContainerLaunch-Context takes a map of resources with a `java.lang.String` as the key and an `org.apache.hadoop.yarn.api.records.LocalResource` as the value. The map key is translated into a symbolic link in the file system visible to the container. More details on this aspect will follow, but for now, let's describe the code in Listing 10.4 that builds the map of LocalResources for the ApplicationMaster ContainerLaunch-Context. First, we create the ContainerLaunchContext as a YARN record.

```
ContainerLaunchContext amContainer =
    Records.newRecord(ContainerLaunchContext.class);

Map<String, LocalResource> localResources =
    new HashMap<String, LocalResource>();
```

One of the command-line options allows the user to give a path on the local file system where the ApplicationMaster jar file is located. This path is on the local file system where the user invokes the client. The problem we immediately face is that a YARN cluster doesn't have visibility to the client's local file system; thus we have to put the jar file in a location where each container has access. The best way to do so is to use HDFS. The first thing we do after creating the map of LocalResources is to have our client copy the jar file from the local file system to HDFS. The LocalResource object for the ApplicationMaster jar file is defined as LocalResourceType.FILE so that it will be copied to a container's file system without being unarchived.

After defining the resource type, we define the resource visibility by exposing the resource as LocalResourceVisibility.APPLICATION, which means only the application will have access to this resource. We could define other visibility settings to make the resource available to all the applications on the container's node or to all the applications of the same user on the node, but in our example, we'll take the most secure approach and limit the use of the jar file to our own application.

After defining resource visibility, for verification purposes, we let YARN know the timestamp of the file as well as the file size. The resource is then added to the LocalResource map, with the map subsequently being added to the ContainerLaunch-Context. The section of Listing 10.4 that handles these tasks is shown next.

```
FileSystem fs = FileSystem.get(conf);
Path src = new Path(appJar);
String pathSuffix = appName + File.separator +
    appId.getId() + File.separator + "JBossApp.jar";

Path dst = new Path(fs.getHomeDirectory(),
    pathSuffix);

jbossAppUri = dst.toUri().toString();
fs.copyFromLocalFile(false, true, src, dst);
FileStatus destStatus = fs.getFileStatus(dst);

LocalResource amJarRsrc =
Records.newRecord(LocalResource.class);

amJarRsrc.setType(LocalResourceType.FILE);
amJarRsrc.setVisibility(
    LocalResourceVisibility.APPLICATION);

amJarRsrc.setResource(
    ConverterUtils.getYarnUrlFromPath(dst));

amJarRsrc.setTimestamp(
    destStatus.getModificationTime());

amJarRsrc.setSize(destStatus.getLen());
```

```
localResources.put("JBossApp.jar", amJarRsrc);
amContainer.setLocalResources(localResources);
```

After adding the local resources to the ContainerLaunchContext, we add optional environment settings and the command to launch the ApplicationMaster. In setting the environment for the ApplicationMaster, we get the class path of the client, get the class path of the client's YARN environment, and build the class path string from those values. The environment variables to set consist of a map of java.lang.Strings to which we add the class path we just built with the key of CLASSPATH.

```
Map<String, String> env =
    new HashMap<String, String>();

StringBuilder classPathEnv = new StringBuilder(
    Environment.CLASSPATH.$()).append(
    File.pathSeparatorChar).append("./*");

for (String c : conf.getStrings(
    YarnConfiguration.YARN_APPLICATION_CLASSPATH,
 YarnConfiguration.DEFAULT_YARN_APPLICATION_CLASSPATH))
{
    classPathEnv.append(File.pathSeparatorChar);
    classPathEnv.append(c.trim());
}

env.put("CLASSPATH", classPathEnv.toString());
amContainer.setEnvironment(env);
```

Next, we build the command to launch the ApplicationMaster; many of the options we pass to that command are the options the user specified on the client's command line. As you can see from the example, we build a standard Java command. In doing so, YARN provides a convenience method with the org.apache.hadoop.yarn.api.ApplicationConstants.Environment class. Through the use of Environment.JAVA_HOME.$(), YARN formats the environment variable appropriately for a Windows environment by using the "%" character before and after the environment variable; it uses the "$" character before the variable in a Linux environment. The rest of the parameters for the Java command are what we would expect. The command is appended with log files to which we redirect stdout and stderr. Here we can define any directory and file to which the YARN application has write permissions. Using our example, we hard-code a directory but we could use the YarnConfiguration object to get the yarn.log.dir value with conf.get("yarn.log.dir");.

A ContainerLaunchContext can take a java.util.List of commands from which YARN will build the shell script to launch the container. For the ApplicationMaster, we need only a single command. Thus, after adding the Java command we just built to the list, we use the list to specify the ContainerLaunchContext commands. The following code segment from Listing 10.4 builds the ApplicationMaster launch command and adds the command to the ContainerLaunchContext.

```
Vector<CharSequence> vargs = new
      Vector<CharSequence>(30);

vargs.add(Environment.JAVA_HOME.$() + "/bin/java");
vargs.add("-Xmx" + amMemory + "m");
vargs.add(appMasterMainClass);
vargs.add("--container_memory " +
   String.valueOf(containerMemory));

vargs.add("--num_containers " +
   String.valueOf(numContainers));

vargs.add("--priority " + String.valueOf(priority));
vargs.add("--admin_user " + adminUser);
vargs.add("--admin_password " + adminPassword);
vargs.add("--jar " + jbossAppUri);

if (debugFlag) {
   vargs.add("--debug");
}

vargs.add("1>" +
   JBossConstants.JBOSS_CONTAINER_LOG_DIR
   + "/JBossApplicationMaster.stdout");

vargs.add("2>" +
   JBossConstants.JBOSS_CONTAINER_LOG_DIR
   + "/JBossApplicationMaster.stderr");

StringBuilder command = new StringBuilder();
for (CharSequence str : vargs) {
   command.append(str).append(" ");
}

List<String> commands = new ArrayList<String>();
commands.add(command.toString());
amContainer.setCommands(commands);
```

After we set the commands on the ContainerLaunchContext, we're ready to let the ApplicationSubmissionContext know that the ContainerLaunchContext we just built is the ApplicationMaster container. Recall that the ApplicationMaster is launched as a container. Because there is only one, however, YARN has a specific method for defining this ContainerLaunchContext as the ApplicationMaster.

```
appContext.setAMContainerSpec(amContainer);
```

After defining the ContainerLaunchContext and adding it to the ApplicationSub-missionContext, we're ready to turn our attention back to the remaining configura-tion of the ApplicationSubmissionContext. One of the important tasks in building the ApplicationSubmissionContext is to specify the resource capability of the application. Typically, one of the most important resources in a YARN application is memory. The example illustrates the standard way to define a memory resource and to add that resource to the ApplicationSubmissionContext. Other important parts of the Applica-tionSubmissionContext are the queue and priority for the application. These values go somewhat hand-in-hand. YARN, like MapReduce version 1, supports the concept of schedulers—for example, the Capacity scheduler. Schedulers are pluggable and defin-able in `yarn-site.xml` and help to manage the concurrent job environment of a typi-cal YARN cluster. If your YARN cluster is a typical cluster, you'll have many YARN applications running simultaneously, which in turn means managing those jobs above and beyond assigning resources will be an administrative concern. Schedulers help with this management by providing queues to which YARN applications are submit-ted and priority values that the queue will assign the application. Chapter 8, "Capacity Scheduler in YARN," addresses this functionality in greater detail. The code to make these settings is shown in the following snippet.

```
Resource capability =
    Records.newRecord(Resource.class);
    capability.setMemory(amMemory);
    appContext.setResource(capability);

Priority pri = Records.newRecord(Priority.class);
    pri.setPriority(amPriority);
    appContext.setPriority(pri);

    appContext.setQueue(amQueue);
```

After we finish defining the scheduler queue and priority of the application, we're ready for the YarnClient to actually submit the application. In the client code, the method call to submit the application blocks until the ResourceManager returns an application state of ACCEPTED.

```
yarnClient.submitApplication(appContext);
```

The last thing we show in the sample application is how to monitor the application from a client perspective (Listing 10.5).

Listing 10.5   **Monitoring a YARN application**

```
private boolean monitorApplication(ApplicationId appId)
                    throws YarnException, IOException {

    while (true) {

        try {
```

```
      Thread.sleep(1000);
   } catch (InterruptedException e) {
   }

   ApplicationReport report =
      yarnClient.getApplicationReport(appId);

   LOG.info("Got application report from ASM for" + ",
      appId=" + appId.getId() + ", clientToAMToken=" +
      report.getClientToAMToken() + ", appDiagnostics="
      + report.getDiagnostics() + ", appMasterHost="
      + report.getHost() + ", appQueue=" +
      report.getQueue() + ", appMasterRpcPort=" +
      report.getRpcPort() + ", appStartTime=" +
      report.getStartTime() + ", yarnAppState="

      + report.getYarnApplicationState().toString()
      + ", distributedFinalState="
      + report.getFinalApplicationStatus().toString()
      + ", appTrackingUrl=" + report.getTrackingUrl()
      + ", appUser=" + report.getUser());

   YarnApplicationState state =
      report.getYarnApplicationState();

   FinalApplicationStatus jbossStatus = report
      .getFinalApplicationStatus();

   if (YarnApplicationState.FINISHED == state) {
      if (FinalApplicationStatus.SUCCEEDED ==
         jbossStatus) {
            LOG.info("Application has completed successfully. Breaking monitoring
➥loop");

            return true;
      } else {
         LOG.info("Application did finished
            unsuccessfully."
            + " YarnState=" + state.toString()
            + ", JBASFinalStatus="
            + jbossStatus.toString()
            + ". Breaking monitoring loop");

         return false;
      }

   } else if (YarnApplicationState.KILLED ==
```

```
      state || YarnApplicationState.FAILED == state)
  {
    LOG.info("Application did not finish." + "
      YarnState=" + state.toString() + ",
      JBASFinalStatus=" + jbossStatus.toString() +
      ". Breaking monitoring loop");

    return false;
  }
 }
}
```

In the monitoring method, shown in Listing 10.5, we simply get the metadata of the application through the YarnClient. The application metadata is encapsulated in an object of type ApplicationReport that we get every second. The ApplicationReport has various convenience methods to get metadata like the application ID, but also more interesting data like the application's state and final status. These metadata values are logged to the console until the application either finishes successfully or is killed by the ResourceManager.

The ApplicationMaster

After creating the client to manage the YARN application submission and application monitoring, we can turn our attention to writing the ApplicationMaster. A newly created application registers itself with the ResourceManager. The ApplicationMaster then performs data processing by requesting resources that are issued as containers from the ResourceManager. The ApplicationMaster then communicates with the NodeManager to start the containers and then to monitor running containers that were previously requested for data processing. This process is described in Figure 10.2.

Like the client, our ApplicationMaster is a Java main method class. Almost identical to the way we set up the YARN application client, we can specify global variables and a main method to kick off the ApplicationMaster, as shown in Listing 10.6.

Listing 10.6   **Developing a YARN ApplicationMaster**

```
public class JBossApplicationMaster {

  private static final Logger LOG =
    Logger.getLogger(
      JBossApplicationMaster.class.getName());

  private Configuration conf;

  private AMRMClientAsync resourceManager;
  private NMClientAsync nmClientAsync;
  private NMCallbackHandler containerListener;
```

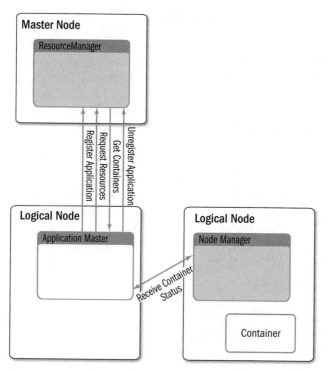

Figure 10.2 ApplicationMaster communication pathways between the
ResourceManager and the NodeManagers

```
private ApplicationAttemptId appAttemptID;

private String appMasterHostname = "";
private int appMasterRpcPort = 0;
private String appMasterTrackingUrl = "";

private int numTotalContainers;
private int containerMemory;
private int requestPriority;

private String adminUser;
private String adminPassword;

private AtomicInteger numCompletedContainers =
   new AtomicInteger();
private AtomicInteger numAllocatedContainers =
   new AtomicInteger();
private AtomicInteger numFailedContainers =
   new AtomicInteger();
```

```
private AtomicInteger numRequestedContainers =
   new AtomicInteger();

private Map<String, String> shellEnv =
   new HashMap<String, String>();

private String jbossHome;
private String appJar;
private String domainController;

private volatile boolean done;
private volatile boolean success;

private List<Thread> launchThreads =
   new ArrayList<Thread>();

private Options opts;

public static void main(String[] args) {

   boolean result = false;
   try {
      JBossApplicationMaster appMaster =
         new JBossApplicationMaster();

      boolean doRun = appMaster.init(args);
      if (!doRun) {
         System.exit(0);
      }
      result = appMaster.run();
         } catch (Throwable t) {
            LOG.log(Level.SEVERE, "Error running
               JBossApplicationMaster", t);
            System.exit(1);
            }
        if (result) {
          LOG.info("Application Master completed
              successfully. exiting");
           System.exit(0);
             } else {
          LOG.info("Application Master failed.
            exiting");
           System.exit(2);
             }
      }
 . . .
}
```

As was the case with the client, we have a default constructor for our JBossApplicationMaster that we use in the main method (Listing 10.7). Also, as was the case with the client constructor, we do some ApplicationMaster setup in the constructor.

Listing 10.7   YARN ApplicationMaster constructor

```
public JBossApplicationMaster() throws Exception {
   conf = new YarnConfiguration();
   opts = new Options();

   opts.addOption("admin_user", true,
      "User id for initial administrator user");

   opts.addOption("admin_password", true,
      "Password for initial administrator user");

   opts.addOption("container_memory", true,
      "Amount of memory in MB to be requested to run
      the shell command");

   opts.addOption("num_containers", true,
      "No. of containers on which the shell command
      needs to be executed");

   opts.addOption("jar", true,
      "JAR file containing the application");

   opts.addOption("priority", true,
      "Application Priority. Default 0");

   opts.addOption("debug", false,
      "Dump out debug information");

   opts.addOption("help", false, "Print usage");
}
```

Like the development flow in the client, the ApplicationMaster flow follows a constructor, initialization, and run sequence. We show the similarity with the client constructor by creating a YarnConfiguration object that encapsulates the YARN environment where the ApplicationMaster container is launched, and by defining command-line options. As with the client, after the constructor, we add a method to do some initialization (Listing 10.8).

Listing 10.8   YARN ApplicationMaster initialization

```
public boolean init(String[] args) throws ParseException, IOException {

   CommandLine cliParser =
```

```
      new GnuParser().parse(opts, args);

  if (args.length == 0) {
    printUsage(opts);
    throw new IllegalArgumentException(
      "No args specified for application master to
        initialize");
  }

  if (cliParser.hasOption("help")) {
    printUsage(opts);
    return false;
  }

  if (cliParser.hasOption("debug")) {
    dumpOutDebugInfo();
  }

  containerMemory =
    Integer.parseInt(cliParser.getOptionValue(
      "container_memory", "1024"));

  numTotalContainers = Integer.parseInt(
    cliParser.getOptionValue("num_containers", "2"));

  adminUser = cliParser.getOptionValue(
    "admin_user", "yarn");

  adminPassword = cliParser.getOptionValue(
    "admin_password", "yarn");

  appJar = cliParser.getOptionValue("jar");

  if (numTotalContainers == 0) {
    throw new IllegalArgumentException(
      "Cannot run JBoss Application Master with no
        containers");
  }

  requestPriority = Integer.parseInt(
    cliParser.getOptionValue("priority", "0"));

  return true;
}
```

Thus far, the pattern follows much of what we did with the client. In the init method shown in Listing 10.8, we code the same type of logic as was used in the client to parse the command-line options. Remember, these are the command-line options for the command you built in the client. Accordingly, you can include some error checking and other validation for the command in the ApplicationMaster code. It's probably best to do the bulk of that validation in the client, because your client code should be the only thing to invoke the ApplicationMaster's command, any command line errors should be caught prior to this step.

The code to run the ApplicationMaster has some significant differences from the code to run the client and introduces a few key concepts of YARN application development. To start, the following code is the run method we'll add to our Application-Master in Listing 10.7.

Listing 10.9   Running a YARN ApplicationMaster

```
public boolean run() throws YarnException, IOException {

    AMRMClientAsync.CallbackHandler allocListener =
        new RMCallbackHandler();

    resourceManager =
        AMRMClientAsync.createAMRMClientAsync(
        1000, allocListener);

    resourceManager.init(conf);
    resourceManager.start();

    containerListener = new NMCallbackHandler();
    nmClientAsync =
        new NMClientAsyncImpl(containerListener);

    nmClientAsync.init(conf);
    nmClientAsync.start();

    RegisterApplicationMasterResponse response =
        resourceManager.registerApplicationMaster(
        appMasterHostname, appMasterRpcPort,
        appMasterTrackingUrl);

    int maxMem = response.getMaximumResourceCapability()
        .getMemory();

    if (containerMemory > maxMem) {
        containerMemory = maxMem;
    }

    for (int i = 0; i < numTotalContainers; ++i) {
        ContainerRequest containerAsk =
            setupContainerAskForRM();
```

```
      resourceManager.addContainerRequest(containerAsk);
   }
   numRequestedContainers.set(numTotalContainers);

   while (!done) {
      try {
         Thread.sleep(200);
      } catch (InterruptedException ex) {
      }
   }
   finish();

   return success;
}
```

Let's break down the flow of the run logic into some easily digested steps.
Here's what needs to happen in your application code to have a fully functional
ApplicationMaster:

- Develop a callback handler to listen for ResourceManager events
- Create an object using the YARN APIs that will encapsulate the YARN
  ResourceManager client in the ApplicationMaster
- Develop a callback handler to listen for NodeManager events
- Create an object using the YARN APIs that will encapsulate the YARN Node-
  Manager client in the ApplicationMaster
- Develop a class to launch a container

In Listing 10.9, we see references to the objects that we need to either instantiate or
develop on our own. The code snippet that follows instantiates our ResourceManager
callback handler and then uses that object to create a client object that is a YARN
library for asynchronous communication between the ApplicationMaster and the
ResourceManager. The class to launch the container will be used by our Resource-
Manager callback handler. Thus, when we review the steps we need to develop that
functionality, we'll show how to develop that class.

```
AMRMClientAsync.CallbackHandler allocListener = new RMCallbackHandler();
resourceManager = AMRMClientAsync.createAMRMClientAsync(1000, allocListener);
resourceManager.init(conf);
resourceManager.start();
```

We saw the same YARN service life cycle in developing the client—that is, call
an init method using a YarnConfiguration object as the argument followed by the
start method call. Likewise, the code snippet from Listing 10.9 that follows shows the
instantiation of a NodeManager callback handler. This object will be used to create the client object for asynchronous communication between the NodeManagers of

the application and the ApplicationMaster. Again, note the YARN service life-cycle method invocation.

```
containerListener = new NMCallbackHandler();
nmClientAsync = new NMClientAsyncImpl(containerListener);
nmClientAsync.init(conf);
nmClientAsync.start();
```

After setting up the callback handlers and the asynchronous clients, it's time to register the ApplicationMaster with the ResourceManager.

```
RegisterApplicationMasterResponse response =
➥resourceManager.registerApplicationMaster(appMasterHostname, appMasterRpcPort,
➥appMasterTrackingUrl);
```

When you register your ApplicationMaster with the ResourceManager, you supply it with basic information such as the ApplicationMaster hostname, the RPC port, and a tracking URL. The tracking URL can be defined by the programmer and is used in several places—most notably the built-in YARN web user interface that will display a link to this URL. After a successful registration, the heartbeat thread between the ResourceManager and the ApplicationManager begins.

The rest of the code in Listing 10.9 should look familiar, as we needed to put similar logic in our client (e.g., code to validate the requested memory for the containers and code to set up the container resource requests).

In the beginning of the run thread, we introduced the callback handlers and the container launch code. One of the first callbacks in the ApplicationMaster's run method is a reference to RMCallbackHandler. Listing 10.10 shows the code we need to create such a handler. We have added this class as a private class to the Application-Master we're building, but it could just as easily be a standard external class.

Listing 10.10   ResourceManager callback handler

```
private class RMCallbackHandler implements
AMRMClientAsync.CallbackHandler {

  public void onContainersCompleted(
    List<ContainerStatus> completedContainers) {

    for (ContainerStatus containerStatus :
      completedContainers) {

      assert (containerStatus.getState() ==
        ContainerState.COMPLETE);

      int exitStatus =
        containerStatus.getExitStatus();

      if (0 != exitStatus) {
```

```
        if (ContainerExitStatus.ABORTED
          != exitStatus) {

          numCompletedContainers.incrementAndGet();
          numFailedContainers.incrementAndGet();

        } else {
          numAllocatedContainers.decrementAndGet();
          numRequestedContainers.decrementAndGet();
        }
      } else {
        numCompletedContainers.incrementAndGet();
      }
    }

    int askCount = numTotalContainers -
    numRequestedContainers.get();
    numRequestedContainers.addAndGet(askCount);

    if (askCount > 0) {
      for (int i = 0; i < askCount; ++i) {
        ContainerRequest containerAsk =
          setupContainerAskForRM();

        resourceManager.
          addContainerRequest(containerAsk);
      }
    }

  if (numCompletedContainers.get() ==
      numTotalContainers) {
      done = true;
  }
}

public void onContainersAllocated(
  List<Container> allocatedContainers) {
  numAllocatedContainers.addAndGet(
    allocatedContainers.size());

  for (Container allocatedContainer :
    allocatedContainers) {

    LaunchContainerRunnable
    runnableLaunchContainer =
    new LaunchContainerRunnable(
      allocatedContainer, containerListener);
```

```
        Thread launchThread = new
            Thread(runnableLaunchContainer);

        launchThreads.add(launchThread);
        launchThread.start();
    }
}

public void onShutdownRequest() {
    done = true;
}

public void onNodesUpdated(
    List<NodeReport> updatedNodes) {
            }

public void onError(Throwable e) {
    done = true;
    resourceManager.stop();
}
}
```

The methods that we use here are all specified in the AMRMClientAsync
.CallbackHandler interface that the RMCallbackHandler implements. The methods
are easy enough to follow, but let's focus on the onContainersAllocated method.
Once a container has been allocated by the ResourceManager, we'll start that container with the LaunchContainerRunnable class that we develop as a thread by implementing java.lang.Runnable. This class is shown in Listing 10.11.

Listing 10.11   Launching a container

```
private class LaunchContainerRunnable implements Runnable {

    Container container;
    NMCallbackHandler containerListener;

    public LaunchContainerRunnable(Container lcontainer, NMCallbackHandler
➥containerListener) {
        this.container = lcontainer;
        this.containerListener = containerListener;
    }

    public void run() {

        String containerId = container.getId().toString();

        ContainerLaunchContext ctx =
            Records.newRecord(ContainerLaunchContext.class);
```

```
        Map<String, LocalResource> localResources = new HashMap<String,
➥LocalResource>();

        String applicationId =
➥container.getId().getApplicationAttemptId().getApplicationId().toString();

    try {
        FileSystem fs = FileSystem.get(conf);
        LocalResource jbossDist =
            Records.newRecord(LocalResource.class);

        jbossDist.setType(LocalResourceType.ARCHIVE);
        jbossDist.setVisibility(
            LocalResourceVisibility.APPLICATION);

        Path jbossDistPath = new Path(new URI(
            JBossConstants.JBOSS_DIST_PATH));

        jbossDist.setResource(ConverterUtils
            .getYarnUrlFromPath(jbossDistPath));

        jbossDist.setTimestamp(
            fs.getFileStatus(jbossDistPath)
          .getModificationTime());
        jbossDist.setSize(
            fs.getFileStatus(jbossDistPath).getLen());

        localResources.put(JBossConstants.JBOSS_SYMLINK,
            jbossDist);

        LocalResource jbossConf =
            Records.newRecord(LocalResource.class);

        jbossConf.setType(LocalResourceType.FILE);
        jbossConf.setVisibility(
            LocalResourceVisibility.APPLICATION);

        Path jbossConfPath = new Path(new URI(appJar));

        jbossConf.setResource(
            ConverterUtils.getYarnUrlFromPath(
            jbossConfPath));

        jbossConf.setTimestamp(
            fs.getFileStatus(jbossConfPath).
            getModificationTime());
        jbossConf.setSize(
            fs.getFileStatus(jbossConfPath).getLen());
```

```
      localResources.put(
        JBossConstants.JBOSS_ON_YARN_APP, jbossConf);
    } catch (Exception e) {
      LOG.log(Level.SEVERE,
          "Problem setting local resources", e);

      numCompletedContainers.incrementAndGet();
      numFailedContainers.incrementAndGet();
      return;
    }

    ctx.setLocalResources(localResources);

    List<String> commands = new ArrayList<String>();

    String host = container.getNodeId().getHost();

    String containerHome =
        conf.get("yarn.nodemanager.local-dirs")
          + File.separator + ContainerLocalizer.USERCACHE
          + File.separator +
        System.getenv().get(Environment.USER.toString())
          + File.separator + ContainerLocalizer.APPCACHE
          + File.separator + applicationId + File.separator
          + containerId;

    jbossHome = containerHome + File.separator
        + JBossConstants.JBOSS_SYMLINK + File.separator
        + JBossConstants.JBOSS_VERSION;

    String jbossPermissionsCommand =
      String.format("chmod -R 777 %s", jbossHome);

    int portOffset = 0;
    int containerCount =
        containerListener.getContainerCount();

    if (containerCount > 1) {
        portOffset = containerCount * 150;
    }

    String domainControllerValue;

    if (domainController == null) {
        domainControllerValue = host;
    } else {
        domainControllerValue = domainController;
    }
```

```
        String jbossConfigurationCommand =
            String.format("%s/bin/java -cp %s %s --home %s --server_group %s
➥--server %s --port_offset %s --admin_user %s --admin_password %s
➥--domain_controller %s --host %s",
            Environment.JAVA_HOME.$(),
            "/opt/hadoop-2.2.0/share/hadoop/common/lib/*" + File.pathSeparator
            + containerHome + File.separator +
            JBossConstants.JBOSS_ON_YARN_APP,
            JBossConfiguration.class.getName(),
            jbossHome,

            applicationId, containerId,
            portOffset, adminUser,
            adminPassword, domainControllerValue, host);

        String jbossCommand =
            String.format("%s%sbin%sdomain.sh
              -Djboss.bind.address=%s
              -Djboss.bind.address.management=%s
              -Djboss.bind.address.unsecure=%s",
              jbossHome, File.separator, File.separator,
              host, host, host);

        commands.add(jbossPermissionsCommand);

        commands.add(JBossConstants.COMMAND_CHAIN);
        commands.add(jbossConfigurationCommand);

        commands.add(JBossConstants.COMMAND_CHAIN);
        commands.add(jbossCommand);

        ctx.setCommands(commands);
        containerListener.addContainer(
            container.getId(), container);

        nmClientAsync.startContainerAsync(
            container, ctx);
    }
  }
```

In general, the ApplicationMaster sets up the containers environment, commands, and local resources before submitting it as a ContainerLaunchContext to the Node-Manager. Once these steps are complete, the NodeManager then launches the provided container, as shown in Figure 10.3.

The container launcher contains many steps. The following is a list of the actions that take place when we start our JBoss application:

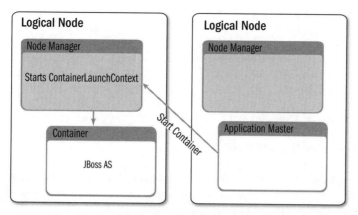

Figure 10.3 ApplicationManager communication with the NodeManager
starting a container for data processing

- We create a map of LocalResources in the same way we did with the client.
- The LocalResource map has two resources added to it: the JBoss AS distribution and the jar file that contains our entire YARN application.
- We create commands to change the permissions of the unarchived JBoss AS file, do some editing of the JBoss AS configuration files, and run the JBoss AS instance.
- We start the container.

Each of these steps will now be discussed in greater detail. The map of Local-Resources has the JBoss AS distribution as a `tar.gz` file. This file is automatically unarchived by YARN and given the symbolic link as the string specified as the map key. Using our example, the JBoss AS distribution can be found in HDFS at the following location: hdfs://yarn1.apps.hdp:9000/apps/jboss/dist/jboss-as-7.1.1.Final.tar.gz.

If the file is in HDFS, we can create a LocalResource with the convenience method `ConverterUtils.getYarnUrlFromPath`. The code from Listing 10.11 to accomplish all this is shown in the following snippet.

```
LocalResource jbossDist =
   Records.newRecord(LocalResource.class);

jbossDist.setType(LocalResourceType.ARCHIVE);
jbossDist.setVisibility(
   LocalResourceVisibility.APPLICATION);

Path jbossDistPath = new Path(
   new URI("hdfs://yarn1.apps.hdp:9000/apps/jboss/dist/jboss-as-7.1.1.Final.tar.
➥gz"));
```

```
jbossDist.setResource(ConverterUtils
    .getYarnUrlFromPath(jbossDistPath));

jbossDist.setTimestamp(fs.getFileStatus(jbossDistPath)
    .getModificationTime());

jbossDist.setSize(
    fs.getFileStatus(jbossDistPath).getLen());

localResources.put("jboss", jbossDist);
```

We also add the application jar file to the container's LocalResource map and then begin building our commands to work with the container. To accomplish this, we need to define the location of our unarchived JBoss AS distribution.

The root of each container's local file system is defined by the property `yarn.nodemanager.local-dirs`, which is specified in `yarn-site.xml`. In our example, we've given this property the value of `/var/data/yarn`. From this base directory, the NodeManager will create subdirectories where each container will have its own file system. Notably, this directory structure will be deleted once the container is stopped, which can make application development difficult. Fortunately, YARN lets us configure how long a container's local directory structure can live before it is deleted by the NodeManager. By specifying the `yarn.nodemanager.delete.debug-delay-sec` property in `yarn-site.xml`, we can give a value in seconds defining how long the container's directory will live before being deleted. For debugging YARN applications, it's best to set this property to a suitably high value so you monitor your container's file system.

Next we need the command to start the JBoss AS instances. The code includes some logic to do a couple of things specific to JBoss AS. Although a complete description of JBoss AS configuration is beyond the scope of this book, we note that we need to configure port numbers and a domain mode. JBoss AS is a server process that will open specific sockets on a number of ports. With YARN, we always have the possibility of running more than one instance of an application container on the same host. Thus, if your application launches a container that might conflict with another running container on the same host, some tweaks are needed. In our case, we need to increment port numbers in the JBoss AS instance if another container is launched by the same NodeManager. Fortunately, JBoss AS offers a quick and easy way to do this—simply specify the value by which to increment all ports in a configuration file.

Also, JBoss AS supports the concept of a domain mode, which means that all server instances in the same domain can be managed by a single UI instance. Since YARN is by nature a clustered application platform, we will take advantage of JBoss AS's domain mode and configure each instance of JBoss AS accordingly. In domain mode, one server instance acts as the domain controller; the remaining instances are slave nodes that communicate to the domain controller with configurable RPC and security settings. All of this configuration takes place before the actual JBoss AS server instance is launched, and all of the source code for this configuration can be found at this book's repository (see Appendix A).

The first command added to the ContainerLaunchContext is easy to understand. It changes the permissions in the container's file system so we can easily write the configuration. The next commands are shown in the following snippet.

```
String jbossConfigurationCommand =
    String.format("%s/bin/java -cp %s %s --home %s --server_group %s --server %s --
➥port_offset %s --admin_user %s --admin_password %s --domain_controller %s --
➥host %s",
    Environment.JAVA_HOME.$(),
    "/opt/hadoop-2.2.0/share/hadoop/common/lib/*"
    + File.pathSeparator + containerHome
    + File.separator + JBossConstants.JBOSS_ON_YARN_APP,
    JBossConfiguration.class.getName(), jbossHome,
    applicationId, containerId, portOffset, adminUser,
    adminPassword, domainControllerValue, host);

String jbossCommand =
    String.format("%s%sbin%sdomain.sh
    -Djboss.bind.address=%s
    -Djboss.bind.address.management=%s
    -Djboss.bind.address.unsecure=%s",
    jbossHome, File.separator, File.separator,
    host, host, host);
```

These commands configure and launch JBoss AS, respectively. When they are added to the ContainerLaunchContext, the only thing left for our container launch class to do is to start the container. Let's start the container by wrapping everything we've created into a single jar file and enter command-line options so that we can parse with the client and propagate to the ApplicationMaster.

```
# java -cp $(hadoop classpath):/etc/hadoop/*:/opt/jboss-on-yarn-0.0.1-SNAPSHOT.jar
➥org.yarnbook.JBossClient -jar /opt/jboss-on-yarn-0.0.1-SNAPSHOT.jar
➥-admin_user yarn -admin_password yarn -num_containers 2
```

When we enter this command, the steps described previously begin execution. Communication with the ResourceManager begins, our jar file is copied to the appropriate location, a certain number of containers are allocated and prepared, and a container directory structure is created on the local file system as shown in Figure 10.4.

Notice the symbolic links representing the LocalResource map that we created for the container and the directory naming convention that we created as the variable containerHome in the LaunchContainerRunnable.run method. If we list the directory contents of the jboss symbolic link, we can see the unarchived contents of the JBoss AS tar.gz file distribution as well as the directory and file permission change we performed with the first command added to the ContainerLaunchContext. An example is given in Figure 10.5.

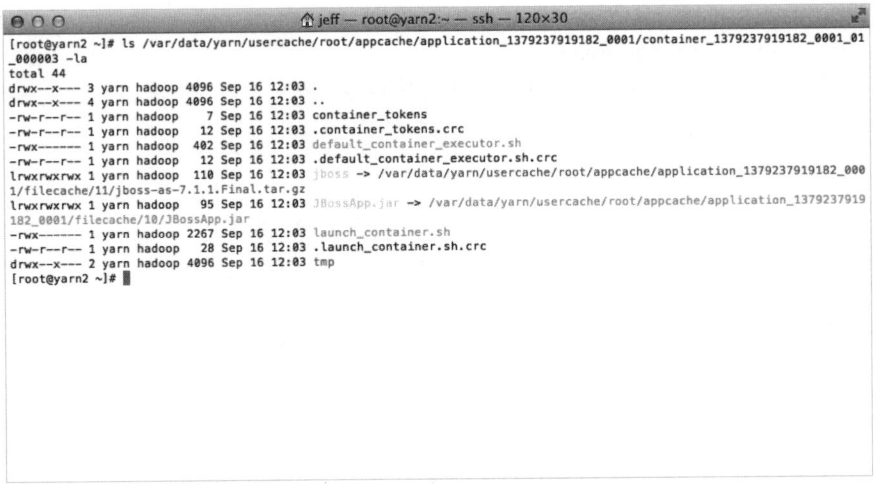

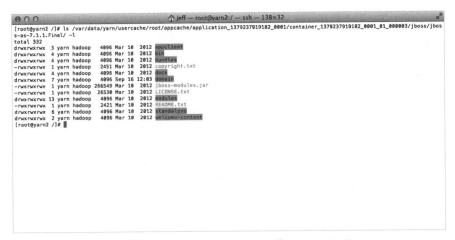

Figure 10.4 Application container directory structure

Figure 10.5 Unarchived resource directory structure

Continuing to examine Figure 10.4, we also see a script called
launch_container.sh. A listing of this script is provided in Figure 10.6.

The launch_container.sh file sets environment variables and the commands that we
propagate to the containers. YARN generates and places the commands into this shell
script and, after the container successfully transitions to a state called LOCALIZED, executes the shell script to start the container. In our case, we have a container that launches
JBoss AS server instances. The use of a run script illustrates that YARN can manage virtually any application written in any language. Figure 10.7 shows what our application,
JBoss on YARN, looks like in the YARN web user interface.

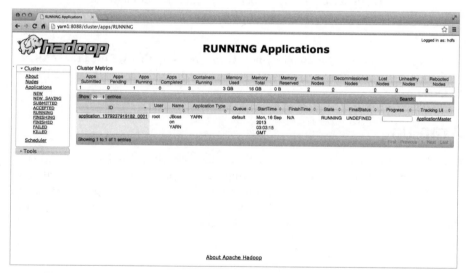

Figure 10.6   Contents of launch_container.sh script

Figure 10.7   JBoss AS YARN application in the YARN web user interface

Next, let's take a look at the JBoss AS domain controller user interface (Figure 10.8) and make sure we have the two instances of JBoss AS up and running—the two instances we specified with the num_containers argument to our client. We should have one master and one slave.

We can see from the JBoss AS UI that we have a master and a slave, and by virtue of their visibility in the management console, we know that we've configured the

Figure 10.8   JBoss AS domain controller user interface

communication between the two instances correctly. Note that we used the YARN application ID as the JBoss AS server group name and the container ID as the JBoss AS server name.

Wrap-up

YARN application development involves creating both a client and an Application-Master. As illustrated in this chapter, creating a non-MapReduce application takes some coding, but much of the code can be reused for other applications. The example developed in this chapter can be easily expanded to a larger number of containers by adjusting the command-line arguments. A full code listing is available from the book code repository mentioned in Appendix A.

11

Using Apache Hadoop YARN Distributed-Shell

The Hadoop YARN project includes the Distributed-Shell application, which is an example of a non-MapReduce application built on top of YARN. Distributed-Shell is a simple mechanism for running shell commands and scripts in containers on multiple nodes in a Hadoop cluster. There are multiple existing implementations of a distributed shell that administrators typically use to manage a cluster of machines, and this application is a way to demonstrate how such a utility can be implemented on top of YARN.

More than just providing a parallel execution application, Distributed-Shell can be used as a starting point for exploring and building Hadoop YARN applications. This chapter is intended to be a guide to how one can use the Distributed-Shell application and, more than that, play with it so as to understand more about how a YARN application can be written as well as how it interacts with YARN for its execution.

Using the YARN Distributed-Shell

For the purpose of examples in the remainder of this chapter, we assume the following installation path of the Distributed-Shell application:

```
$ export YARN_DS=$YARN_HOME/share/hadoop/yarn
```

$YARN_HOME should point to the installation directory of YARN. In addition, the Distributed-Shell examples that follow have a version tag defined using the environment variable "$YARN_VERSION." Change this value to match your installation.

```
$ export YARN_VERSION=2.2.0
```

Distributed-Shell exposes various options that can be found by running the following:

```
$ yarn org.apache.hadoop.yarn.applications.distributedshell.Client -jar \
$YARN_DS/hadoop-yarn-applications-distributedshell-$YARN_VERSION.jar -help
```

The output of this command follows; we will explore some of these options in the examples illustrated in this chapter.

```
usage: Client
 -appname <arg>                  Application Name. Default value -
                                 DistributedShell
 -container_memory <arg>         Amount of memory in MB to be requested to run
                                 the shell command
 -debug                          Dump out debug information
 -help                           Print usage
 -jar <arg>                      Jar file containing the application master
 -log_properties <arg>           log4j.properties file
 -master_memory <arg>            Amount of memory in MB to be requested to run
                                 the application master
 -num_containers <arg>           No. of containers on which the shell command
                                 needs to be executed
 -priority <arg>                 Application Priority. Default 0
 -queue <arg>                    RM Queue in which this application is to be
                                 submitted
 -shell_args <arg>               Command line args for the shell script
 -shell_cmd_priority <arg>       Priority for the shell command containers
 -shell_command <arg>            Shell command to be executed by the
                                 Application Master
 -shell_env <arg>                Environment for shell script. Specified as
                                 env_key=env_val pairs
 -shell_script <arg>             Location of the shell script to be executed
 -timeout <arg>                  Application timeout in milliseconds
```

A Simple Example

The simplest use-case for the Distributed-Shell application is to run an arbitrary shell command in a container. We will demonstrate the use of the uptime command as an example. This command can be run on the cluster using Distributed-Shell as follows:

```
$ yarn org.apache.hadoop.yarn.applications.distributedshell.Client -jar \
$YARN_DS/hadoop-yarn-applications-distributedshell-$YARN_VERSION.jar \
-shell_command uptime
```

By default, Distributed-Shell spawns only one instance of a given shell command. When this command is run, one can see log messages on the screen. If the shell command succeeds, the following should appear at the end of the output:

```
13/10/16 19:34:23 INFO distributedshell.Client: Application completed successfully
```

If the shell command did not work for whatever reason, the following message will be displayed:

```
13/10/16 19:36:15 ERROR distributedshell.Client: Application failed to
➥complete successfully
```

The next step is to examine the output for the application. Distributed-Shell redirects the output of the individual shell commands run on the cluster nodes into the log files, which are found either on the individual nodes or aggregated on to HDFS depending on whether log aggregation is enabled.

Assuming log aggregation is not enabled, the results for each instance of the command are listed by container under an application-id directory. For example, if the contents of the application-id directory are listed, two containers' directories can be seen:

```
$ ls $YARN_HOME/logs/userlogs/application_1381961205352_0005
container_1381961205352_0005_01_000001  container_1381961205352_0005_01_000002
```

Recall that the first container (.._000001) is the ApplicationMaster (the head process). The second container (.._000002) is where the actual command output resides. Within each directory, there are two files, stdout and stderr. For example,

```
$ ls $YARN_HOME/logs/userlogs/application_1381961205352_0005/
➥container_1381961205352_0005_01_000002/
stderr  stdout
```

If we print the contents of the stdout file, we find the expected result for the uptime command.

```
19:44:30 up 1 day,  6:53,  6 users,  load average: 0.00, 0.00, 0.00
```

Similarly, one can look for the following output if log aggregation is enabled:

```
$ yarn logs -applicationId application_1388537987294_0001
```

This command will show the output for all containers in a single output stream.

Using More Containers

Distributed-Shell can run commands to be executed on any number of containers by way of the -num_containers argument. For example, to see on which nodes the Distributed-Shell command was run, we can use the following:

```
$ yarn org.apache.hadoop.yarn.applications.distributedshell.Client –jar \
$YARN_DS/hadoop-yarn-applications-distributedshell-$YARN_VERSION.jar \
 -shell_command hostname -num_containers 4
```

If we now examine the results for this job, there will be five containers' log directories, each containing its own stdout and stderr files.

```
$ ls $YARN_HOME/logs/userlogs/application_1381961205352_0006/
container_1381961205352_0006_01_000001
container_1381961205352_0006_01_000002
container_1381961205352_0006_01_000003
container_1381961205352_0006_01_000004
container_1381961205352_0006_01_000005
```

Containers with IDs ranging from 2 to 5 will have in their stdout file the hostname of the machine where the job was run.

Distributed-Shell Examples with Shell Arguments

Arguments can be added to the shell command using the `-shell_args` option. For example, to do a `ls -l` in the directory from where the shell command was run, we can use the following commands:

```
$ yarn org.apache.hadoop.yarn.applications.distributedshell.Client -jar \
$YARN_DS/hadoop-yarn-applications-distributedshell-$YARN_VERSION.jar \
 -shell_command ls -shell_args -l
```

The resulting output is as follows:

```
total 16
-rw-r--r-- 1 hdfs hadoop    7 Oct 16 20:17 container_tokens
-rwx------ 1 hdfs hadoop  382 Oct 16 20:17 default_container_executor.sh
-rwx------ 1 hdfs hadoop 1303 Oct 16 20:17 launch_container.sh
drwx--x--- 2 hdfs hadoop 4096 Oct 16 20:17 tmp
```

As you can see, the resulting files are new and not located anywhere in our hdfs or local file system. If we explore a little more using a Distributed-Shell `pwd` command, we find that these files are in directories of the kind

```
/hdfs/tmp/usercache/doug/appcache/application_1381961205352_0008/container_1381961
➥205352_0008_01_000002
```

on the node that executed the shell command.

However, once the application finishes, if we log into the node and search for these files, they may not exist. These transient files are used by YARN to run the Distributed-Shell application and are removed once the application finishes. You can preserve these files for a specific interval by adding the following to the `yarn-site.xml` configuration file and restarting YARN. You can choose the delay in seconds to suit your needs—these files will be retained on the individual nodes only for the duration of the specified delay.

```
<property>
    <name>yarn.nodemanager.delete.debug-delay-sec</name>
    <value>10000000</value>
</property>
```

These files—in particular, `launch_container.sh`—are important when debugging YARN applications. Let's use the Distributed-Shell itself to dig into what this file is about. We can examine the `launch_container.sh` file with the following command:

```
$ yarn org.apache.hadoop.yarn.applications.distributedshell.Client -jar \
$YARN_DS/hadoop-yarn-applications-distributedshell-$YARN_VERSION.jar \
 -shell_command cat -shell_args launch_container.sh
```

This command outputs the `launch_container.sh` file that is created and run by YARN before executing the user-supplied shell utility. The contents of the file are shown in Listing 11.1. The file basically exports some important YARN variables and then, at the end, "execs" the command directly and sends the output to the `stdout` and `stderr` files mentioned earlier.

Listing 11.1   Distributed-Shell launch_container.sh file

```
#!/bin/bash

export NM_HTTP_PORT="8042"
export LOCAL_DIRS="/hdfs/tmp/usercache/doug/appcache/application_1381856870533_0040"
export HADOOP_COMMON_HOME="/opt/yarn/hadoop-$YARN_VERSION"
export JAVA_HOME="/usr/lib/jvm/java-1.6.0-openjdk.x86_64"
export HADOOP_YARN_HOME="/opt/yarn/hadoop-$YARN_VERSION"
export
➥HADOOP_TOKEN_FILE_LOCATION="/hdfs/tmp/usercache/doug/appcache/application_138185687
➥0533_0040/container_1381856870533_0040_01_000002/container_tokens"
export NM_HOST="n2"
export JVM_PID="$$"
export USER="doug"
export HADOOP_HDFS_HOME="/opt/yarn/hadoop-$YARN_VERSION"
export
➥PWD="/hdfs/tmp/usercache/doug/appcache/application_1381856870533_0040/container_138
➥1856870533_0040_01_000002"
export CONTAINER_ID="container_1381856870533_0040_01_000002"
export NM_PORT="45176"
export HOME="/home/"
export LOGNAME="doug"
export HADOOP_CONF_DIR="/opt/yarn/hadoop-$YARN_VERSION/etc/hadoop"
export MALLOC_ARENA_MAX="4"
export LOG_DIRS="/opt/yarn/hadoop-
➥$YARN_VERSION/logs/userlogs/application_1381856870533_0040/container_1381856870533_
➥0040_01_000002"
exec /bin/bash -c "cat launch_container.sh 1>/opt/yarn/hadoop-
➥$YARN_VERSION/logs/userlogs/application_1381856870533_0040/container_1381856870533_
➥0040_01_000002/stdout 2>/opt/yarn/hadoop-
➥$YARN_VERSION/logs/userlogs/application_1381856870533_0040/container_1381856870533_
➥0040_01_000002/stderr "
```

There are more options for the Distributed-Shell that you can play with. However, as we mentioned earlier, some other existing utilities (such as the `pdsh` utility) provide easy and feature-rich tools for running simple commands and scripts across the cluster. The real value of the Distributed-Shell application is its showcasing of applications that can run within the Hadoop YARN infrastructure.

We will now delve a little more into the internal details of how Distributed-Shell itself works and how you can modify it, enhance it, or even use it as a scaffolding to write your own YARN applications.

Internals of the Distributed-Shell

The Distributed-Shell is the "hello-world.c" for Hadoop 2. That is, it demonstrates the basic functionality of a YARN application. Once its internal workings are understood, it can be used as a starting point for writing new YARN applications. The source code for the Distributed-Shell can be found in `$YARN_HOME/share/hadoop/yarn/sources`. These source files can be extracted by running

```
jar -xf hadoop-yarn-applications-distributedshell-$YARN_VERSION-sources.jar
```

Three main classes make up (and so can be changed to use it as a template for your own YARN application) the main package of Distributed-Shell—that is, the `org.apache.hadoop.yarn.applications.distributedshell` package. These classes are:

1. Client
2. ApplicationMaster
3. DSConstants

In addition to making changes to the existing Distributed-Shell application, you may want to write more complex logic than just invoking shell commands. A large share of the code can be reused with minimal changes, allowing for quick prototyping of bare-bones YARN applications. To help you in getting started with understanding the internals as well as to provide templates that you can use with subsequent modification, selective fragments of code will be highlighted here. The goals of this approach are twofold: to explain the workings of the application and to allow simple modification or duplication of existing code so that you can quickly get a prototype application running.

Application Constants

The DSConstants class offers a simple way to keep track of information as environment keys that will be used in containers later. In its native form, it is designed to be a shell script run as part of Distributed-Shell. To reuse the code in Listing 11.2, simply make copies of the three string variables for each file (local resource) you plan on using in your containers.

Listing 11.2   **Metadata for the DistributedShellScript public class DSConstants**

```
public class DSConstants {

  /**
   * Environment key name pointing to the shell script's location
   */
  public static final String DISTRIBUTEDSHELLSCRIPTLOCATION =
➥"DISTRIBUTEDSHELLSCRIPTLOCATION";
  /**
   * Environment key name denoting the file timestamp for the shell script.
```

```
    * Used to validate the local resource.
    */
  public static final String DISTRIBUTEDSHELLSCRIPTTIMESTAMP =
➥"DISTRIBUTEDSHELLSCRIPTTIMESTAMP";
  /**
    * Environment key name denoting the file content length for the shell script.
    * Used to validate the local resource.
    */
  public static final String DISTRIBUTEDSHELLSCRIPTLEN =
➥"DISTRIBUTEDSHELLSCRIPTLEN";
}
```

Strictly speaking, these environment variables are just a simple way of passing static information like file timestamps and file lengths to the ApplicationMaster so that it can, in turn, set the same information as part of launching containers. A more complex application may have more static data as well as dynamic information that needs to be passed. Using environment variables is one way of achieving this outcome. Other possibilities are to use configuration files that are distributed as local resources and shared services (like HDFS) that the client and ApplicationMaster can access.

Client

The Client class is fundamentally responsible for launching the ApplicationMaster, which will then schedule and run the shell commands in each container. The Client class performs three major tasks to get user-supplied executables to run in their own containers:

1. Launch the Client CLI (command-line interface)
2. Manage additional local resources
3. Set up the ApplicationMaster environment

The Client CLI obtains the application jar file, the location of a user shell script, a custom log-configuration file, and other information from the user. Listing 11.3 checks whether a jar file was passed to the CLI and adds its results to a variable.

Listing 11.3 Adding the appMasterJar to the CLI

```
  if (!cliParser.hasOption("jar")) {
      throw new IllegalArgumentException("No jar file specified for application
➥master");
      }
      appMasterJar = cliParser.getOptionValue("jar");
```

The CLI parsing code can be modified if necessary to add more libraries for execution as containers. By duplicating how the ApplicationMaster jar file is added from the command-line parser, you can quickly add new configuration features to the Client class.

After checking for valid input from the CLI, the client needs to connect to the ResourceManager for application submission. At this point, the client can request additional cluster information like the maximum container size, together with a new ApplicationId. In the Distributed-Shell application, the YarnClient library is used to create an instance of YarnClientApplication that encompasses this information.

The client then creates an ApplicationSubmissionContext that specifies the application details such as ApplicationId, an application name, the priority assigned to the application, and the submission queue's name. The ApplicationSubmissionContext record also requires a ContainerLaunchContext that describes the container under which the ApplicationMaster itself is launched. Inside the ContainerLaunchContext, we define the resource requirements for the ApplicationMaster container; the local resources (jar files, configuration files), the execution environment for the container, and the commands that must be executed to start the ApplicationMaster container.

Because the ApplicationMaster does not make use of the libraries required by the containers that run the user scripts, there is no need to make them available to the ApplicationMaster container itself; they need only be uploaded to HDFS. An example is the way Distributed-Shell makes a shell script available to the actual containers. Listing 11.4 is a simple snippet that shows how to upload your container libraries into HDFS.

Listing 11.4   Code to upload your container libraries to HDFS

```
String hdfsShellScriptLocation = "";
long hdfsShellScriptLen = 0;
long hdfsShellScriptTimestamp = 0;
if (!shellScriptPath.isEmpty()) {
  Path shellSrc = new Path(shellScriptPath);
  String shellPathSuffix =
      appName + "/" + appId.getId() + "/"
          + (Shell.WINDOWS ? windowBatPath : linuxShellPath);
  Path shellDst =
      new Path(fs.getHomeDirectory(), shellPathSuffix);
  // Copy the file to DFS
  fs.copyFromLocalFile(false, true, shellSrc, shellDst);
  // Record its metadata
  hdfsShellScriptLocation = shellDst.toUri().toString();
  FileStatus shellFileStatus = fs.getFileStatus(shellDst);
  hdfsShellScriptLen = shellFileStatus.getLen();
  hdfsShellScriptTimestamp = shellFileStatus.getModificationTime();
}
```

Although the ApplicationMaster does not use the libraries itself, it will be launching the final containers that use these libraries. Because of this, the ApplicationMaster needs to know the metadata—that is, where the libraries are on HDFS, the last modification time of the file, and the file content length. After the Client uploads the libraries, this metadata can be collected and made available as environmental properties in the ApplicationMaster's container (or via separate configuration files, as we hinted earlier). The DSConstants class is used to manage these environment properties. Listing 11.5 shows how the shell script's metadata is stored into the container environment.

Listing 11.5   **Code for storing the shell script's metadata into the container environment**

```
Map<String, String> env = new HashMap<String, String>();
    // put location of shell script into env
    // using the env info, the application master will create the correct local
➡resource for the
    // eventual containers that will be launched to execute the shell scripts
    env.put(DSConstants.DISTRIBUTEDSHELLSCRIPTLOCATION, hdfsShellScriptLocation);
    env.put(DSConstants.DISTRIBUTEDSHELLSCRIPTTIMESTAMP,
Long.toString(hdfsShellScriptTimestamp));
    env.put(DSConstants.DISTRIBUTEDSHELLSCRIPTLEN,
Long.toString(hdfsShellScriptLen));
```

The resources needed by the AM container itself can be added to the local resources in the ApplicationSubmissionContext as shown in Listing 11.6.

Listing 11.6   **Adding local resources to the AM container**

```
    if (!shellCommand.isEmpty()) {
      addToLocalResources(fs, null, shellCommandPath, appId.getId(),
          localResources, shellCommand);
    }

  private void addToLocalResources(FileSystem fs, String fileSrcPath,
      String fileDstPath, int appId, Map<String, LocalResource> localResources,
      String resources) throws IOException {
    [ . . . . ]
    FileStatus scFileStatus = fs.getFileStatus(dst);
    LocalResource scRsrc =
        LocalResource.newInstance(
            ConverterUtils.getYarnUrlFromURI(dst.toUri()),
            LocalResourceType.FILE, LocalResourceVisibility.APPLICATION,
            scFileStatus.getLen(), scFileStatus.getModificationTime());
    localResources.put(fileDstPath, scRsrc);
  }
```

Finally, the ApplicationSubmissionContext is submitted to the ResourceManager and the client then monitors the application by requesting a periodic ApplicationReport from the ResourceManager (Listing 11.7).

Listing 11.7 Monitoring the progress of the application

```
private boolean monitorApplication(ApplicationId appId)
    throws YarnException, IOException {
  while (true) {

    // Check app status every 1 second
    Thread.sleep(1000);

    // Get application report for the appId we are interested in
    ApplicationReport report = yarnClient.getApplicationReport(appId);

    YarnApplicationState state = report.getYarnApplicationState();
    if (YarnApplicationState.FINISHED == state) {
      LOG.info("Application has completed successfully. Breaking monitoring loop");
        return true;
    }
  [ . . . ]
  }
}
```

Mimicking existing distributed-shell utilities, if the application is taking an excessive amount of time to execute, the client kills the application.

> **Note**
>
> If you want to create a long-running application that is not killed via the built-in distributed shell timeout, comment out the code in Listing 11.8 in the client.

Listing 11.8 **Application Timeout code block**

```
    if (System.currentTimeMillis() > (clientStartTime + clientTimeout)) {
        LOG.info("Reached client specified timeout for application. Killing
➥application");
        forceKillApplication(appId);
        return false;
    }
```

ApplicationMaster

The ApplicationMaster begins by registering itself with the ResourceManager (Listing 11.9), and then sends a heartbeat to the ResourceManager at regular intervals to indicate that it is up and alive. When you are writing your own application, it is important that the ApplicationMaster register itself immediately so that the ResourceManager does not think it has failed to start and, therefore, kill the AM container.

Listing 11.9   **Registration with the ResourceManager**

```
AMRMClientAsync.CallbackHandler allocListener = new RMCallbackHandler();
amRMClient = AMRMClientAsync.createAMRMClientAsync(1000, allocListener);
amRMClient.init(conf);
amRMClient.start();

RegisterApplicationMasterResponse response = amRMClient
    .registerApplicationMaster(appMasterHostname, appMasterRpcPort,
        appMasterTrackingUrl);
```

The ApplicationMaster's init method initializes the DistributedShellScript variables by accessing the parameters set in its own environment by the Client class. These parameters are then later used in creating LocalResources for the final containers that are launched by the ApplicationMaster. The code in Listing 11.10 initializes metadata for LocalResources used in the final containers.

Listing 11.10   **Initializing metadata for LocalResources used in the final containers**

```
if (envs.containsKey(DSConstants.DISTRIBUTEDSHELLSCRIPTLOCATION)) {
    shellScriptPath = envs.get(DSConstants.DISTRIBUTEDSHELLSCRIPTLOCATION);

    if (envs.containsKey(DSConstants.DISTRIBUTEDSHELLSCRIPTTIMESTAMP)) {
        shellScriptPathTimestamp = Long.valueOf(envs
            .get(DSConstants.DISTRIBUTEDSHELLSCRIPTTIMESTAMP));
    }
    if (envs.containsKey(DSConstants.DISTRIBUTEDSHELLSCRIPTLEN)) {
        shellScriptPathLen = Long.valueOf(envs
            .get(DSConstants.DISTRIBUTEDSHELLSCRIPTLEN));
    }
}
```

To perform the requisite processing, the ApplicationMaster must request containers from the ResourceManager. This request is made using a ResourceRequest with specific entries for each resource—the node location, memory, or CPU needs of the container. Most of this information is user input that already exists as part of the Distributed-Shell Client CLI parameters that eventually get passed to the Application-Master. The ResourceManager responds with a set of newly allocated containers, as well as current state of freely available resources.

For each allocated container, the ApplicationMaster then sets up the necessary launch context via ContainerLaunchContext to specify the allocated container ID, local resources required by the executable, the environment to be set up for the executable, commands to execute, and so on.

Inside the run() method of the ApplicationMaster, the ContainerLaunchContext sets up its Environment and LocalResources for the final containers. One can modify the code used for the DistributedShellScript and adjust it so that it points to the libraries' metadata that was populated from the DSConstants environmental variables.

You can also easily add new environment parameters (e.g., the ApplicationMaster hostname) by creating an instance of HashMap<String, String>, populating it with key-value pairs, and finally calling setEnvironment(HashMapObj), thereby adding the parameters to the final containers' environment. If you are using jar, zip, or tar files that require expansion inside the container, changing the LocalResourceType.FILE to ARCHIVE will automatically decompress the archive into a folder named after the file. The code in Listing 11.11 adds environment and file data to the final container.

Listing 11.11   Adding environment and file data to the final container resources

```
// Set the environment
     ctx.setEnvironment(shellEnv);


 // Set the local resources
     Map<String, LocalResource> localResources = new HashMap<String,
➡LocalResource>();

     // The container for the eventual shell commands needs its own local
     // resources too.
     // In this scenario, if a shell script is specified, we need to have it
     // copied and made available to the container.
     if (!shellScriptPath.isEmpty()) {
       LocalResource shellRsrc = Records.newRecord(LocalResource.class);
       shellRsrc.setType(LocalResourceType.FILE);
       shellRsrc.setVisibility(LocalResourceVisibility.APPLICATION);
       try {
         shellRsrc.setResource(ConverterUtils.getYarnUrlFromURI(new URI(
            shellScriptPath)));
       } catch (URISyntaxException e) {
         LOG.error("Error when trying to use shell script path specified"
            + " in env, path=" + shellScriptPath);
         e.printStackTrace();

         // A failure scenario on bad input such as invalid shell script path
         // We know we cannot continue launching the container
         // so we should release it.
         numCompletedContainers.incrementAndGet();
         numFailedContainers.incrementAndGet();
         return;
       }
       shellRsrc.setTimestamp(shellScriptPathTimestamp);
       shellRsrc.setSize(shellScriptPathLen);
       localResources.put(Shell.WINDOWS ? ExecBatScripStringtPath :
            ExecShellStringPath, shellRsrc);
       shellCommand = Shell.WINDOWS ? windows_command : linux_bash_command;
     }
     ctx.setLocalResources(localResources);
```

The last potential area for modification of the ApplicationMaster code lies in the container launch commands. It is here that setting up particular class libraries, running code, and performing other actions can be taken inside the containers. Anything that can be run from the Linux or Windows command line can be run as a command in the containers. If, for example, you wanted to run a Runnable.jar that you have uploaded as a library up to this point, you can do so with the following code:

```
vargs.add(Environment.JAVA_HOME.$() + "/bin/java -jar Runnable.jar");
```

Note

Multiple commands can be stacked for execution when the container starts. To run multiple commands in sequence, run the commands by making use of semicolons. Other shell syntax will work as well. For example, this multistep command can be set up to run at container launch:

```
'cd UnTarDirectory; mkdir testDir; mv cmd1.sh testDir/; cd testDir; sh cmd1.sh'
```

Listing 11.12 adds the actual application commands to the launch containers.

Listing 11.12 **Adding commands to the launch containers**

```
// Set the necessary command to execute on the allocated container
  Vector<CharSequence> vargs = new Vector<CharSequence>(5);

  // Set executable command
  vargs.add(shellCommand);
  // Set shell script path
  if (!shellScriptPath.isEmpty()) {
    vargs.add(Shell.WINDOWS ? ExecBatScripStringtPath
        : ExecShellStringPath);
  }

  // Set args for the shell command if any
  vargs.add(shellArgs);
  // Add log redirect params
  vargs.add("1>" + ApplicationConstants.LOG_DIR_EXPANSION_VAR + "/stdout");
  vargs.add("2>" + ApplicationConstants.LOG_DIR_EXPANSION_VAR + "/stderr");

  // Get final command
  StringBuilder command = new StringBuilder();
  for (CharSequence str : vargs) {
    command.append(str).append(" ");
  }
  List<String> commands = new ArrayList<String>();
  commands.add(command.toString());
  ctx.setCommands(commands);
```

The ApplicationMaster finally talks to the appropriate NodeManager to launch the container (Listing 11.13). It uses the NMClient library to do so.

Listing 11.13   **Launching the container**

```
containerListener = createNMCallbackHandler();
nmClientAsync = new NMClientAsyncImpl(containerListener);
nmClientAsync.init(conf);
nmClientAsync.start();
[ . . . ]


containerListener.addContainer(container.getId(), container);
nmClientAsync.startContainerAsync(container, ctx);
```

The ApplicationMaster can monitor the launched container by either querying the ResourceManager using ApplicationMasterProtocol.allocate() API to get updates on completed containers or using the ContainerManagementProtocol.getContainerStatus() API to query for the status of the allocated container's ContainerId. Most applications, including Distributed-Shell, do the former.

After its work is completed, similar to application registration, the AM container sends a FinishApplicationMasterRequest to the ResourceManager to inform it about the container's status.

Final Containers

The final containers launched by the ApplicationMaster can be anything that the Container start-up commands can execute—for example, Python programs, Perl, Java, C++, shell commands, and more. Often, the real challenge is not launching the containers to execute the code, but rather coordinating the distributed nature of the containers. Numerous applications can be made to operate in a distributed parallel fashion with minimal changes. This aspect promotes reuse of existing codebases to run as YARN applications. In many cases, only the parallelism logic needs to be created and added to the main application code.

Wrap-up

The Distributed-Shell represents one of the first YARN application frameworks that does not run as a MapReduce application. Although it might not add a lot of real-world utility to existing parallel-shell utilities, it serves as an excellent starting point for building new Hadoop YARN applications. Using the code examples provided in this chapter, you can easily modify the Distributed-Shell application and explore writing your own YARN applications. In addition, using Distributed-Shell to probe the YARN execution process itself helps provide insight into how YARN runs distributed applications.

12

Apache Hadoop YARN
Frameworks

One of the most exciting aspects of YARN is its ability to support multiple programming models and application frameworks. In Hadoop version 1, the only processing model available to users is MapReduce. In Hadoop version 2, MapReduce is separated from the resource management layer of Hadoop and placed into its own application framework. YARN forms a resource management platform, which provides services such as scheduling, fault monitoring, data locality, and more to MapReduce and other frameworks.

The following is a brief survey of emerging open-source frameworks that are being developed to run under YARN. As of this writing, there are many YARN frameworks under active development and the framework landscape is expected to change rapidly. Commercial vendors are also taking advantage of the YARN platform. Each of the following frameworks is under various stages of development and deployment; please consult the Framework webpage for full details.

Distributed-Shell

Distributed-Shell is an example application that demonstrates how to write applications on top of YARN. It is covered in detail in Chapter 11, "Using Apache Hadoop YARN Distributed-Shell," and represents a simple method for running shell commands and scripts in containers in parallel on a Hadoop YARN cluster.

Hadoop MapReduce

As mentioned earlier, MapReduce was the first YARN framework and drove many of YARN's requirements. As described in previous chapters, MapReduce works well, is of production quality, has almost the same feature set as before, and provides full compatibility, with a few minor exceptions, with Hadoop version 1. In addition, it has been thoroughly tested on a large scale, and is integrated tightly with the rest of the Hadoop ecosystem projects, such as Apache Pig, Apache Hive, and Apache Oozie.

One important aspect of the YARN design is the increased "user agility" in choosing different versions of MapReduce to use on a cluster. Indeed, with YARN it is possible to have production jobs using a stable MapReduce algorithm, even as test versions of MapReduce are running concurrently. These test versions allow developers to fix issues, develop new features, and fully test new versions of MapReduce on the same cluster.

Apache Tez

One great example of a new YARN framework that exploits its power is Apache Tez. Many Hadoop jobs consist of executing a complex directed acyclic graph (DAG) of tasks using separate MapReduce stages. Apache Tez generalizes this process and allows these tasks spread across stages to be run as a single, all-encompassing job. For example, a reduce task of a traditional MapReduce job can feed directly into another reduce task without an intermediate (pass-through) map task. The end result is faster processing of jobs and the promotion of what was previously a batch-oriented job to an interactive query.

Tez can be used as a MapReduce replacement for projects such as Apache Hive and Apache Pig. It provides them with a more natural model for their execution plans, together with faster response times and extreme throughput at a petabyte scale. The Apache Tez project is part of the Stinger Initiative, a broad, community-based effort to drive the future of Apache Hive, delivering 100-times performance improvements at a petabyte scale with familiar SQL semantics.

Recently, Tez released a technical preview as part of the Stinger Initiative Phase 3 release. Hortonworks reported that besides Apache Hive, Apache Pig and Cascading are moving toward using Tez. Users are able to run jobs with and without Tez to get an understanding of how much performance gain is possible. The Tez preview can be run in the Hortonworks Sandbox VM or with a full Hortonworks Data Platform-based Apache Hadoop cluster.

For more information, see http://tez.incubator.apache.org/, http://hortonworks.com/hadoop/tez/, and http://hortonworks.com/labs/stinger/.

Apache Giraph

Apache Giraph is an iterative graph processing system built for high scalability. This open-source implementation is based on Google's Pregel, which is used to calculate page rank (pages are vertices connected by edges that represent hyperlinks). It is used by Facebook, Twitter, and LinkedIn to create social graphs of users. Both Giraph and Pregel are based on the Bulk Synchronous Parallel (BSP) model of distributed computation, which was introduced by Leslie Valiant. Giraph adds several features beyond the basic Pregel model, including master computation, shared aggregators, edge-oriented input, out-of-core computation, and more.

Giraph was originally written to run on standard Hadoop version 1, using the MapReduce framework, but is inefficient and totally unnatural for various reasons. It runs as a map-only job where each map is special (breaking typical MapReduce assumptions) and interacts with other maps (vertices). The native Giraph implementation under YARN provides the user with an iterative processing model not directly available with MapReduce.

Support for YARN has been present in Giraph since its own version 1.0 release. Giraph's YARN-related abstraction is easy to extend or use as a template for new projects. Giraph takes advantage of the ApplicationMaster to perform a more natural job control, which includes the ability to spawn and retire tasks as part of each BSP step. In addition, using the flexibility of YARN, Giraph plans on implementing its own web interface to monitor job progress.

For more information, see http://giraph.apache.org/.

Hoya: HBase on YARN

The Hoya project creates dynamic and elastic Apache HBase clusters on top of YARN. It does so with a client application that creates the persistent configuration files, sets up the HBase cluster XML files, and then asks YARN to create an ApplicationMaster. YARN copies all files listed in the client's application-launch request from HDFS into the local file system of the chosen server, and then executes the command to start the ApplicationMaster.

When the Hoya ApplicationMaster starts, it starts an HBase Master on the local machine, which is the sole HBase Master that Hoya currently manages. In parallel with the Master start-up, Hoya asks YARN for a number of containers matching the number of HBase region servers it needs. For each of these containers, Hoya provides the commands to start the region server and does not run any Hoya-specific code on the worker nodes. The Hoya ApplicationMaster points YARN at those files that need to be on the worker nodes and the necessary commands. YARN then does the rest of the work. Because HBase clusters use Apache ZooKeeper to find each other, as do HBase clients, the HBase services locate each other automatically with neither Hoya nor YARN getting involved.

For more information, see http://hortonworks.com/blog/introducing-hoya-hbase-on-yarn/.

Dryad on YARN

Similar to Apache Tez, Microsoft's Dryad provides a DAG as the abstraction of execution flow. It is ported to run natively on YARN. Dryad on YARN is fully compatible with its non-YARN version.

The ported code is written completely in native C++ and C# for worker nodes. The ApplicationMaster leverages a thin layer of Java interfacing with the Resource-Manager for the native Dryad graph manager to schedule work. Eventually, the Java layer will be substituted by direct interaction with protocol-buffer interfaces. Overall, this project demonstrates, as-an-aside, YARN's enablement of writing applications in programming languages of choice.

For more information, see http://research.microsoft.com/en-us/projects/dryad/.

Apache Spark

Spark was initially developed for applications where keeping data in memory helps performance, such as iterative algorithms, which are common in machine learning, and interactive data mining.

Spark is often compared to MapReduce because it provides parallel processing over HDFS and other Hadoop input sources. Spark differs from MapReduce in two important ways, however. First, Spark holds intermediate results in memory, rather than writing them to disk—an approach that drastically decreases query response times. Second, Spark supports more than just MapReduce functions, greatly expanding the set of possible analyses that can be executed over HDFS data stores. Spark offers a general execution model that can optimize arbitrary operator graphs, and it supports in-memory computing, which lets it query data faster than disk-based engines like MapReduce. It also provides clean, concise APIs in Scala, Java, and Python. Users can also use Spark interactively from the Scala and Python shells to rapidly query big data sets.

Since 2013, Spark has been running on production YARN clusters at Yahoo!. The advantage of porting and running Spark on top of YARN is the common resource management and a single underlying data fabric. Spark users can continue to use the same data for building models and share the same physical resources with other Hadoop frameworks.

For more information, see http://spark.incubator.apache.org.

Apache Storm

Apache Storm allows processing of unbounded streams of data in real time. It is designed to be used in any programming language. The basic Storm use cases are real-time analytics, online machine learning, continuous computation, distributed RPC (remote procedure call), ETL (extract, transform, load), and more. Storm provides fast performance, is scalable, is fault tolerant, and gives processing guarantees.

Traditional MapReduce jobs are expected to eventually finish, but Storm continuously processes messages until it is stopped. This behavior makes it ideal for a YARN cluster. There are two kinds of nodes on a Storm cluster: the master node and the worker nodes, which can be fully implemented with an ApplicationMaster. The master node runs a daemon called "Nimbus" that is responsible for distributing code around the cluster, assigning tasks to machines, and monitoring for failures. Each worker node runs a daemon called the "Supervisor," which listens for work assigned to its machine and starts and stops worker processes as necessary based on what Nimbus has assigned to it. Each worker process executes a subset of a topology; a running topology consists of many worker processes spread across many machines.

Efforts are under way to run Storm directly under YARN and take advantage of the common resource management substrate.

For more information, see http://storm-project.net/documentation.html.

REEF: Retainable Evaluator Execution Framework

YARN's flexibility sometimes requires significant effort on the part of application implementers. Writing a custom application on YARN includes building one's own ApplicationMaster, performing client and container management, and handling aspects of fault tolerance, execution flow, coordination, and other concerns. The REEF project by Microsoft recognizes this challenge and factors out several components that are common to many applications, such as storage management, data caching, fault detection, and checkpoints. Framework designers can build on top of REEF more easily than they can build directly on YARN, and can reuse these common services/libraries. REEF's design makes it suitable for both MapReduce and DAG-like executions as well as iterative and interactive computations.

Hamster: Hadoop and MPI on the Same Cluster

The Message Passing Interface (MPI) is widely used in high-performance computing (HPC). MPI is primarily a set of optimized message-passing library calls for C, C++, and Fortran that operate over popular server interconnects such as Ethernet and InfiniBand. Because users have full control of their YARN containers, there is no reason why MPI applications cannot run within a Hadoop cluster. The Hamster effort is a work-in-progress that provides a good discussion of the issues involved in mapping MPI to a YARN cluster (see https://issues.apache.org/jira/browse/MAPREDUCE-2911). Currently, an alpha version of MPICH2 is available for YARN that can be used to run MPI applications.

For more information, see https://github.com/clarkyzl/mpich2-yarn.

Wrap-up

Application frameworks for Apache Hadoop YARN are emerging and evolving at a rapid pace. This area is expected to see large amounts of growth as developers create more applications that move beyond MapReduce and take full advantage of the data services and capabilities offered by a shared Hadoop YARN cluster. Indeed, like many successful data processing platforms in use today, Apache Hadoop YARN will eventually migrate to be a behind-the-scenes layer and allow users to move away from execution management and closer to their big data applications and the subsequent discoveries they provide.

A

Supplemental Content and Code Downloads

Available Downloads

Supplemental content and all of the code and examples mentioned in this book can be downloaded from `http:yarn-book.com`.

Please see the README available on that site file for a full description of the files.

B

YARN Installation Scripts

The following is a listing of the installation scripts discussed in Chapter 5, "Installing Apache Hadoop YARN." They can be used to help follow the installation discussion. All of the scripts are available from the download page listed in Appendix A.

install-hadoop2.sh

```
#!/bin/bash
#
# Install Hadoop 2 using pdsh/pdcp where possible.
#
# Command can be interactive or file-based. This script sets up
# a Hadoop 2 cluster with basic configuration. Modify data, log, and pid
# directories as desired. Further configure your cluster with ./conf-hadoop2.sh
# after running this installation script.
#

# Basic environment variables. Edit as necessary
HADOOP_VERSION=2.2.0
HADOOP_HOME="/opt/hadoop-${HADOOP_VERSION}"
NN_DATA_DIR=/var/data/hadoop/hdfs/nn
SNN_DATA_DIR=/var/data/hadoop/hdfs/snn
DN_DATA_DIR=/var/data/hadoop/hdfs/dn
YARN_LOG_DIR=/var/log/hadoop/yarn
HADOOP_LOG_DIR=/var/log/hadoop/hdfs
HADOOP_MAPRED_LOG_DIR=/var/log/hadoop/mapred
YARN_PID_DIR=/var/run/hadoop/yarn
HADOOP_PID_DIR=/var/run/hadoop/hdfs
HADOOP_MAPRED_PID_DIR=/var/run/hadoop/mapred
HTTP_STATIC_USER=hdfs
YARN_PROXY_PORT=8081
```

```
source hadoop-xml-conf.sh
CMD_OPTIONS=$(getopt -n "$0"  -o hif --long "help,interactive,file"  -- "$@")

# Take care of bad options in the command
if [ $? -ne 0 ];
then
  exit 1
fi
eval set -- "$CMD_OPTIONS"

all_hosts="all_hosts"
nn_host="nn_host"
snn_host="snn_host"
dn_hosts="dn_hosts"
rm_host="rm_host"
nm_hosts="nm_hosts"
mr_history_host="mr_history_host"
yarn_proxy_host="yarn_proxy_host"

install()
{
        echo "Copying Hadoop $HADOOP_VERSION to all hosts..."
        pdcp -w ^all_hosts hadoop-"$HADOOP_VERSION".tar.gz /opt

        echo "Copying JDK 1.6.0_31 to all hosts..."
        pdcp -w ^all_hosts jdk-6u31-linux-x64-rpm.bin /opt

        echo "Installing JDK 1.6.0_31 on all hosts..."
        pdsh -w ^all_hosts chmod a+x /opt/jdk-6u31-linux-x64-rpm.bin
        pdsh -w ^all_hosts /opt/jdk-6u31-linux-x64-rpm.bin -noregister 1>&- 2>&-

        echo "Setting JAVA_HOME and HADOOP_HOME environment
➥variables on all hosts..."
        pdsh -w ^all_hosts 'echo export JAVA_HOME=/usr/java/jdk1.6.0_31 >
➥/etc/profile.d/java.sh'
        pdsh -w ^all_hosts "source /etc/profile.d/java.sh"
        pdsh -w ^all_hosts "echo export HADOOP_HOME=$HADOOP_HOME >
➥/etc/profile.d/hadoop.sh"
        pdsh -w ^all_hosts 'echo export HADOOP_PREFIX=$HADOOP_HOME >>
➥/etc/profile.d/hadoop.sh'
        pdsh -w ^all_hosts "source /etc/profile.d/hadoop.sh"

        echo "Extracting Hadoop $HADOOP_VERSION distribution on all hosts..."
        pdsh -w ^all_hosts tar -zxf /opt/hadoop-"$HADOOP_VERSION".tar.gz -C /opt

        echo "Creating system accounts and groups on all hosts..."
        pdsh -w ^all_hosts groupadd hadoop
        pdsh -w ^all_hosts useradd -g hadoop yarn
```

```
        pdsh -w ^all_hosts useradd -g hadoop hdfs
        pdsh -w ^all_hosts useradd -g hadoop mapred

        echo "Creating HDFS data directories on NameNode host,
➥Secondary NameNode host, and DataNode hosts..."
        pdsh -w ^nn_host "mkdir -p $NN_DATA_DIR && chown hdfs:hadoop $NN_DATA_DIR"
        pdsh -w ^snn_host "mkdir -p $SNN_DATA_DIR && chown hdfs:hadoop
➥$SNN_DATA_DIR"
        pdsh -w ^dn_hosts "mkdir -p $DN_DATA_DIR && chown hdfs:hadoop
➥$DN_DATA_DIR"

        echo "Creating log directories on all hosts..."
        pdsh -w ^all_hosts "mkdir -p $YARN_LOG_DIR && chown yarn:hadoop
➥$YARN_LOG_DIR"
        pdsh -w ^all_hosts "mkdir -p $HADOOP_LOG_DIR && chown hdfs:hadoop
➥$HADOOP_LOG_DIR"
        pdsh -w ^all_hosts "mkdir -p $HADOOP_MAPRED_LOG_DIR && chown mapred:hadoop
➥$HADOOP_MAPRED_LOG_DIR"

        echo "Creating pid directories on all hosts..."
        pdsh -w ^all_hosts "mkdir -p $YARN_PID_DIR && chown yarn:hadoop
➥$YARN_PID_DIR"
        pdsh -w ^all_hosts "mkdir -p $HADOOP_PID_DIR && chown hdfs:hadoop
➥$HADOOP_PID_DIR"
        pdsh -w ^all_hosts "mkdir -p $HADOOP_MAPRED_PID_DIR && chown mapred:hadoop
➥$HADOOP_MAPRED_PID_DIR"

        echo "Editing Hadoop environment scripts for log directories on all
➥hosts..."
        pdsh -w ^all_hosts echo "export HADOOP_LOG_DIR=$HADOOP_LOG_DIR >>
➥$HADOOP_HOME/etc/hadoop/hadoop-env.sh"
        pdsh -w ^all_hosts echo "export YARN_LOG_DIR=$YARN_LOG_DIR >>
➥$HADOOP_HOME/etc/hadoop/yarn-env.sh"
        pdsh -w ^all_hosts echo "export
➥HADOOP_MAPRED_LOG_DIR=$HADOOP_MAPRED_LOG_DIR >>
➥$HADOOP_HOME/etc/hadoop/mapred-env.sh"

        echo "Editing Hadoop environment scripts for pid directories on all
➥hosts..."
        pdsh -w ^all_hosts echo "export HADOOP_PID_DIR=$HADOOP_PID_DIR >>
➥$HADOOP_HOME/etc/hadoop/hadoop-env.sh"
        pdsh -w ^all_hosts echo "export YARN_PID_DIR=$YARN_PID_DIR >>
➥$HADOOP_HOME/etc/hadoop/yarn-env.sh"
        pdsh -w ^all_hosts echo "export
➥HADOOP_MAPRED_PID_DIR=$HADOOP_MAPRED_PID_DIR >>
➥$HADOOP_HOME/etc/hadoop/mapred-env.sh"

        echo "Creating base Hadoop XML config files..."
        create_config --file core-site.xml
        put_config --file core-site.xml --property fs.default.name
➥--value "hdfs://$nn:9000"
```

```
        put_config --file core-site.xml --property hadoop.http.staticuser.user
➡--value "$HTTP_STATIC_USER"

        create_config --file hdfs-site.xml
        put_config --file hdfs-site.xml --property dfs.namenode.name.dir
➡--value "$NN_DATA_DIR"
        put_config --file hdfs-site.xml --property fs.checkpoint.dir
➡--value "$SNN_DATA_DIR"
        put_config --file hdfs-site.xml --property fs.checkpoint.edits.dir
➡--value "$SNN_DATA_DIR"
        put_config --file hdfs-site.xml --property dfs.datanode.data.dir
➡--value "$DN_DATA_DIR"
        put_config --file hdfs-site.xml --property dfs.namenode.http-address
➡--value "$nn:50070"
        put_config --file hdfs-site.xml
➡--property dfs.namenode.secondary.http-address --value "$snn:50090"


        create_config --file mapred-site.xml
        put_config --file mapred-site.xml --property mapreduce.framework.name
➡--value yarn
        put_config --file mapred-site.xml --property mapreduce.jobhistory.address
➡--value "$mr_hist:10020"
        put_config --file mapred-site.xml
➡--property mapreduce.jobhistory.webapp.address --value "$mr_hist:19888"
        put_config --file mapred-site.xml
➡--property yarn.app.mapreduce.am.staging-dir --value /mapred


        create_config --file yarn-site.xml
        put_config --file yarn-site.xml --property yarn.nodemanager.aux-services
➡--value mapreduce.shuffle
        put_config --file yarn-site.xml --property yarn.nodemanager.aux-
➡services.mapreduce.shuffle.class --value org.apache.hadoop.mapred.ShuffleHandler
        put_config --file yarn-site.xml --property yarn.web-proxy.address
➡--value "$yarn_proxy:$YARN_PROXY_PORT"
        put_config --file yarn-site.xml --property yarn.resourcemanager
➡.scheduler.address
➡--value
➡"$rmgr:8030"
        put_config --file yarn-site.xml --property yarn.resourcemanager.resource-
➡tracker.address --value "$rmgr:8031"
        put_config --file yarn-site.xml
➡--property yarn.resourcemanager.address --value "$rmgr:8032"
        put_config --file yarn-site.xml
➡--property yarn.resourcemanager.admin.address --value "$rmgr:8033"
        put_config --file yarn-site.xml
➡--property yarn.resourcemanager.webapp.address --value "$rmgr:8088"

        echo "Copying base Hadoop XML config files to all hosts..."
        pdcp -w ^all_hosts core-site.xml hdfs-site.xml mapred-site.xml
➡yarn-site.xml $HADOOP_HOME/etc/hadoop/
```

```
echo "Creating configuration, command, and script links on all hosts..."
pdsh -w ^all_hosts "ln -s $HADOOP_HOME/etc/hadoop /etc/hadoop"
pdsh -w ^all_hosts "ln -s $HADOOP_HOME/bin/* /usr/bin"
pdsh -w ^all_hosts "ln -s $HADOOP_HOME/libexec/* /usr/libexec"

echo "Formatting the NameNode..."
pdsh -w ^nn_host "su - hdfs -c '$HADOOP_HOME/bin/hdfs namenode -format'"

echo "Copying startup scripts to all hosts..."
pdcp -w ^nn_host hadoop-namenode /etc/init.d/
pdcp -w ^snn_host hadoop-secondarynamenode /etc/init.d/
pdcp -w ^dn_hosts hadoop-datanode /etc/init.d/
pdcp -w ^rm_host hadoop-resourcemanager /etc/init.d/
pdcp -w ^nm_hosts hadoop-nodemanager /etc/init.d/
pdcp -w ^mr_history_host hadoop-historyserver /etc/init.d/
pdcp -w ^yarn_proxy_host hadoop-proxyserver /etc/init.d/

echo "Starting Hadoop $HADOOP_VERSION services on all hosts..."
pdsh -w ^nn_host "chmod 755 /etc/init.d/hadoop-namenode && chkconfig
➥hadoop-namenode on && service hadoop-namenode start"
pdsh -w ^snn_host "chmod 755 /etc/init.d/hadoop-secondarynamenode &&
➥chkconfig hadoop-secondarynamenode on && service hadoop-secondarynamenode start"
pdsh -w ^dn_hosts "chmod 755 /etc/init.d/hadoop-datanode && chkconfig
➥hadoop-datanode on && service hadoop-datanode start"
pdsh -w ^rm_host "chmod 755 /etc/init.d/hadoop-resourcemanager &&
➥chkconfig hadoop-resourcemanager on && service hadoop-resourcemanager start"
pdsh -w ^nm_hosts "chmod 755 /etc/init.d/hadoop-nodemanager && chkconfig
➥hadoop-nodemanager on && service hadoop-nodemanager start"

pdsh -w ^yarn_proxy_host "chmod 755 /etc/init.d/hadoop-proxyserver
➥&& chkconfig hadoop-proxyserver on && service hadoop-proxyserver start"

echo "Creating MapReduce Job History directories..."
su - hdfs -c "hadoop fs -mkdir -p /mapred/history/done_intermediate"
su - hdfs -c "hadoop fs -chown -R mapred:hadoop /mapred"
su - hdfs -c "hadoop fs -chmod -R g+rwx /mapred"

pdsh -w ^mr_history_host "chmod 755 /etc/init.d/hadoop-historyserver &&
➥chkconfig hadoop-historyserver on && service hadoop-historyserver start"

echo "Running YARN smoke test..."
pdsh -w ^all_hosts "usermod -a -G hadoop $(whoami)"
su - hdfs -c "hadoop fs -mkdir -p /user/$(whoami)"
su - hdfs -c "hadoop fs -chown $(whoami):$(whoami) /user/$(whoami)"
source /etc/profile.d/java.sh
source /etc/profile.d/hadoop.sh
source /etc/hadoop/hadoop-env.sh
source /etc/hadoop/yarn-env.sh
```

```
        hadoop jar $HADOOP_HOME/share/hadoop/mapreduce/hadoop-mapreduce-examples-
➥$HADOOP_VERSION.jar pi
➥-Dmapreduce.clientfactory.class.name=org.apache.hadoop.mapred.YarnClientFactory
➥-libjars $HADOOP_HOME/share/hadoop/mapreduce/hadoop-mapreduce-client-jobclient-
➥$HADOOP_VERSION.jar 16 10000
}

interactive()
{
        echo -n "Enter NameNode hostname: "
        read nn
        echo -n "Enter Secondary NameNode hostname: "
        read snn
        echo -n "Enter ResourceManager hostname: "
        read rmgr
        echo -n "Enter Job History Server hostname: "
        read mr_hist
        echo -n "Enter YARN Proxy hostname: "
        read yarn_proxy
        echo -n "Enter DataNode hostnames (comma-separated or hostlist syntax): "
        read dns
        echo -n "Enter NodeManager hostnames (comma-separated or hostlist
➥syntax): "
        read nms

        echo "$nn" > "$nn_host"
        echo "$snn" > "$snn_host"
        echo "$rmgr" > "$rm_host"
        echo "$mr_hist" > "$mr_history_host"
        echo "$yarn_proxy" > "$yarn_proxy_host"
        dn_hosts_var=$(sed 's/\,/\n/g' <<< $dns)
        nm_hosts_var=$(sed 's/\,/\n/g' <<< $nms)
        echo "$dn_hosts_var" > "$dn_hosts"
        echo "$nm_hosts_var" > "$nm_hosts"
        echo "$(echo "$nn $snn $rmgr $mr_hist $yarn_proxy
➥$dn_hosts_var $nm_hosts_var" | tr ' ' '\n' | sort -u)" > "$all_hosts"
}

file()
{
        nn=$(cat nn_host)
        snn=$(cat snn_host)
        rmgr=$(cat rm_host)
        mr_hist=$(cat mr_history_host)
        yarn_proxy=$(cat yarn_proxy_host)
        dns=$(cat dn_hosts)
        nms=$(cat nm_hosts)
```

```
        echo "$(echo "$nn $snn $rmgr $mr_hist $dns $nms"
➥| tr ' ' '\n' | sort -u)" > "$all_hosts"
}


help()
{
cat << EOF
install-hadoop2.sh

This script installs Hadoop 2 with basic data, log, and pid directories.

USAGE:  install-hadoop2.sh [options]

OPTIONS:
    -i, --interactive       Prompt for fully qualified domain names (FQDN) of the
➥NameNode,
                            Secondary NameNode, DataNodes,
➥ResourceManager, NodeManagers,
                            MapReduce Job History Server, and YARN
➥Proxy server. Values
                            entered are stored in files in the same
➥directory as this command.

    -f, --file              Use files with fully qualified domain names
➥(FQDN), newline
                            separated. Place files in the same directory
➥as this script.
                            Services and file name are as follows:
                            NameNode = nn_host
                            Secondary NameNode = snn_host
                            DataNodes = dn_hosts
                            ResourceManager = rm_host
                            NodeManagers = nm_hosts
                            MapReduce Job History Server = mr_history_host
                            YARN Proxy Server = yarn_proxy_host

   -h, --help              Show this message.

EXAMPLES:
   Prompt for host names:
     install-hadoop2.sh -i
     install-hadoop2.sh --interactive

   Use values from files in the same directory:
     install-hadoop2.sh -f
     install-hadoop2.sh --file

EOF
}
```

```
while true;
do
  case "$1" in

    -h|--help)
      help
      exit 0
      ;;
    -i|--interactive)
      interactive
      install
      shift
      ;;
    -f|--file)
      file
      install
      shift
      ;;
    --)
      shift
      break
      ;;
  esac
done
```

uninstall-hadoop2.sh

```
#!/bin/bash

HADOOP_VERSION=2.0.5-alpha
HADOOP_HOME="/opt/hadoop-${HADOOP_VERSION}"
NN_DATA_DIR=/var/data/hadoop/hdfs/nn
SNN_DATA_DIR=/var/data/hadoop/hdfs/snn
DN_DATA_DIR=/var/data/hadoop/hdfs/dn
YARN_LOG_DIR=/var/log/hadoop/yarn
HADOOP_LOG_DIR=/var/log/hadoop/hdfs
HADOOP_MAPRED_LOG_DIR=/var/log/hadoop/mapred

echo "Stopping Hadoop 2 services..."
pdsh -w ^dn_hosts "service hadoop-datanode stop"
pdsh -w ^snn_host "service hadoop-secondarynamenode stop"
pdsh -w ^nn_host "service hadoop-namenode stop"
pdsh -w ^mr_history_host "service hadoop-historyserver stop"
pdsh -w ^yarn_proxy_host "service hadoop-proxyserver stop"
pdsh -w ^nm_hosts "service hadoop-nodemanager stop"
pdsh -w ^rm_host "service hadoop-resourcemanager stop"
```

```
echo "Removing Hadoop 2 services from run levels..."
pdsh -w ^dn_hosts "chkconfig --del hadoop-datanode"
pdsh -w ^snn_host "chkconfig --del hadoop-secondarynamenode"
pdsh -w ^nn_host "chkconfig --del hadoop-namenode"
pdsh -w ^mr_history_host "chkconfig --del hadoop-historyserver"
pdsh -w ^yarn_proxy_host "chkconfig --del hadoop-proxyserver"
pdsh -w ^nm_hosts "chkconfig --del hadoop-nodemanager"
pdsh -w ^rm_host "chkconfig --del hadoop-resourcemanager"

echo "Removing Hadoop 2 startup scripts..."
pdsh -w ^all_hosts "rm -f /etc/init.d/hadoop-*"

echo "Removing Hadoop 2 distribution tarball..."
pdsh -w ^all_hosts "rm -f /opt/hadoop-2*.tar.gz"

echo "Removing JDK 1.6.0_31 distribution..."
pdsh -w ^all_hosts "rm -f /opt/jdk*"

echo "Removing JDK 1.6.0_31 artifacts..."
pdsh -w ^all_hosts "rm -f sun-java*"
pdsh -w ^all_hosts "rm -f jdk*"

echo "Removing Hadoop 2 home directory..."
pdsh -w ^all_hosts "rm -Rf $HADOOP_HOME"

echo "Removing Hadoop 2 bash environment setting..."
pdsh -w ^all_hosts "rm -f /etc/profile.d/hadoop.sh"

echo "Removing Java bash environment setting..."
pdsh -w ^all_hosts "rm -f /etc/profile.d/java.sh"

echo "Removing /etc/hadoop link..."
pdsh -w ^all_hosts "unlink /etc/hadoop"

echo "Removing Hadoop 2 command links..."
pdsh -w ^all_hosts "unlink /usr/bin/container-executor"
pdsh -w ^all_hosts "unlink /usr/bin/hadoop"
pdsh -w ^all_hosts "unlink /usr/bin/hdfs"
pdsh -w ^all_hosts "unlink /usr/bin/mapred"
pdsh -w ^all_hosts "unlink /usr/bin/rcc"
pdsh -w ^all_hosts "unlink /usr/bin/test-container-executor"
pdsh -w ^all_hosts "unlink /usr/bin/yarn"

echo "Removing Hadoop 2 script links..."
pdsh -w ^all_hosts "unlink /usr/libexec/hadoop-config.sh"
pdsh -w ^all_hosts "unlink /usr/libexec/hdfs-config.sh"
pdsh -w ^all_hosts "unlink /usr/libexec/httpfs-config.sh"
```

```
pdsh -w ^all_hosts "unlink /usr/libexec/mapred-config.sh"
pdsh -w ^all_hosts "unlink /usr/libexec/yarn-config.sh"

echo "Uninstalling JDK 1.6.0_31 RPM..."
pdsh -w ^all_hosts "rpm -ev jdk-1.6.0_31-fcs.x86_64"

echo "Removing NameNode data directory..."
pdsh -w ^nn_host "rm -Rf $NN_DATA_DIR"

echo "Removing Secondary NameNode data directory..."
pdsh -w ^snn_host "rm -Rf $SNN_DATA_DIR"

echo "Removing DataNode data directories..."
pdsh -w ^dn_hosts "rm -Rf $DN_DATA_DIR"

echo "Removing YARN log directories..."
pdsh -w ^all_hosts "rm -Rf $YARN_LOG_DIR"

echo "Removing HDFS log directories..."
pdsh -w ^all_hosts "rm -Rf $HADOOP_LOG_DIR"

echo "Removing MapReduce log directories..."
pdsh -w ^all_hosts "rm -Rf $HADOOP_MAPRED_LOG_DIR"

echo "Removing HDFS account..."
pdsh -w ^all_hosts "userdel -r hdfs"

echo "Removing MapReduce system account..."
pdsh -w ^all_hosts "userdel -r mapred"

echo "Removing YARN system account..."
pdsh -w ^all_hosts "userdel -r yarn"

echo "Removing Hadoop system group..."
pdsh -w ^all_hosts "groupdel hadoop"
```

hadoop-xml-conf.sh

```
#!/bin/bash
#
# Utility functions for processing Hadoop 2 XML configuration files.
#
# Depends on Python built-in XML processing and libxml2 for formatting.
#
installed=false
if [ -f /etc/profile.d/hadoop.sh ]; then
```

```
      source /etc/profile.d/hadoop.sh
      source $HADOOP_HOME/etc/hadoop/hadoop-env.sh
      installed=true
fi


create_config()
{
      local filename=

      case $1 in
          '')     echo $"$0: Usage: create_config --file"
                  return 1;;
          --file)
                  filename=$2
                  ;;
      esac

      python - <<END
from xml.etree import ElementTree
from xml.etree.ElementTree import Element

conf = Element('configuration')

conf_file = open("$filename",'w')
conf_file.write(ElementTree.tostring(conf))
conf_file.close()
END
      write_file $filename
}

put_config()
{
      local filename= property= value=

      while [ "$1" != "" ]; do
      case $1 in
          '')     echo $"$0: Usage: put_config --file --property --value"
                  return 1;;
          --file)
                  filename=$2
                  shift 2
                  ;;
          --property)
                  property=$2
                  shift 2
                  ;;
```

```
                --value)
                     value=$2
                     shift 2
                     ;;
        esac
        done

        python - <<END
from xml.etree import ElementTree
from xml.etree.ElementTree import Element
from xml.etree.ElementTree import SubElement

def putconfig(root, name, value):
        for existing_prop in root.getchildren():
                if existing_prop.find('name').text == name:
                        root.remove(existing_prop)
                        break
        property = SubElement(root, 'property')
        name_elem = SubElement(property, 'name')
        name_elem.text = name
        value_elem = SubElement(property, 'value')
        value_elem.text = value

path = ''
if "$installed" == 'true':
        path = "$HADOOP_CONF_DIR" + '/'

conf = ElementTree.parse(path + "$filename").getroot()
putconfig(root = conf, name = "$property", value = "$value")

conf_file = open("$filename",'w')
conf_file.write(ElementTree.tostring(conf))
conf_file.close()
END
        write_file $filename
}

del_config()
{
        local filename= property=

        while [ "$1" != "" ]; do
        case $1 in
            '')     echo $"$0: Usage: del_config --file --property"
                    return 1;;
            --file)
                    filename=$2
```

```
                        shift 2
                        ;;
                --property)
                        property=$2
                        shift 2
                        ;;
        esac
        done


        python - <<END
from xml.etree import ElementTree
from xml.etree.ElementTree import Element
from xml.etree.ElementTree import SubElement

def delconfig(root, name):
        for existing_prop in root.getchildren():
                if existing_prop.find('name').text == name:
                        root.remove(existing_prop)
                        break

path = ''
if "$installed" == 'true':
        path = "$HADOOP_CONF_DIR" + '/'

conf = ElementTree.parse(path + "$filename").getroot()
delconfig(root = conf, name = "$property")

conf_file = open("$filename",'w')
conf_file.write(ElementTree.tostring(conf))
conf_file.close()
END
        write_file $filename
}


write_file()
{
        local file=$1
        xmllint --format "$file" > "$file".pp && mv "$file".pp "$file"
}
```

C
YARN Administration Scripts

The following is a listing of the administration scripts discussed in Chapter 6, "Apache Hadoop YARN Administration." They can be used to help follow the administration discussion. All of the scripts are available from the download page listed in Appendix A.

configure-hadoop2.sh

```
#!/bin/bash

HADOOP_VERSION=2.0.5-alpha
HADOOP_HOME=/opt/hadoop-"${HADOOP_VERSION}"

source hadoop-xml-conf.sh

op=
file=
property=
value=
refresh=false

delete()
{
        del_config --file $file --property $property
}

put()
{
        put_config --file $file --property $property --value $value
}

deploy()
```

```
{
        echo "Deploying $file to the cluster..."
        pdcp -w ^all_hosts "$file" $HADOOP_HOME/etc/hadoop/
}

restart_hadoop()
{
        echo "Restarting Hadoop 2..."
        pdsh -w ^dn_hosts "service hadoop-datanode stop"
        pdsh -w ^snn_host "service hadoop-secondarynamenode stop"
        pdsh -w ^nn_host "service hadoop-namenode stop"
        pdsh -w ^mr_history_host "service hadoop-historyserver stop"
        pdsh -w ^yarn_proxy_host "service hadoop-proxyserver stop"
        pdsh -w ^nm_hosts "service hadoop-nodemanager stop"
        pdsh -w ^rm_host "service hadoop-resourcemanager stop"

        pdsh -w ^nn_host "service hadoop-namenode start"
        pdsh -w ^snn_host "service hadoop-secondarynamenode start"
        pdsh -w ^dn_hosts "service hadoop-datanode start"
        pdsh -w ^rm_host "service hadoop-resourcemanager start"
        pdsh -w ^nm_hosts "service hadoop-nodemanager start"
        pdsh -w ^yarn_proxy_host "service hadoop-proxyserver start"
        pdsh -w ^mr_history_host "service hadoop-historyserver start"
}

process()
{
        if [ "$op" == "delete" ]
        then
          delete
        fi

        if [ "$op" == "put" ]
        then
          put
        fi

        deploy

        if $refresh;
        then
         restart_hadoop
        fi
}

help()
{
```

```
    cat << EOF
    configure-hadoop2.sh

    This script edits Hadoop 2 XML configuration files. Assumes an existing
    ➥Hadoop installation.

    USAGE:  configure-hadoop2.sh [options]

    OPTIONS:
        -o, --operation       Valid values are 'put' and 'delete'. A 'put'
                              operation writes the property and value if it
                              doesn't exist and overwrites it if it does exist.
                              A 'delete' operation removes the property.

        -f, --file            The name of the configuration file.

        -p, --property        The name of the Hadoop configuration property

        -v, --value           The value of the Hadoop configuration property.
                              Required for a 'put' operation, ignored for a
                              'delete' operation.

        -r, --restart         Flag to restart Hadoop. Configuration files are
                              deployed to the cluster automatically to
                              \$HADOOP_HOME/etc/hadoop.

        -h, --help            Show this message.

    EXAMPLES:
        Add or edit a Hadoop configuration property:
            configure-hadoop2.sh -f hdfs-site.xml -p dfs.namenode.name.dir -v
    ➥/path/to/nn/data

        Delete a Hadoop configuration property:
            configure-hadoop2.sh -f hdfs-site.xml -p dfs.namenode.name.dir

        Add or edit a Hadoop configuration property and restart Hadoop:
            configure-hadoop2.sh -f hdfs-site.xml -p dfs.namenode.name.dir
    ➥-v /path/to/nn/data -r

    EOF
    }

    while :
    do
      case $1 in

        -h | --help)
          help
```

```
        exit 0
       ;;
   -o | --operation)
      if [ -n "$2" ];
      then
         if [ "$2" != "put" ] && [ "$2" != "delete" ]
         then
            echo "Operation (-o | --operation)  must be either 'put' or 'delete'"
            exit 1
         fi
         op="$2"
      fi
      shift 2
       ;;
   -f | --file)
      if [ -n "$2" ];
      then
         file="$2"
      fi
      shift 2
       ;;
   -p | --property)
      if [ -n "$2" ];
      then
         property="$2"
      fi
      shift 2
       ;;
   -v | --value)
      value="$2"
      shift 2
       ;;
   -r | --restart)
      refresh=true
      shift
       ;;
   --)
      shift
      break
       ;;
   -*)
      echo "WARN: Unknown option (ignored): $1" >&2
      shift
       ;;
   *)
      break
       ;;
```

```
    esac
done

if [ "$op" == "" ]; then
    echo "ERROR: option '-o | --operation' not given. See --help" >&2
    exit 1
fi

if [ "$file" == "" ]; then
    echo "ERROR: option '-f | --file' not given. See --help" >&2
    exit 1
fi

if [ "$property" == "" ]; then
    echo "ERROR: option '-p | --property' not given. See --help" >&2
    exit 1
fi

if [ "$op" == "put" ] && [ "$value" == "" ]; then
    echo "ERROR: option '-o | --operation' given with option '-v | --value' not
given. See --help" >&2
    exit 1
fi

process
```

D
Nagios Modules

The following is a selective listing of the Nagios modules described in Chapter 6, "Apache Hadoop YARN Administration." They can be used to help follow the Nagios installation discussion. All the Nagios modules are available from the download page listed in Appendix A.

check_resource_manager.sh

```
#!/bin/bash
# Licensed to the Apache Software Foundation (ASF) under one or more
# contributor license agreements. See the NOTICE file distributed with
# this work for additional information regarding copyright ownership.
# The ASF licenses this file to You under the Apache License, Version 2.0
# (the "License"); you may not use this file except in compliance with
# the License. You may obtain a copy of the License at
#
#     http://www.apache.org/licenses/LICENSE-2.0
#
# Unless required by applicable law or agreed to in writing, software
# distributed under the License is distributed on an "AS IS" BASIS,
# WITHOUT WARRANTIES OR CONDITIONS OF ANY KIND, either express or implied.
# See the License for the specific language governing permissions and
# limitations under the License.

VERSION="Version 1.0"

PROGNAME=`/bin/basename $0`

# Exit codes
STATE_OK=0
STATE_CRITICAL=2
```

```
version() {
    echo "$PROGNAME - $VERSION"
}

usage() {
    echo "Usage: $PROGNAME [-v] -w <limit> -c <limit>"
}

help() {
    version
    echo "Check the ResourceManager process\n"
    usage
}

while [ "$1" ]; do
    case "$1" in
        -h | --help)
            help
            exit $STATE_OK
            ;;
        -V | --version)
            version
            exit $STATE_OK
            ;;
        -v | --verbose)
            : $(( verbosity++ ))
            shift
            ;;
        -?)
            usage
            exit $STATE_OK
            ;;
        *)
            echo "$PROGNAME: Invalid option '$1'"
            usage
            exit $STATE_UNKNOWN
            ;;
    esac
done

status=$(/sbin/service hadoop-resourcemanager status)

if echo "$status" | grep --quiet running ; then
    echo "ResourceManager OK - $status"
    exit $STATE_OK
else
```

```
    echo "ResourceManager CRITICAL - $status"

    exit $STATE_CRITICAL
fi
```

check_data_node.sh

```
#!/bin/bash

# Licensed to the Apache Software Foundation (ASF) under one or more
# contributor license agreements. See the NOTICE file distributed with
# this work for additional information regarding copyright ownership.
# The ASF licenses this file to You under the Apache License, Version 2.0
# (the "License"); you may not use this file except in compliance with
# the License. You may obtain a copy of the License at
#
#     http://www.apache.org/licenses/LICENSE-2.0
#
# Unless required by applicable law or agreed to in writing, software
# distributed under the License is distributed on an "AS IS" BASIS,
# WITHOUT WARRANTIES OR CONDITIONS OF ANY KIND, either express or implied.
# See the License for the specific language governing permissions and
# limitations under the License.

VERSION="Version 1.0"

PROGNAME=`/bin/basename $0`

# Exit codes
STATE_OK=0
STATE_CRITICAL=2

version() {
    echo "$PROGNAME - $VERSION"
}

usage() {
    echo "Usage: $PROGNAME [-v] -w <limit> -c <limit>"
}

help() {
    version
    echo "Check the DataNode process\n"
    usage
}

while [ "$1" ]; do
```

```
    case "$1" in
        -h | --help)
            help
            exit $STATE_OK
            ;;
        -V | --version)
            version
            exit $STATE_OK
            ;;
        -v | --verbose)
            : $(( verbosity++ ))
            shift
            ;;
        -?)
            usage
            exit $STATE_OK
            ;;
        *)
            echo "$PROGNAME: Invalid option '$1'"
            usage
            exit $STATE_UNKNOWN
            ;;
    esac
done

status=$(/sbin/service hadoop-datanode status)

if echo "$status" | grep --quiet running ; then
    echo "DataNode OK - $status"
    exit $STATE_OK
else
    echo "DataNode CRITICAL - $status"
    exit $STATE_CRITICAL
fi
```

check_resource_manager_old_space_pct.sh

```
#!/bin/bash

# Licensed to the Apache Software Foundation (ASF) under one or more
# contributor license agreements. See the NOTICE file distributed with
# this work for additional information regarding copyright ownership.
# The ASF licenses this file to You under the Apache License, Version 2.0
# (the "License"); you may not use this file except in compliance with
# the License. You may obtain a copy of the License at
#
```

```
#        http://www.apache.org/licenses/LICENSE-2.0
#
# Unless required by applicable law or agreed to in writing, software
# distributed under the License is distributed on an "AS IS" BASIS,
# WITHOUT WARRANTIES OR CONDITIONS OF ANY KIND, either express or implied.
# See the License for the specific language governing permissions and
# limitations under the License.

VERSION="Version 1.0"

PROGNAME=`/bin/basename $0`

# Exit codes
STATE_OK=0
STATE_WARNING=1
STATE_CRITICAL=2
STATE_UNKNOWN=3

source /etc/profile.d/hadoop.sh
source /etc/profile.d/java.sh
source /etc/rc.d/init.d/functions
source ${HADOOP_HOME}/etc/hadoop/hadoop-env.sh
source ${HADOOP_HOME}/etc/hadoop/yarn-env.sh

PIDFILE="${YARN_PID_DIR}/yarn-yarn-resourcemanager.pid"

version() {
    echo "$PROGNAME - $VERSION"
}

usage() {
    echo "Usage: $PROGNAME [-v] -w <limit> -c <limit>"
}

help() {
    version
    echo "Check the ResourceManager Heap Old Space % used\n"
    usage
}

warn=
critical=

while [ "$1" ]; do
    case "$1" in
        -h | --help)
            help
```

```
            exit $STATE_OK
            ;;
    -V | --version)
        version
        exit $STATE_OK
        ;;
    -v | --verbose)
        : $(( verbosity++ ))
        shift
        ;;
    -w | --warning | -c | --critical)
        if [[ -z "$2" || "$2" = -* ]] ; then
            echo "$PROGNAME: Option '$1' requires an argument"
            print_usage
            exit $STATE_UNKNOWN
        elif [[ "$2" = +([0-9]) ]] ; then
            thresh=$2
        else
            echo "$PROGNAME: Threshold must be integer or percentage"
            print_usage
            exit $STATE_UNKNOWN
        fi
        [[ "$1" = *-w* ]] && warn=$thresh || critical=$thresh
        shift 2
        ;;
    -?)
        usage
        exit $STATE_OK
        ;;
    *)
        echo "$PROGNAME: Invalid option '$1'"
        usage
        exit $STATE_UNKNOWN
        ;;
    esac
done

if [[ -z "$warn" || -z "$critical" ]]; then
    echo "$PROGNAME: Threshold not set"
    usage
    exit $STATE_UNKNOWN
elif [[ "$critical" -lt "$warn" ]]; then
    echo "$PROGNAME: Warning Old Space % should be more than critical Old Space %"
    usage
    exit $STATE_UNKNOWN
fi
```

```
pct=$("$JAVA_HOME"/bin/jstat -gcutil $(cat "$PIDFILE") | awk 'FNR == 2 {print $4}')

if [ "$pct" > "$critical" ] ; then
    printf "ResourceManager Heap Old Space %% used %s - %g" CRITICAL "$pct"
    exit $STATE_CRITICAL
elif [ "$pct" > "$warn" ]; then
    printf "ResourceManager Heap Old Space %% used %s - %g" WARN "$pct"
    exit $STATE_WARNING
else
    printf "ResourceManager Heap Old Space %g%% used is %s" "$pct" OK
    exit $STATE_OK
fi
```

E

Resources and Additional Information

Apache Hadoop is an open-source project and is part of the Apache Foundation (http://www.apache.org/). Community involvement is encouraged and information about the Apache Hadoop project can be found at the project website: http://hadoop.apache.org.

In addition, an active discussion can be found in Apache's JIRA issue tracker system. Issues, ideas, and many important discussions take place on this site. You can see all the Hadoop JIRAs by consulting the following:

```
https://issues.apache.org/jira/secure/BrowseProjects.jspa#10292
```

In addition to the project website and the JIRA issue tracker, you may wish to consult the following resources for further information.

1. Vinod Kumar Vavilapalli, Arun C. Murthy, Chris Douglas, Sharad Agarwal, Mahadev Konar, Robert Evans, Thomas Graves, Jason Lowe, Hitesh Shah, Siddharth Seth, Bikas Saha, Carlo Curino, Owen O'Malley, Sanjay Radia, Benjamin Reed, and Eric Baldeschwieler. *Apache Hadoop YARN: Yet Another Resource Negotiator*. ACM Symposium on Cloud Computing 2013. http://www.socc2013.org/home/program/a5-vavilapalli.pdf.

2. J. Dean and S. Ghemawat. MapReduce: Simplified data processing on large clusters. *Communications of the ACM*, 51(1), January 2008.

3. K. Shvachko, H. Kuang, S. Radia, and R. Chansler. The Hadoop Distributed File System. In *Proceedings of the 2010 IEEE 26th Symposium on Mass Storage Systems and Technologies (MSST)*, MSST '10. Washington, DC: IEEE Computer Society, 2010.

4. O. O'Malley. Hadoop. In *Hadoop: The Definitive Guide*. O'Reilly Media, 2012.

5. Apache Storm: http://storm-project.net/documentation.html.

6. T. Graves. GraySort and MinuteSort at Yahoo! on Hadoop 0.23. 2013. http://sortbenchmark.org/Yahoo2013Sort.pdf.

7. Apache TEZ. http://incubator.apache.org/projects/tez.html.

8. M. Isard, M. Budiu, Y. Yu, A. Birrell, and D. Fetterly. Dryad: Distributed data-parallel programs from sequential building blocks. In *Proceedings of the 2nd ACM SIGOPS/EuroSys European Conference on Computer Systems 2007,* EuroSys '07. New York, NY: ACM, 2007.

9. S. Loughran, D. Das, and E. Baldeschwieler. *Introducing Hoya: HBase on YARN.* 2013. http://hortonworks.com/blog/introducing-hoya-hbase-on-yarn.

10. C. Olston, B. Reed, U. Srivastava, R. Kumar, and A. Tomkins. Pig Latin: A not-so-foreign language for data processing. In *Proceedings of the 2008 ACM SIGMOD International Conference on Management of Data,* SIGMOD '08. New York, NY: ACM, 2008.

11. A. Thusoo, J. S. Sarma, N. Jain, Z. Shao, P. Chakka, N. Zhang, S. Anthony, H. Liu, and R. Murthy. Hive: A petabyte scale data warehouse using Hadoop. In F. Li, M. M. Moro, S. Ghandeharizadeh, J. R. Haritsa, G. Weikum, M. J. Carey, F. Casati, E. Y. Chang, I. Manolescu, S. Mehrotra, U. Dayal, and V. J. Tsotras, eds., *Proceedings of the 26th International Conference on Data Engineering, ICDE 2010, March 1-6, 2010, Long Beach, California, USA.* IEEE, 2010.

12. B. Hindman, A. Konwinski, M. Zaharia, A. Ghodsi, A. D. Joseph, R. Katz, S. Shenker, and I. Stoica. Mesos: A platform for fine-grained resource sharing in the data center. In *Proceedings of the 8th USENIX Conference on Networked Systems Design and Implementation,* NSDI '11. Berkeley, CA: USENIX Association, 2011.

F

HDFS Quick Reference

This appendix is intended for those readers who have little or no experience with the Hadoop Distributed File System (HDFS). The following discussion is intended to provide minimal background on a few commands that will help get you started with Apache Hadoop HDFS. It is not a full description of HDFS and may be missing many of the important commands and features. In addition to this Quick Start, you are strongly advised to consult these two resources:

- http://hadoop.apache.org/docs/stable1/hdfs_design.html
- http://developer.yahoo.com/hadoop/tutorial/module2.html

The following is a quick command reference that may help you get started with HDFS. Be aware that there are alternative options for each command and that the examples given here are simple use-cases.

Quick Command Reference

To interact with HDFS, you must use the `hdfs` command. The following options are available. Only a few of these will be demonstrated here.

```
Usage: hdfs [--config confdir] COMMAND
       where COMMAND is one of:
  dfs                  run a file system command on the file systems supported in
➥Hadoop.
  namenode -format     format the DFS file system
  secondarynamenode    run the DFS secondary namenode
  namenode             run the DFS namenode
  journalnode          run the DFS journalnode
  zkfc                 run the ZK Failover Controller daemon
  datanode             run a DFS datanode
  dfsadmin             run a DFS admin client
  haadmin              run a DFS HA admin client
  fsck                 run a DFS filesystem checking utility
```

```
balancer              run a cluster balancing utility
jmxget                get JMX exported values from NameNode or DataNode
oiv                   apply the offline fsimage viewer to an fsimage
oev                   apply the offline edits viewer to an edits file
fetchdt               fetch a delegation token from the NameNode
getconf               get config values from configuration
groups                get the groups which users belong to
snapshotDiff          diff two snapshots of a directory or diff the
                      current directory contents with a snapshot
lsSnapshottableDir    list all snapshottable dirs owned by the current user
                                           Use -help to see options
portmap               run a portmap service
nfs3                  run an NFS version 3 gateway
```

Most commands print help when invoked w/o parameters.

Starting HDFS and the HDFS Web GUI

HDFS must be started and running on the cluster before it can used. See Chapter 5, "Installing Apache Hadoop YARN," for information on how to start and verify HDFS on your cluster.

Get an HDFS Status Report

A status report, similar to what is summarized on the web GUI, can be obtained by entering the following command (the output is truncated here).

$ hdfs dfsadmin -report

```
Configured Capacity: 747576360960 (696.23 GB)
Present Capacity: 675846991872 (629.43 GB)
DFS Remaining: 302179352576 (281.43 GB)
DFS Used: 373667639296 (348.01 GB)
DFS Used%: 55.29%
Under replicated blocks: 13
Blocks with corrupt replicas: 0
Missing blocks: 0


-----------------------------------------------
Datanodes available: 4 (4 total, 0 dead)

Live datanodes:
 .
 .
 .
```

Perform an FSCK on HDFS

The health of HDFS can be checked by using the `fsck` (file system check) option.

```
$ hdfs fsck /
```

```
Connecting to namenode via http://headnode:50070
FSCK started by hdfs (auth:SIMPLE) from /10.0.0.1 for path / at
➥Fri Jan 03 16:32:16 EST 2014
Status: HEALTHY
 Total size:    110594648065 B
 Total dirs:    311
 Total files:   528
 Total symlinks:            0
 Total blocks (validated):  1341 (avg. block size 82471773 B)
 Minimally replicated blocks:  1341 (100.0 %)
 Over-replicated blocks:    0 (0.0 %)
 Under-replicated blocks:   13 (0.9694258 %)
 Mis-replicated blocks:     0 (0.0 %)
 Default replication factor:  3
 Average block replication:  2.9888144
 Corrupt blocks:            0
 Missing replicas:          78 (1.9089574 %)
 Number of data-nodes:      4
 Number of racks:           1
FSCK ended at Fri Jan 03 16:32:16 EST 2014 in 74 milliseconds
```

General HDFS Commands

HDFS provides a series of commands similar to those found in a standard POSIX file system. A list of those commands can be obtained by issuing the following command. A few of these commands will be highlighted here.

```
$ hdfs dfs
```

```
Usage: hadoop fs [generic options]
        [-appendToFile <localsrc> ... <dst>]
        [-cat [-ignoreCrc] <src> ...]
        [-checksum <src> ...]
        [-chgrp [-R] GROUP PATH...]
        [-chmod [-R] <MODE[,MODE]... | OCTALMODE> PATH...]
        [-chown [-R] [OWNER][:[GROUP]] PATH...]
        [-copyFromLocal [-f] [-p] <localsrc> ... <dst>]
        [-copyToLocal [-p] [-ignoreCrc] [-crc] <src> ... <localdst>]
        [-count [-q] <path> ...]
        [-cp [-f] [-p] <src> ... <dst>]
        [-createSnapshot <snapshotDir> [<snapshotName>]]
        [-deleteSnapshot <snapshotDir> <snapshotName>]
```

```
[-df [-h] [<path> ...]]
[-du [-s] [-h] <path> ...]
[-expunge]
[-get [-p] [-ignoreCrc] [-crc] <src> ... <localdst>]
[-getmerge [-nl] <src> <localdst>]
[-help [cmd ...]]
[-ls [-d] [-h] [-R] [<path> ...]]
[-mkdir [-p] <path> ...]
[-moveFromLocal <localsrc> ... <dst>]
[-moveToLocal <src> <localdst>]
[-mv <src> ... <dst>]
[-put [-f] [-p] <localsrc> ... <dst>]
[-renameSnapshot <snapshotDir> <oldName> <newName>]
[-rm [-f] [-r|-R] [-skipTrash] <src> ...]
[-rmdir [--ignore-fail-on-non-empty] <dir> ...]
[-setrep [-R] [-w] <rep> <path> ...]
[-stat [format] <path> ...]
[-tail [-f] <file>]
[-test -[defsz] <path>]
[-text [-ignoreCrc] <src> ...]
[-touchz <path> ...]
[-usage [cmd ...]]
```

```
Generic options supported are
-conf <configuration file>     specify an application configuration file
-D <property=value>            use value for given property
-fs <local|namenode:port>      specify a namenode
-jt <local|jobtracker:port>    specify a job tracker
-files <comma-separated list of files>    specify comma separated files to
➡be copied to the map reduce cluster
-libjars <comma separated list of jars>    specify comma separated jar files to
➡include in the class path
-archives <comma separated list of archives>    specify comma separated
➡archives to be unarchived on the compute machines.
```

```
The general command-line syntax is
bin/hadoop command [genericOptions] [commandOptions]
```

List Files in HDFS

To list the files in the root HDFS directory, enter the following command:

$ hdfs dfs -ls /

```
Found 8 items
drwxr-xr-x   - hdfs   hdfs        0 2013-02-06 21:17 /apps
drwxr-xr-x   - hdfs   hadoop      0 2014-01-01 14:17 /benchmarks
```

```
drwx------   - mapred hdfs          0 2013-04-25 16:20 /mapred
drwxr-xr-x   - hdfs   hdfs          0 2013-12-17 12:57 /system
drwxrwxr--   - hdfs   hadoop        0 2013-11-21 14:07 /tmp
drwxrwxr-x   - hdfs   hadoop        0 2013-10-31 11:13 /user
drwxr-xr-x   - doug   hdfs          0 2013-10-11 16:24 /usr
drwxr-xr-x   - hdfs   hdfs          0 2013-10-31 21:25 /yarn
```

To list files in your home directory, enter the following command:

$ hdfs dfs -ls

```
Found 16 items
drwx------   - doug hadoop          0 2013-04-26 02:00 .Trash
drwxr-xr-x   - doug hadoop          0 2013-10-16 20:25 DistributedShell
-rw-------   3 doug hadoop        488 2013-04-24 16:01 NOTES.txt
drwxr-xr-x   - doug hadoop          0 2013-11-21 14:34
➥QuasiMonteCarlo_1385061734722_747204430
drwxr-xr-x   - doug hadoop          0 2014-01-02 12:48 TeraGen
drwxr-xr-x   - doug hadoop          0 2014-01-01 16:31 TeraGen-output
-rw-------   3 doug hadoop 1083049567 2013-02-07 01:10 acces_log
drwx------   - doug hadoop          0 2013-04-25 15:01 bin
-rw-r--r--   3 doug hadoop         31 2013-10-16 17:09 ds-test.sh
drwxr-xr-x   - doug hadoop          0 2013-04-25 15:44 id.out
-rw-------   3 doug hadoop       2246 2013-04-25 15:43 passwd
drwxr-xr-x   - doug hadoop          0 2013-05-14 17:07 test
drwxr-xr-x   - doug hadoop          0 2013-05-14 17:23 test-output
drwx------   - doug hadoop          0 2013-05-15 11:21 war-and-peace
drwxr-xr-x   - doug hadoop          0 2013-02-06 15:14 wikipedia
drwxr-xr-x   - doug hadoop          0 2013-08-27 15:54 wikipedia-output
```

The same result can be obtained by issuing the following command:

$ hdfs dfs -ls /user/doug

Make a Directory in HDFS

To make a directory in HDFS, use the following command. As with the -ls command, when no path is supplied, the user's home directory is used (e.g., /users/doug).

$ hdfs dfs -mkdir stuff

Copy Files to HDFS

To copy a file from your current local directory into HDFS, use the following command. Note that if a full path is not supplied, your home directory on HDFS is assumed. In this case, the file test is placed in the directory stuff that was created previously.

```
$ hdfs dfs -put test stuff
```

The file transfer can be confirmed by using the -ls command:

```
$ hdfs dfs -ls stuff
```

```
Found 1 items
-rw-r--r--   3 doug hadoop          0 2014-01-03 17:03 stuff/test
```

Copy Files from HDFS

Files can be copied back to your local file system using the following command. In this case, the file we copied into HDFS, test, will be copied back to the current local directory with the name test-local.

```
$ hdfs dfs -get stuff/test test-local
```

Copy Files within HDFS

The following command will copy a file in HDFS.

```
$ hdfs dfs -cp stuff/test test.hdfs
```

Delete a File within HDFS

The following command will delete the HDFS file test.dhfs that was created previously.

```
$ hdfs dfs -rm test.hdfs
```

```
Deleted test.hdfs
```

Delete a Directory in HDFS

The following command will delete the HDFS directory stuff and all its contents.

```
$ hdfs dfs -rm -r stuff
```

```
Deleted stuff
```

Decommissioning HDFS Nodes

This task is done by the HDFS administrator. To remove an active HDFS node, perform the following steps. The procedure for removing a YARN node running the NodeManager daemons is given in Chapter 6, "Apache Hadoop YARN

Administration." Depending on your installation, these may be the same or different nodes on which HDFS is running.

1. Add the following file path property to the `hdfs-site.xml` file. In this example, the file name `hdfs.excludes` is used.

```
<property>
    <name> dfs.hosts.exclude</name>
    <value>/opt/yarn/hadoop-2.2.0/etc/hadoop/hdfs.excludes</value>
</property>
```

2. Stop and restart the NameNode daemon.

3. To decommission a node, add the node name (or IP address) to the `hdfs.excludes` file.

4. Run the following to decommission the node:

```
hdfs dfsadmin -refreshNodes
```

5. HDFS will then begin decommissioning the node. Do not shut down or remove the node until this process is complete. The decommission status can be found by running `hdfs dfsadmin -report`. The report for the decommissioned nodes should have the following line:

```
Decommission Status : Decommission in progress
```

Once the task is complete, issuing the command `hdfs dfsadmin -report` will produce the following output:

```
Decommission Status : Decommissioned
```

It is now safe to remove the node. To add the node back, simply remove the node from the `hdfs.excludes` file and rerun `hdfs dfsadmin -refreshNodes`.

Consult the HDFS documentation for additional information.

Index

M

FREE
Online Edition

Your purchase of *Apache Hadoop™ YARN* includes access to a free online edition for 45 days through the **Safari Books Online** subscription service. Nearly every Addison-Wesley Professional book is available online through **Safari Books Online**, along with thousands of books and videos from publishers such as Cisco Press, Exam Cram, IBM Press, O'Reilly Media, Prentice Hall, Que, Sams, and VMware Press.

Safari Books Online is a digital library providing searchable, on-demand access to thousands of technology, digital media, and professional development books and videos from leading publishers. With one monthly or yearly subscription price, you get unlimited access to learning tools and information on topics including mobile app and software development, tips and tricks on using your favorite gadgets, networking, project management, graphic design, and much more.

Activate your FREE Online Edition at
informit.com/safarifree

STEP 1:   Enter the coupon code: WDQEQGA.

STEP 2:   New Safari users, complete the brief registration form.
Safari subscribers, just log in.

If you have difficulty registering on Safari or accessing the online edition,
please e-mail customer-service@safaribooksonline.com